EYE CLINIC
WAITING ROOM
This is an eye clinic. I am blind. Please tell me you are not pointing?!

Published by Aye Aye Publishing

Website: www.WingingItBlind.com

Printed in the United Kingdom

Cover design and layout
by www.spiffingcovers.com

Paperback ISBN-13: 978-1-9164463-6-6
.epub eBook ISBN-13: 978-1-9164463-7-3

WINGING IT BLIND!

OR CHANGING WHAT YOU THINK IS POSSIBLE

FEAR NOT THE TASK, CELEBRATE WHAT YOU HAVE ALREADY ACHIEVED

SIMON MAHONEY

Contents

DEDICATION

In memory of Kelly my wife, Chris my son, dear friends Eileen and Dennis, and fellow blind veterans.

ACKNOWLEDGEMENTS

My thanks go to my many friends and companions who put up with my questions and flights of fancy.

To Denise, who keeps me on the straight and narrow and without whose help and humour things would be very different.

To Beverley, Carrie and Sylvia for reading early drafts and your encouragement.

To the team at SpiffingCovers who have wrought their usual magic.

To my patient and wonderful editor, Kimberley Miller, for her editorial skills and the brilliant cartoon.

To the RM and Blind Veterans (which used to be called St. Dunstains), both of which have made a tremendous impact on my life.

My thanks to Liz for everlasting good humour and support

THE TEN RULES OF ENGAGEMENT WITH SIGHT LOSS

1. Accept your sight loss.
2. Obstacles are an opportunity to improvise, adapt and overcome.
3. Learn or improve a skill every day.
4. Listen carefully, judge slowly.
5. Sight loss is nothing to be ashamed of. Do not be embarrassed.
6. Get organised. Have a place for everything.
7. Apply the 'broken glass' principle: Sort out hazards and problems as you come to them.
8. Ask for help. Remember, you are the one with the problem.
9. Check everything, and go at your own pace. Rushing plus blindness equals chaos!
10. Do not be offended by references to sight.

CAVEAT

Throughout all my writing I prate about the need to be independent, assertive, and not stand for any nonsense. Whether I would be quite so gung-ho without the astonishing and immense help of Blind Veterans is another matter! The charity has provided a wonderful platform, or haven, which has enabled me to rebuild my life. Whilst my connection with the charity is strong, I must make it clear that the thoughts, opinions and ideas in this book are mine and in no way reflect those of Blind Veterans UK., and that the techniques and methods work for me and may not be suitable for everyone.

FOREWORD

I first met Simon approximately fifteen years ago when my sister-in-law said, "I want you to meet someone really special." At that time Simon still had his vision but, needless to say, he was still the witty and 'go for it guy' we all know and love today.

Having advocated and supported people with sensory loss, including sight loss, for over twenty-five years of my working career in both the United States and Great Britain, I feel I can confidently say that the work, insight and courage Simon has shown during his journey into darkness has amazed and impressed me.

While reading the proofs for *Winging it Blind* it came to mind that having a book with this much information, self-experience and trial and error, written by a person who was actually going through the experience of losing his sight, would have been a godsend to me as I was beginning, and indeed throughout, my career. *Winging it Blind* would also be a perfect addition to reading material for both students in college going into the field of support for those with sensory loss and for those who already work there.

While people may initially feel that the book

is for those who are losing their sight, I feel it would also greatly benefit friends and family who support a loved one who is undergoing their own *Descent into Darkness*, Simon's first book, as well as those who have been newly diagnosed with a sight loss condition.

Simon has a true gift for portraying the loneliness sight loss brings, while simultaneously encouraging those who are travelling this path, letting them know and understand that anything can be accomplished as long as one perseveres, takes small steps, and remembers that it's okay to laugh!

Simon is the best and biggest advocate and supporter for the blind who I have met in both my career and private life. His books are packed with knowledge and information, including how to go about getting assistance and where best to find it. I would encourage everyone who wants to gain knowledge, information and insight into the world of the blind to read his books.

Sylvia Welford

PS. Simon, remember the spectacular smash accompanied by flying roast turkey (I know, turkeys can't fly), Brussels sprouts and red wine at our family Christmas a few years ago? Perfect story to describe proprioception and spatial awareness (or the lack of it)!

In the middle of Christmas dinner for eleven guests, Simon, who had been gradually losing his sight, raised a glass of red wine, flailing it around at the precise moment I, sitting on his right, was passing a plate full of Christmas dinner to his wife, sitting on his left. The collision was spectacular! Simon piped up with, "Did I do that?"

The nine other faces around the table didn't know whether to put their head down or burst out laughing, and I calmly said, "Yup, that was you."

How far you have come, my friend.

INTRODUCTION

'We look through, not at, our eyes.'
– Harley Mason 2019

Losing your sight is a major life event and, as with many such events, we have to make a choice. The majority of people choose to retire from life. It seems that only a few fight to get their lives back.

There are at least sixteen million people in the UK who have imperfect eyesight. Anyone who thinks that sight loss is no concern of theirs is living in a fool's paradise: complete or partial blindness is a concern for everybody.

Sight loss is amongst us in greater numbers than most people imagine, and the numbers are set to rise year on year. The reasons for this are many, complex, and intricately bound up with each other. The most likely suspects are the toxic nature of our modern environment and lifestyle in combination with ever-increasing longevity.

There is, however, I believe, another significant figure lurking in the wings. This is the way in which we regard our eyes, which may be far and away the most influential contributor to the increasing frequency of unnecessary sight loss. Our attitude to our eyes is somewhat removed. There appears to be no ability to make the link between our eyes and what they do. It is almost as if our eyes were not a part of us. This may be because we see through, rather than at, our eyes and rarely see them. This seems to operate at an institutional as well as an individual level.

Whilst our disregard of our eyes is an important factor, it cannot be denied that the disconnect between eye care and support for sight loss also plays an important part. The ensuing delays result in people being cast adrift at a crucial time. Many do not recover from this.

The majority of people who have severe sight loss or blindness choose to be inactive. This is partly due to the taboo nature of the condition. Very few people think or talk about sight loss until it happens to them, and even then there is a great degree of denial and refusal to accept it. When sight loss hits it takes a huge amount of work, support and luck to rise above it and claim your life back.

I believe the issue is important, and not only for the mental health, social and personal consequences for individuals and their loved ones. It is also important for the potential economic consequences for the country as a whole. If current trends continue, a substantial proportion of the population will either have, or be looking after someone with, sight loss. These people will on the whole be economically inactive.

It is the not knowing what to expect that is the true horror. As such it can be totally disenabling, as fear of the unknown can be paralysing. Indeed, in many ways, it can be almost as bad as the condition itself.

This book is an attempt to provide a framework, skills set and information to manage losing your sight. The contents are based on my experience of going blind, overcoming many of its limitations, and coming through the process relatively sane and upbeat. It is intended as a guide and comfort for all those who are and will face the unknown terrors of not being able to see.

Simon Mahoney
Ashbourne, 2020

LEVEL ONE

ESSSENTIAL FOUNDATION KNOWLEDGE

First contact – the shock of engagement
The great disconnect
Registration, or putting yourself on the map
Stress – the enemy within
Rules of engagement – prop or weapon
The totality of sight loss
Getting it back together again

CHAPTER ONE

FIRST CONTACT - THE SHOCK OF ENGAGEMENT

'Change what we think is possible.'
– Ministry of Defence

Sight loss is a unique and highly personal event for everyone. There are as many ways of experiencing and perceiving it as there are people with the condition.

The ancient Hindu parable of the elephant and the blind men, with some adaptation, provides a simple and clear illustration of this.

Thousands of years ago an elephant was brought into the royal court. Nobody, including the King, had any idea of what kind of beast the elephant may be. Accordingly the King sent for some blind people to determine the nature of the animal. Six appeared, all blind, five of whom were beggars – and a right motley crew of slovens they were too. They were told to examine the beast.

The first person shuffled over and found the tail. He whimpered that it was a whip, and it would scourge him in his infirmity out of court.

The second stumbled into the legs and cried, "It is an impenetrable barrier, just like my lack of sight!"

The third walked into the side. He protested that it was huge, featureless, and beyond understanding – in the same way as his sight loss.

The fourth discovered the trunk and whined it was a snake and, that like his disability, would either consume or injure him.

The fifth fell over the tusks. He whispered that they were mighty weapons and begged not to be impaled upon them for his helplessness.

The sixth remained standing somewhat removed from the creature.

The King, now thoroughly dispirited by the circus of ineptitude and dismal catalogue of woe, wearily looked at the last blind person. He asked them if they were going to examine the animal.

The sixth replied that they already had. To the King's astonishment he realised that it was a young woman before him. She was neatly dressed, proud of bearing, and clearly at the peak of physical fitness and health. Looking directly at the King she explained that she was, in spite of her blindness, a tracker. She had examined its footprints and dung, which had determined the beast was female, healthy, ate only plants, was very big, could live and work in almost any type of country, and would make a good beast of burden.

The King was, of course, delighted with this analysis. The tracker was rewarded accordingly.

However, he was curious how it was that a blind person could be a tracker and, on being asked, she declared it was not a problem. She went on to explain that she could hear, she could smell, and she could feel. These three, with a positive attitude, patience and application, were quite sufficient for her needs. (See Note 1)

A positive attitude, patience and application are invaluable in managing our sight loss. In the early days, however, there is a major hurdle to clear. When we first learn we are going to lose our sight we are immediately faced with choices, and those that we make will be largely determined by our emotions, the most pressing of which will be fear. Fear of the unknown.

Fear of the unknown is primordial, basic, and hardwired into our DNA. It is a major factor in behaviour. When you lose your sight the fear of the unknown is suddenly very real. You can smell it. You can taste it. You can hear it. You can feel it. And it can paralyse you. Nonetheless, we have no option but to ride into it headlong.

But we do have a choice in how we take

that ride. We can sit there like a startled rabbit and let the fear overwhelm us. That way lies disaster, surrender, and a featureless wait for death.

Alternatively, we can choose to embrace the fear, use it as a motivating force to fight the disabling effects of sight loss. Here lies the road to acceptance, moving on, and eventual renaissance.

To do this requires emotional stability, knowledge, method, patience and determination. It demands the direct application of qualities of which you may have had no previous awareness. But the qualities are there within all of us. It is just a matter of digging them out.

It is important that you constantly search for knowledge about your sight loss. Knowledge is power and removes much of the fear of the unknown. As far as knowledge is concerned, be prepared to be told nothing by the eye clinics. They may understand eye care, but they have no idea about sight loss. This book, the RNIB (the Royal National Institute of Blind People), and other people in the same position will provide much of the information you need. How you use that information, of course, is another matter.

When you lose your sight there will be a period when you will be disabled. If you are to move beyond the initial shock of engagement you have to constantly challenge, and indeed change, what you think is possible. Only by doing this can you progress. Be aware, however, that in making this challenge you are also making others question dearly held stereotypes about people with sight loss. You can expect furious resistance.

There is no suggestion that sight loss should be tackled in a berserker rage, tempting though that may be. Dealing with sight loss requires hard work, patience, and above all method.

The method

The method is universal and can be used at every activity and stage of the battle to regain your life. There is one overriding principal and five sequential stages. Each stage is important, and to miss one can imperil whatever you are trying to do.

The overriding principal is the old chestnut that forms the mnemonic **KISS**, or **Keep It Simple Stupid.**

Life is complicated enough without adequate sight, and there is no point in adding to the problems. Therefore, keep things as simple as possible and avoid overthinking things.

The five sequential stages are **safety, lazy person principle, organisation, preparation** and **execution**. This reduces every activity to a drill which enables you to focus on what you are doing. The method is explained fully in chapter fifteen, 'Cooking without fear'.

Method and structure are vital. When you lose your sight you are not only trying to challenge, and change, what is possible, you are also attempting to rebuild your life. As with any structure it has to be built from the ground up. There are no shortcuts. You have to rebuild your life a brick at a time.

If you choose to engage with your sight loss it is important that you have no illusions about the magnitude of the battle. You will, in effect, spend the rest of your life adjusting what you think is possible. It is important that you understand from the outset that each adjustment of the possible only leads to the next apparently impossible objective. For all practical purposes, this trail of apparent impossibilities has no end. The task of achieving acceptance, moving on and renaissance, and then maintaining it is one which will take up the rest of your life. (See Note 2)

If this sounds heavy and dispiriting, then you have an understanding of the scope of the battle. Nothing worthwhile comes easy. Getting your life back after sight loss has to be up there among the ranks of worthwhile objectives. The good news is that it is perfectly doable, but it will require your active involvement. Sitting there like a chick on a perch waiting to be fed will achieve nothing.

However, before becoming disheartened, is what has been described really that different to what we have all experienced all our lives? After all, we have spent our entire existence developing and learning, and each step has changed what we think is possible.

Apart from application of knowledge and method, when it comes to sight loss, you also need to understand yourself. Psychological understanding will come with interpersonal skills, communication and assertiveness training. You also need to develop the skill of careful and thoughtful listening, yet unfortunately this kind of training is not generally available. Maybe one day. One can only hope. In any event, actively seeking to understand yourself and listening carefully will make a major contribution to your resources.

As a start there are elements of interpersonal, communication and assertion skills throughout the book. Bearing in mind the all-embracing nature of sight loss, how could there not be?

The battle with sight loss involves every aspect of your life. It is multi-facetted, multi-dimensional and interminable. If you think otherwise, you are fooling yourself and you will fail.

The question for all of us is very simple. Are we, like the five blind men, so sunk in our blindness we cannot see beyond it? Or, like the tracker, are we going above our blindness, not allowing it to restrict us and see the bigger picture? We all have the capacity to be either. We just have to ask ourselves which route we are to choose and why.

What follows in this book will help with that choice. It cannot make the choice for you. That is both your privilege and your burden.

Note 1

As I understand it the original parable demonstrates how a faith could be described in different ways, and yet remain true to itself. Here I have used the same idea to look at sight loss. There are different ways of describing it, all of which are true for the describer, but all are describing the same thing. In doing this it is not my intention to offend anyone.

Note 2

The Royal Marines, at the time of writing, were running the following advertisement: Fear of the unknown is a primal instinct. A Royal Marine rides head long into the unknown. All a Royal Marine does is change what he thinks is possible. This is a brilliant summary of sight loss.

As far as the advertisement goes, I agree entirely with the first and third lines. The Corps are the ultimate professionals. The only way a Marine would ride headlong into the unknown would be if they missed the O Group (a meeting held to pass across orders), or briefing, if he was not listening, or if it was one of those occasional right royal Charlie Foxtrots.

In the case of sight loss, we are hurled headlong into the unknown because it is rare to be told anything about sight loss until it happens. (See the next chapter, 'The great disconnect'.)

Fear of the unknown is with us always. Therefore we have to constantly change what we think is possible.

CHAPTER TWO

THE GREAT DISCONNECT

'This is an eye clinic. I am blind.
Please tell me you are not pointing.'
– Author, 2018

I started to lose my sight in 2013 and was stone-blind within four years. Writing about it has been hugely instrumental in coming to an understanding of vision loss in general, and blindness in particular, and I was extremely fortunate as I was referred to, and picked up by, Blind Veterans UK within weeks of registration.

After going to their centre in Sheffield, I wrote that for the first time I was in an environment which was entirely dedicated to sight loss and blindness. I carried on writing, but then was brought up short by a sense of surprise, almost shock. I had spent the previous eighteen months attending eye clinics almost on a monthly basis and had endured a number of examinations and procedures. In spite of this, there was no feeling whatsoever that my sight loss itself had been addressed.

2.1 Incomprehension of sight loss

The NHS staff were in general warm and personable, although somewhat removed. Looking back it seemed that the treatment was almost formulaic. The overall impression was that the eyes were apparently disembodied from their owners and their difficulties, and there was no awareness of the challenges that lay ahead. There was certainly no connection with the consequences of the conditions they were treating, and no comprehension beyond general eye care.

I have now included three simple examples that demonstrate this disconnect between eye care and dealing with loss of sight.

Example 1

One day I walked into the eye clinic and found my way to the desk. After the usual interrogation about who had brought me in, the subsequent gasps of horror at finding that I had come on public transport on my own, I asked for the location of a chair. There was a rustle of clothing and a disembodied voice said, "Over there."

I leant toward the voice and said, "This is an eye clinic. I am blind. Please tell me you are not pointing."

This clearly had an impact. When they see me now I am immediately grabbed and taken to a chair.

The fact remains, however, that this experience indicated to me a lack of training, and even thoughtlessness, and a definite disconnect from the patient group. It also seemed to apply that there was (and is) no expectation that blind people can find their way around without an escort or carer. In short, there is a presumption of helplessness, even though on that occasion the helplessness was ignored.

Example 2

One day I was talking to my consultant about hallucinations, referred to as Charles Bonnet Syndrome or CBS. I asked him why I had not been warned about these alarming hallucinations by the eye clinic. He replied that there were leaflets on the subject. There was an embarrassed silence, and I looked towards him. Finally he commented that perhaps that was "not appropriate".

There are a couple of points that can be made concerning this. Firstly, without awareness of CBS, the blind would have no reason to take a leaflet, even if they could actually see where they were and read the thing. Secondly, my consultant is a lovely chap, intelligent and caring, but it had never occurred to him that people might find it helpful to be warned about the possibility of CBS.

Example 3

When I asked my consultant whether my eyes warranted registration his reply left me somewhat aghast: "Oh. You want to be registered, do you?"

This was an interesting response at a number of levels. Firstly, because it seemed to indicate he had no idea how helpful registration could be. This is discussed in the next chapter. Secondly, there seemed to be surprise that anyone should want to officially be seen as disabled, almost as if it was something of which to be ashamed, which I will be looking at this later in the book too. Thirdly, it seemed to indicate the disconnect between eye care and dealing with sight loss.

Finally, it made me wonder if there is a policy of under registration in order to conceal the real extent of the frequency of sight impairment. As we all know, once a problem is recognised something has to be done about it. (There is, of course, minimal chance of finding out whether this is the case.)

2.2 Lack of information

It is clear, in hindsight, how much I had to find out for myself. It was surprising how little the medical centres could, or would, tell me. It seems that unless you are well informed and are able to ask the relevant questions you are told nothing or very little.

Looking back, it is now obvious that the medical focus was extremely narrow. They concentrated on my eyes and ignored my impending sight loss. There was even a degree of incredulity that I should inquire about registration.

There was no attempt to prepare me to cope with the consequences of my deteriorating condition, which would culminate in blindness. Yet the potential consequences are many, including physical, social, psychological, psychiatric and economic, to name the more obvious. I go into much more detail about this in chapter four.

There was no warning of the initial lack of balance. Perhaps it was assumed that I would find out when I kept falling over! Likewise there was no mention of loss of confidence in the proprioceptive sense. Presumably the trail of wreckage was considered a sufficient cause for caution.

There was no warning of the crushing tiredness

brought on by the need to concentrate all the time. There was no suggestion that counselling, particularly bereavement counselling, might be helpful if not necessary.

Other areas, such as having to completely rebuild communication skills, regain social inclusion, and develop resistance to the inevitable limiting effects of labelling were not even mentioned let alone discussed.

Perhaps the most serious omission was not informing me of the possibility of hallucinations that can accompany some sight loss. These hallucinations, the previously mentioned Charles Bonnet Syndrome or CBS, are harmless provided you know about them. If you are unaware of CBS, you could find your mental equilibrium highly disrupted. To put it another way, you can begin to think you're going crazy. Indeed, until relatively recently, CBS was treated with anti-hallucinatory drugs.

In the case of those with significant sight loss this lack of information can be catastrophic. It can lead to people being cast adrift in an alien and frightening environment, and the fear generated by this situation can be as disabling as the condition itself. The proportion of people who fail to engage with sight loss may well be a consequence of this.

2.3 The role of the eye clinics

We can all recognise that medical services are under monstrous pressure. At the end of the day their focus is a medical one. It would be unreasonable to expect them to broaden their scope to a wider social function, even though this may well make a significant contribution to recovery from medical intervention.

It may be that the problem is an institutional and cultural one across the NHS. The role of medics is to deal with tangible complaints. Generally there are no shades of grey; something is or it isn't. I feel that this very black and white framework must make it extraordinarily difficult to open themselves up to consider more ephemeral issues, such as lack of confidence, fear, stress and isolation. This combined with the growth of specialism, where individuals know more and more about less and less, must make it very difficult to consider non-medical factors. To put it another way, medics are too busy with facts to be able to consider other more fluffy social factors. This, it is felt, lies at the heart of the apparent lack of continuity between eye care and support for sight loss. After all, training can only go so far in overcoming the habits of a lifetime.

It should also be remembered that medics are human. They too may ignore eyes as something we look through, rather than at.

There is another possible reason. The NHS, like many other large organisations, is driven by key performance indicators, targets and the notion of value for money. In such a culture it may be that consultants are unwilling to parade the failure of eye care to other professionals. No profession is willing to deny its omnipotence.

I discussed this with a friend who happens to be a ROVI – a rehabilitation officer for the visually impaired. She, being much wiser, gentler and considerably less jaundiced than myself, had a rather different take on this. She said, "I have been in this game for a long time. Every person I have met has gone into medicine because they want to help people. It may be that registering people is admitting to both themselves and the patient that they cannot help any more. I think you can understand their reluctance."

I thought about this, and it occurred to me that it must be a bit like a person with sight loss taking up a cane for the first time. It is a crossing of the Rubicon, a declaration of passing a point of no return, something which can be very emotional and requires great fortitude.

2.4 Beyond the clinics

The charitable sector is equipped, geared up and resourced for information-giving and at least some other forms of social intervention. The major organisation is the RNIB, and a call to their helpline is a useful first port of call. They maintain a registry of every organisation which has any connection with sight loss up and down the UK.

In so many cases there is a critical time lag between the initial need for nonmedical intervention and support and its application. Indeed, a recent report by the Guide Dogs for the Blind suggested that as many as seventy percent of people have to wait at least a year for any support. I had to wait eighteen months. Another report by the RNIB suggests that only seventeen percent of people receive any emotional support.

Losing any part of you is a bereavement. And, if possible, is even more so in the case of sight loss. Our sight is so central to living that its loss is nothing short of catastrophic, and I feel the lack of emotional support is criminal. At the very least it is mortgaging future resources. I have no doubt in my mind that eye care and sight loss support should be offered together as a single integrated care package.

2.5 The significance of this disconnect

The disconnect matters both at a personal and a national level. As indicated above, this time lag can be catastrophic for individuals. When people surrender to the horrors of sight loss they gobble up resources in terms of being cared for. In addition to this, many of them cease to contribute to society.

With over two million people with sight loss this may be sustainable. However, that figure is based on the number of people who are registered, under treatment, or thought to be suffering with sight problems without registration. (See Appendix Three, 'Statistics on sight loss'.)

Another estimate quotes four million, and one organisation projects ten million. It seems no one really knows the size of the problem, but numbers like this would be economically unsustainable for any country. Just to add to the confusion, it would appear there is a degree of systemic failure in the eye clinics. It appears that many people are either having to wait so long for treatment, or are not being diagnosed with sight problems at all. Some are ending up with unnecessary loss of vision.

I have discovered that many people are unaware of registration, let alone its importance. As already indicated, the NHS do not seem to fall over themselves to suggest it. As a former social worker, I knew about it. Would I still be waiting if I had not? In addition to that, I had to wait until I was practically blind, and was only registered after insisting.

There may well be individuals who refuse to accept they have sight loss, do not seek help, and remain below the radar. There are others who are so deep in denial they only take their medication prior to seeing their consultant. I knew a chap with glaucoma who did this, and he is now as blind as I am. This could have been avoided with the right intervention, and I find it hard to believe he is the only such case.

In addition to this there are others who choose to 'take a long swim' on hearing of pending sight loss. This is a hidden aspect of the overall picture, and as such there is only anecdotal evidence and certainly no idea of the numbers involved.

It is pretty clear that sight loss is and will continue to be a major issue. Pretending it is not happening and not addressing it will just not cut it. Unless we start to educate people, the unnecessary incidents of sight loss will continue. That combined with the side-lining of those who have it will have catastrophic consequences.

2.6 Some causes of sight problems

When we look at our modern environment, the apparent official indifference or lack of interest, the failure to educate the population about the dangers, and lack of joined-up provision all seem to point to one thing: we are sleepwalking into a sight loss epidemic of almost biblical proportions. (I discuss the causes and consequences at length in Appendix One, 'Sight loss, the lurking menace'.)

It is interesting to note that Microsoft and other tech giants are spending billions on developing access technology. They do this not from the goodness of their hearts. No, they recognise there is a large and rapidly growing market. In other words, they can see that the incidence of sight loss is growing rapidly.

The Covid-19 pandemic may well have a huge influence on the numbers of potential sight loss sufferers. Whilst information is highly edited and sketchy, the disease seems to have targeted many people who could expect to develop, or already have, sight loss. It has, we are told, targeted the elderly, the obese, Type 1 and Type 2 diabetics, cigarette smokers and people living in polluted inner cities.

At the time of writing we have no idea how it will affect the demographics of the population of the UK. Covid-19 might well cause a slight check in the increase in the numbers, but as we have no way of knowing how many of the people who died had sight loss, it is difficult to even begin to assess its impact. However, if nothing is done about the environmental and lifestyle causes of sight loss we will see more and more people developing blindness in the long term.

In the short term, we may see a massive increase. This will be because three lockdowns have meant many people will not have had their regular eye checks, whether in the throes of sight loss or not. It is not rocket science to predict the numbers of people with unnecessary sight loss will increase substantially.

2.7 Accelerating rates of sight loss

When I first started to take an interest in sight loss five years ago the RNIB estimated that between two and three people an hour were joining the ranks of the sight impaired, which translates to between three and five hundred people a week. Or to put it another way, fifteen to twenty-five thousand a year. I found this quite shocking.

The RNIB are now saying that two hundred and fifty people are beginning to lose their sight a day. That is nearly eighteen hundred a week, or over ninety thousand people a year. (Probably a net gain of between fifty and seventy thousand people a year.) The epidemic seems to be gathering pace, not least because we are living much, much longer and therefore developing many more ailments, including sight loss, as we age.

If this rate of increase continues, it may be that three hundred thousand people a year will be losing their sight in five years or so. I am blind already, and I find this horrifying. It is past the time when someone needs to start to take notice.

It is important to appreciate that these are just the people losing their sight. Each person will have others around them whose lives will be impacted. There will also be a considerable cost in mental health, both amongst the carers and those losing their sight.

In addition to the personal cost in terms of blasted hopes and anguish, there will also be an economic cost. It is probable that the vast majority of those with sight loss will become inactive economically, plus there will be a substantial cost attached in terms of reduction of tax revenue and an increase in costs in terms of their ongoing care.

There seems to be little awareness of measures that can be taken to keep people in employment. This implies that the majority of people who develop sight problems could find themselves on the scrapheap in disproportionate numbers.

It is strange that, in spite of the increasing numbers, there is a year on year drop in registrations. It would be nice to attribute this to improved eye care, but I strongly believe this is pushing the bounds of credibility.

Curiously, it is almost as if there is a conspiracy of silence about sight loss. Apart from the occasional 'Guide Dogs for the Blind' advertisement stating that half of sight loss cases are unnecessary, I am unaware of any concerted effort at its prevention. We have to make it possible for people to know, understand, and get themselves in a position to make informed choices. If sight loss is so terrifying that it is taboo, then it should be dragged out, kicking and screaming, into the open. This could start with the schools.

Both the incidents of sight loss and support for those with the condition need to be addressed as a matter of urgency. Apart from the human cost, it is also economically unsustainable. If half of sight loss is unnecessary, why is there not a prominent educational program in force? The cost of such a programme would be an impossibly small fraction of that of treatment, support and loss of economic activity. This should be an absolute priority on just economic grounds. Sadly, I don't believe it ever will be.

2.8 Eliminating the disconnect

The appalling tardiness of support has to be addressed. Somehow this time lag has to be reduced or eliminated. Failure to do this will result in the support for sight loss neither being cost effective or successful in the long term. This has implications for both mental health and the subsequent level of dependency.

An important key to dealing with sight loss at a personal level is to eliminate the ignorance of what could happen as your sight fades. A very simple solution would be to have a basic information video running on a loop in eye clinic waiting rooms. Some doctors' surgeries do something similar, so why not eye clinics? This would be a useful first step in making patients aware of what might happen, which would then lead to exploring other options in order to promote greater involvement with the very real issues embedded within sight loss.

The first option would be to encourage patients to manage their own recovery from major change. There are most likely very few people who would either have the experience to recognise the need, or the presence of mind to insist upon it. As a minimum people should be encouraged to seek registration as soon as possible. This would immediately trigger signposting to support organisations.

The second option would be to ensure that nonmedical intervention is introduced far earlier by much closer liaison between the medical centre and the organisations providing that assistance. As suggested above, the ideal situation would be both eye care and support for vision loss to be running side by side. This could be achieved through the existing system of hospital social workers and eye clinic liaison officers. Medical staff must be trained to recognise the value of social intervention and be prepared to inform their patients of the existence and role of these agencies.

The third option is to actively recruit individuals who have gone through the same life-changing experience, those who could act as mentors or buddies for newly diagnosed individuals. The arguments for and benefits accruing from this idea are outlined further on in the book.

There is a pressing need to recognise the expertise of patients, and acknowledge their implied authority having gone through the process of losing their sight, accepting the implications and rebuilding their lives. In short, people should be encouraged and actively recruited to help and support those with the same condition. This would not only be a valuable and highly relevant addition to current resources, but also extremely cathartic for those involved.

It is clear that all the above is only tinkering with what little already exists. In an ideal world the eye clinics would have a low vision clinic attached to it which would provide a taper between eye care and sight loss provision. The low vision clinic would have a voluntary agencies hub attached to it, which in some respects would perform the role of the eye clinic liaison officer. It would also provide a clear and tangible route from diagnosis of sight loss to registration as being sight impaired.

With clear communication, free access and goodwill between the three elements, it would eliminate the disconnect, remove the delay, and provide timely emotional, physical and psychological help.

Summary

The gap between eye care and provision for sight loss must be closed. Every person has to be encouraged to be more active as a response to the news of impending loss of sight, asking questions and insisting on useable answers. It is important that once you have the diagnosis of sight loss you insist on registration at the earliest moment. Registration not only puts you on the map as far as sight loss provision is concerned, but also has numerous benefits attached to it. These will be outlined in the next chapter.

CHAPTER THREE

REGISTRATION, OR PUTTING YOURSELF ON THE MAP

'Registration is only the beginning of the fight back.'

– Author, 2013

Losing your sight is the ultimate horror in the minds of most people. Its contemplation reduces many to a state of numbness and almost paralysis. It requires a great degree of personal fortitude to come through this life-changing experience and regain some semblance of normal life, as without adapting to this new reality and improvising new rules to engage with our physical and social environment there will be small chance of overcoming the challenges. A recent poll in New York found that the number one personal disaster is losing your site. One has to wonder, however, if they asked anyone who was blind.

Credible and appropriate support should be made available from the outset. Registering as sight impaired or severely sight impaired/blind is the most important step you can take in beginning to get a handle on your sight loss. It is the start of taking charge of what is happening. Without gaining some control of the chaos created by losing some or all of your sight, it is all too easy to become overwhelmed.

As mentioned previously, there seems to be not only a general reluctance to register people who are sight impaired but also to inform them that it is even possible. The process of getting registered is simple enough. First, you have to know about it and, second, persuade your eye consultant to give you the necessary certificate.

3.1 Process of registration

Step 1: Ask your consultant to certify you as sight impaired or severely sight impaired/blind. With any luck he/she will give you a completed certificate.

Step 2: Obtain at least a dozen photocopies of the certificate.

Step 3: Send the original to your local council. You should receive notice of your registration within a few working days. If this does not happen make sure that you follow up. In some areas registration falls far behind the number of certificates.

Step 4: Begin the process of claiming the benefits to which you are entitled. There are several advantages and benefits that come with registration. Below is a list, which is not exhaustive, but will highlight some of the key points.

There seems to be a general feeling that sight loss is something of which we should be ashamed, as if it somehow makes us less of a person. It is important to appreciate from the outset that not being able to see does not mean the rest of you does not work or is worthless. Sometimes it may feel like it, however, which is why it is so important to be positive and active in addressing your sight loss. I cannot emphasise enough that the first step is registration. Without registration a very difficult task becomes almost impossible.

The most important aspect of registration is that you are doing something about your sight loss. You are accepting that it is happening and not just ignoring it. Lost vision may not be recoverable, but it can certainly be managed.

3.2 Advantages and benefits of registration

The most important aspect of registration is that it puts you on the map. You will no longer be ignored and there will be access to support from the various sight-related organisations. What follows is a list of some of the benefits.

- If you are a taxpayer, then registration as severely sight impaired/blind will automatically entitle you to more than £2,000 on your personal tax allowance. This can usually be accessed by a telephone call to your tax office. It works out at more than £400 a year. There are periodic increases in the amount and the exact current figure needs to be checked.
- There is automatic right to a personal blue badge which can be used in any car that transports you. This is obtained by applying to your local county council. They will want to see your certificate or a copy of it.
- A half-price TV licence can be obtained by writing to the TV Licencing Authority with a copy of your certificate. Telephone them first.
- You will have access to help such as Blind Veterans or other appropriate local help and organisations. Your local hospital or Social Services will tell you what is available. Alternatively, never overlook the knowledge of the local radio or paper. Finally, the RNIB helpline is always an excellent fall back resource. Amongst other things they have a register of sight-related organisations throughout the UK.
- A bus pass is obtainable from your local

county council if you do not already have one because of your age. Sometimes local shops will give a discount on production of a bus pass. One of our local pubs offers a twenty percent discount! In some areas you can take someone with you on the bus, and if you tell the driver they are your bus pass assistant they will travel for free. It is worth checking.

- To get your disabled rail card collect a form from your local train station. It costs about twenty pounds a year and allows you to buy rail tickets at two-thirds of the normal price, and a carer can travel free.
- You'll receive free Directory Enquiries if you are with British Telecom.
- You'll have use of a radar key which gives access to disabled toilets. These are usually cleaner, involve less queueing, are more spacious, and are usually free. These keys are obtainable from your local council office.

There are other possible benefits, too, such as attendance or care allowance. You'll need to apply through the Department of Work and Pensions for this. They will probably refuse the application, however, so you'll then need to go to your nearest Citizens Advice Bureau to get help to lodge an appeal. This is something you should try and get, as it is worth at least £2,500 a year, tax-free. As far as I am aware, this is not means tested.

Go to Social Services for any adaptations and welfare rights advice. Some examples of adaptations might be modifications to your domestic lighting,

a rail at the top of the stairs, a frame around the toilet, or a grab rail in the shower, for example. It is important to include all adaptations to your home, not just those for sight loss.

If you do have adaptations made to your home, or have to dedicate one room for storing specialist equipment, then you may be eligible for disability discount on your council tax. If you ring the council tax office of your local council they will send someone out to discuss it with you.

You may also qualify for assisted bin collection. This means that the chaps on the waste wagon will collect and return your bins from where they are stored. Contact your local council to find out.

If you are below retirement age, a host of other benefits kick in. Go to Social Services or a welfare rights expert to find out your full entitlement. Do not rely on the DWP to tell you all you need to know.

3.3 Employment

If you are employed registration will, in theory, give you protection in the workplace. Your employer is required by law to make reasonable provision to enable you to continue in your job. One of the problems, however, is what can be considered reasonable.

If continuing to work is not possible because of health and safety or other factors then they have to retrain you. This is covered by the Equality at Work Act 2010 under the provisions for assisting people to return to work. Many employers may tell you they are unaware of any such provision. They may presume ignorance of the law and seek to terminate your employment on the grounds of inability or incompetence.

The minute they mention discussing your future because of your failing sight you must tell them that you are happy to do so once you have sought advice. If you are a member of a union go to your union representative for help. They should ask the employer for a formal meeting in ten working days. This will achieve four things:

1. It gives notice that you are not going to let the employer just bundle you out of the door without a fight.
2. It gives the representative time to get their act together and consult the union's legal experts.

3. It gives you and the representative time to identify and explore all possible options.
4. It gives the employer time to consult with HR – human resources or personnel – or even their lawyers. Those worthies will inform them of the protections you have.

The subsequent meeting can be used to work out the best solution for you. This may be retraining, provision of specialist equipment or assistance, or it may be a generous severance package.

If you are not a union member you should still seek to put it on a formal basis by asking for a meeting in ten working days. This will give you time to get advice. As far as I understand it, any lawyer has to give you thirty minutes free advice. Make sure you have sorted out what you need to know before going into any such meeting, as time is precious.

A phone call to ACAS mediator services may well be a good move. They also have a very useful website. The RNIB helpline may also be of help.

If you are a veteran you can seek assistance through the Forces Covenant. Any of the forces' charities will be able to guide you on this. As a veteran you should also give serious consideration to joining Blind Veterans UK.

The main thing to remember is that there

is specialised help available, it is just a matter of remaining calm and thinking the problem through. In any event it is important that you have someone with you when you meet members of management. They do not like witnesses, and the presence of someone else keeps the meeting objective. I have accompanied a number of friends to such meetings, and they have always found it helpful.

I fully understand that all of this may be viewed as stressful, but it is vitally important you manage to navigate through registration. This will be priceless in accessing the resources available, and will also boost your confidence beyond all recognition. The next chapter on stress will give you some pointers on how you can achieve this without falling apart, partially or wholly, in the process!

CHAPTER FOUR

STRESS - THE ENEMY WITHIN

'Nobody expects the Spanish Inquisition.'
– Monty Python

Life is full of surprises. Some are pleasant and others can be catastrophic. The acquisition of any impairment, be it physical, mental or social, is most definitely a surprise that can be an additional source of stress in an already stressful life. As a consequence, many of us become overwhelmed and experience an ever-tightening downward spiral of confusion and dismay. This can prevent a successful return to an even keel after such a life-changing event.

If we wish to regain some control over our lives then we have to get a grip on this stress. We have to find the answers to four crucial questions:

1. What is stress?

2. Why can it have such a negative effect?
3. How does it occur?
4. How can we deal with it?

Failure to find coherent answers can have serious consequences.

4.1 What is stress?

Stress readies us for action and has always been part of us. It enables us to be at our physical best to meet a crisis. It is the fight/flight response.

This causes the body to do the following:

- Raise heart rate to increase blood flow to the muscles.
- Increase respiration to flood the blood with oxygen.
- Release adrenalin to maximise awareness and reflexes.
- Dump unnecessary weight such as faeces and urine.
- Close down systems not necessary for fighting and running such as digestive, reproductive and immune systems to save energy.

In effect, stress causes the body to respond so that it is in the very best condition to fight or run. In such a situation we are at our physical optimum. This is ideal in an acute crisis where an immediate physical response is required, but can have a highly negative effect on our health if it is prolonged.

4.2 Why can it have such a negative effect?

In modern life situations tend to be long term, and an intense physical response, however tempting, is inappropriate and indeed harmful. Unfortunately evolution has betrayed us, as it has not enabled us to develop stress responses suitable for long-term situations.

The stress response we have, if prolonged, can become dangerous. We are like a long bow. When strung for action, they are superb. If left strung, they soon deteriorate and lose their power. If we remain 'strung' for too long then we too can deteriorate to an alarming degree. These are just a few of the dangerous responses:

- Constantly elevated heart rate can lead to high blood pressure, damage to the heart, vascular system and some organs.
- Increased respiration can lead to long-term damage to the lungs.
- Constant adrenalin results in the production of toxins and hyperactivity, which is both exhausting and socially unacceptable.
- Closing down the digestive system prevents any food being used effectively and can lead

to damage or problems with the stomach and digestive tract.

- Closing down the immune system leaves you wide open to any infection with limited resources to fight them. This also includes the eyes.
- Closing down the reproductive system can lead to physical, emotional and mental health problems.

Even a cursory glance at the consequences of long-term stress tells us it is something to be avoided, as it is inevitable that such a catalogue of physical deficiencies must also lead to emotional, psychological and mental health issues. Ultimately they can cause illness and, in some cases, death.

It may surprise you to learn that research has found that losing your sight can cause stress. Really? Who would have thought it! What is of much greater interest is that the same research has also found that stress can both exacerbate and cause sight loss. This should not really be a surprise. Being mindful of the catalogue of woes accompanying chronic stress, it would be a little naïve to think that the eyes get a free ride.

4.3 How does it occur?

Modern stress occurs because events overwhelm

people. This happens because they believe one or all of the following:

- They have too much to do.
- Too little time to do it.
- They can see no way through a stressful situation.
- Something has happened which is too enormous.
- The thing cannot be comprehended at any level.

The overwhelm is frequently characterised by feelings of helplessness and dismay, bordering on despair. There is also a general feeling of not being able to cope.

4.4 How can we deal with it?

Here the critical element is belief. By that I mean belief in what resources are available, and in the size or complexity of the task. What we believe about these two things presents us with a clear route to tackle the stress concerned. We can either increase the resources available, or reduce the task to a manageable size or complexity. If we don't do these things, we will be overwhelmed.

In my own case, the onset of sight loss was totally overwhelming. Coming to terms with, let alone living with, sight loss appeared to be utterly beyond any resources I could muster.

The first thing I learned was that learning to live with sight loss was a marathon and not a sprint. In other words, I could select specific elements on which to work. The task was then reduced to manageable, bite-sized chunks.

The second thing I learned was that training and practice increased my resources beyond all recognition, the result being I restored my faith in my ability to meet the demands of the task and adjusted my belief of what the task involved. This was both in terms of size and complexity. In short, I changed what I thought was possible.

To be more specific, one of the features of sight loss was a complete lack of confidence in the sense of proprioception: I had no idea where my hands were or what they were doing. This was not only stressful, as it sapped my confidence in a number of areas of activity, it also created tension with others around me. Thus a simple incapacity caused a rapid deterioration as the stress fed on itself until the problem was blown out of all proportion. I knew I had to do something.

I devised a set of exercises and practiced rigorously until I was able to renew confidence in my sense of proprioception, which enabled me to regain use of my hands. I realised these exercises were an essential part of many of the skills I needed, and practicing them restored my belief in my abilities significantly, and hence my personal resources. The exercises are described later in the book.

I realised that if we use training and practice to increase and improve our available resources, then we can get a grip on one aspect of stress. And by looking at how tasks can be broken down into bite-sized chunks we can tackle the other.

An example of how this works is learning how to use a long cane. The proper use of a long cane requires knowledge, skill and hours of practice. I broke the task down into the following bits:

- Learning the right way to hold the cane and maintain it.
- Learning the right position for the cane.
- Learning the correct arc of swing.
- Swinging the cane in step.

Once I could walk with a cane in a relatively orderly fashion, then the real work started, which was understanding what the cane was telling me. If I had tried to learn the whole thing together it would have been chaos, and seemingly impossible. Breaking it down into chunks of learning meant each chunk led to an understanding of the next. As a consequence, I was not overwhelmed.

It is important to appreciate that mastering the use of a long cane is only one part of independent mobility outside the safety of the home cave, and mobility is only a fraction of the work involved in getting to grips with sight loss.

Mastering sight loss must be viewed as tackling the many elements of daily life. To put it more simply, we are all used to breaking life down into smaller chunks. This is nothing new, but with sight loss we just have to do it more consciously. If we do this, we can manage our belief in our abilities and the task itself. The question remains, however: How do we fight our way clear of the irrationality and chaos caused by stress in the first place? The answer is devastatingly simple.

4.5 Starting the removal of stress

Whenever we start thinking "This is all too much", "I can't hack this" or anything similar, it is time to find someone to talk to. The simple act of talking about the problem and your feelings about it is hugely beneficial for the following reasons:

- It helps put things in perspective.
- It introduces an air of calmness and rationality.

- It allows space to unpick things.
- It will result in a restoration of your belief in yourself and the resources available.

Stress will destroy you if you allow it. It can cause you to give up and lose any hope of coping. That must be avoided as there is only one outcome to that. Being embarrassed about talking to someone is not an option. There is far too much at stake.

There are medical solutions, but these can only be short term. It seems to me that nonmedical interventions are far more effective. It boils down, in the end, to getting things in perspective and believing in yourself.

4.6 The importance of perspective

The value of achieving a sense of perspective cannot be overstated. For me that moment came when I walked into Blind Veterans the first time. Not only was I met with warmth and good humour, and ex-servicemen joshing each other because they could not see, I also learned about perspective. Hearing of a teenage soldier losing limbs as well as being blinded was sobering. Learning he was getting on with his life without complaint was humbling. It made me realise that my sight loss was just not worth moaning about.

I also came to appreciate that I was not alone. The matter-of-fact approach of the staff allowed me to realise there was no need for drama, and the prospect of training restored my optimism. This enabled me to examine my situation in a more rational and thoughtful manner. The never-ending downward spiral of despair and gloom was halted in its tracks, which reduced my stress concerning my impending blindness considerably.

There was nothing mysterious or complicated about this, it was just a new perspective, and it changed everything. This could also work for anyone else. In short, stop the panic and get a handle on what is happening.

4.7 Additional internal resources

There is also another way in which the chaos and stress of the onset of sight loss can be managed. Support, training and talking to other people is immensely helpful. There comes a time, however, when you are left alone with your thoughts and sight loss. It is one thing to be brave in a crowd and quite another when alone in the wee small hours. This can be terrifying if you allow it.

I found that one of the most helpful tactics to control the headlong ride into the unknown and sense of isolation was to devise a set of rules which would keep me grounded. They would also provide a central and consistent point to which I could return. These rules of engagement are listed at the beginning of the book and are discussed in detail in the next chapter.

Once when I was explaining stress to a class, one of the students made what I thought was an important comment: "So you're saying stress is all in the head?" When you think about that it tells us one very important thing. It tells us that just as stress is in our head, then the solution to it lies within us too. All we need is to find the way to deal with it. Knowing there is a way out, even if you do not think there is just at this moment, has to be the most important step of all.

CHAPTER FIVE

RULES OF ENGAGEMENT

'Rules are for the obedience of fools and the guidance of wise men.'

– **Douglas Bader**

Life-changing events involving loss and change occur for everyone. These events are often accompanied by a period of intense emotions, irrationality and mental chaos. Sometimes the individuals involved feel they are losing their mind. The associated turmoil is not a comfortable experience, and medication, talking therapies, or a combination of both may be used to help people find their way.

Clearly talking about feelings and accepting them helps to make sense of the new situation. There is, however, an internal resource which can help to restore some order in a chaotic situation. This is the formulation of and adherence to a set of rules of engagement. These rules can be anything you like provided they are:

- Relevant
- Have meaning for you
- Are achievable
- Are clear
- Are few enough to remember and act upon

Creating the rules was not any kind of prescience on my part: the effects of life-changing events are well known and predictable. As a former social worker it would have been shameful if I had been unaware of them.

On being informed I was going to lose my sight everything changed. I knew I was going to have to completely restructure my life in terms of relationships, leisure pursuits, getting about, in fact most aspects of living. It was going to be chaotic, mentally, emotionally and practically. It was clear I would need some structure to help keep me stable. I needed to create a reliable centre to which I could return and remain grounded. The ten rules I devised, some of which are conceptual whilst others are behavioural, are as follows:

Rule 1. Accept your situation

Acceptance means recognising sight loss is actually happening, and that means not ignoring it in the hope it will go away. Acceptance does not have to involve being manically cheerful. But giving way to self-indulgent misery is not the answer either. Full acceptance may, and most likely will be, a work in progress throughout life. Do not expect it to be easy or even inevitable. Up and down the land there are many people with sight loss who have failed to accept it and move on. Without acceptance nothing else can happen with respect to regaining a normal life. Even now I will finish a task, go to move away and be utterly shocked that I cannot see.

Rule 2. Treat obstacles as an opportunity to improvise, adapt and overcome

This is an unashamed steal of the idea of the power of positive thinking. Regarding problems as the opportunity to find solutions is, I have found, a good way to boost yourself and diminish the obstacle. The phrase 'improvise, adapt and overcome' is a pretty clear mandate to reduce obstacles to their rightful place: something to be dealt with and not allowed to run amok in your life. It is also a familiar mantra to anyone who has undergone basic military training.

Rule 3. Learn or improve a skill every day

This acts as a reminder that the battle to live

with sight loss is a marathon and not a sprint. It is vital that some momentum is maintained, and this includes every aspect of life. When you feel overwhelmed by the enormity of the task, looking at what you can do in comparison to a few weeks ago will restore your motivation to keep improving.

At times it may seem you are banging your head against a brick wall and making no progress. Then one day the penny drops and what you have been trying to learn is ridiculously easy. A good example is acquiring keyboard skills. If someone had told me that I would be happily typing when totally blind I would have thought they were crazy. But here I am, doing exactly that.

Rule 4. Listen carefully, judge slowly, condemn rarely

This is a reminder that with the inability to read non-verbal communication our communication skills are altered drastically. We have to listen harder, assess what is being said more carefully, and be cautious about the conclusions we draw. We must take a more considered and thoughtful approach to our interactions with others. This will be covered at some length later in the book.

Hearing is something we tend to ignore when we can see. Now we have to learn to listen properly for the first time in our lives. We also need to be aware that learning to use other senses when we have been reliant on sight has to be worked at actively. For now, just be aware that our ears are now our eyes. As a consequence of this we are operating on less than a tenth of the information to which we are used.

Rule 5. Your impairment is nothing to be ashamed of

Do not be embarrassed about being blind. Do not feel it is due to some failing in yourself. It happens to far more people than you could ever appreciate. If you feel you are being judged, remember people are too busy with their own affairs to be watching or judging us. If after that you still suspect they are, then consider how well they would cope with sight loss.

Remember that no one is perfect. If they think they are, that in itself is an imperfection!

Rule 6. Get organised

Have a place for everything. This is simple pragmatism. Without sight there is so much we have to remember and any trick or strategy to make life easier should be used. Make sure you know exactly where everything you use is kept. Further to this, make sure the people you live with know that items have to stay in a certain place and not to move them. Ensure people are aware that removal or relocating even a single item can cause our world to become even more chaotic. To be more precise, know the location of everything that affects you, and try to be as consistent as possible with your belongings, and therefore limit how much you have to remember. Even though it is a pain, continually remind people to not move anything. They don't have to remember things the way we now do.

Rule 7. The broken glass principle

The broken glass principle comes from the action you would take if you saw a broken bottle on a beach: you would pick it up immediately to prevent injury. I try to use this principle in the sense that if I come across something that needs doing – like putting a pair of shoes safely to one side – then I will do it immediately.

Just be aware that without sight we do not have the constant reminder provided by our seeing something. It is this simple fact that makes us appear as if our memory is failing. People can become entrenched in the idea of your failing memory that it is all too easy to collude with it. You do not have to accept any explanation that is thrust on you.

Rule 8. Ask for help

Remember, we are the one with the problem. We can be fiercely independent and insist on doing everything without help, in which case good luck (!); or we can be sensible and negotiate for the use of someone else's eyes when we need sight to do something. I feel this is so important as it is a recurring daily theme.

If we are to leave our snug and secure cave and venture back into the real world, we have to rely on other people. You will find that many people are only too pleased to offer help. As someone once commented, "The miserable sods who do not want to help you will not see anyway." (Actually he wasn't as polite as that, but the point is made!) Asking for and refusing help is never really talked about. In this book a whole chapter is devoted to it.

Rule 9. Check everything and go at your own pace

Rushing plus blindness equals chaos. We must check and check again whenever we do anything. And as a quick visual check is no longer possible, we have to be meticulous in physically checking our immediate environment with our hands. To begin with you will be very slow at tasks, but under no circumstances should you allow others to rush you, as therein lies disaster, and disaster will provide an excuse for others to deny you the opportunity to do anything for yourself. The reason will be given as health and safety. The real reason is that they do not want you bumbling about and threatening their peace of mind and chattels!

Rule 10. Do not be offended by references to sight

Phrases such as, "Look at the colour of that sky!" or "Do you see what I mean?" are an integral part of language and people cannot help using them. People do become dreadfully embarrassed, however, and it is down to us to reassure them. The bottom line is very simple: we cannot expect people to change the linguistic habits of a lifetime. However, if someone is giving you directions and they tell you to turn left at the red door, then we have every right to pull them up. I usually do this by holding up my cane and repeating "*Red* door..." with the emphasis fully on red. This often leads to a fairly positive conversation about the limitations of your sight. You then get more useable instructions.

Summary of the rules

These rules were formulated to deal with my sight loss. But the principle of trying to create order out of chaos clearly applies across the board. They are also a fit for how things are now for me. When things change, including my own abilities, it may be necessary to review the rules to see if they are still fit for purpose.

Remember that the rules are for your guidance and not your domination. They are there to help you find your way, not to tell you what to do. Remember the quote at the start that 'rules are for the direction of fools and the guidance of the wise.'

After a number of years of severe sight loss initially, and then blindness, it seems there is one fundamental rule that informs the rest. This overriding rule, or one to rule them all and in the darkness bind them, is, of course, learn to be patient. Patience, we are told, is a virtue. Perhaps that is why I find it so difficult!

Anyone who has an impairment is, by definition, physically inferior to those without. I feel this applies as much to sight loss as any other disability or impairment. Unfortunately it seems that this inferiority is extended to the entire person by a substantial minority of people. Thus we have the somewhat vexing experience of being treated as deaf or imbeciles or both.

A recent investigation of the Department of Work and Pensions by the BBC's Panorama programme (13 March 2020) found that this attitude towards staff with handicaps, disabilities or impairments was pretty extensive – and appalling. They failed consistently to take any notice of their own occupational health department's recommendations and lost thirteen percent of cases brought against them under anti-discrimination legislation. (Typically, only three percent of cases succeed.)

We are expected to put up with being treated as dunderheads. When someone asks us to wait, as we cannot see what they are doing it seems like an age. Everything we do has to be relearned from scratch, and almost every aspect of our lives requires enormous patience.

To my mind patience is the glue that gives meaning and feasibility to the other rules. It also stops us from alienating ourselves from those who are so willing to help us. It is certainly essential if we are ever to accept our situation, and this is discussed in the next chapter. (Appendix Five outlines further rules of engagement.)

CHAPTER SIX

THE TOTALITY OF SIGHT LOSS

'Not being able to see is
only a tiny part of sight loss'
– Author, 2019

When you lose your sight the world stops. The panic and despair is palpable. For many of us there is no support, no information, and no encouragement. It is as if we have been cast adrift in a sinking boat with no coast in sight.

We have, at this point, a choice. We can cry and get nowhere, or we can laugh, climb back on our feet and fight. But think about these two things. First, if we just cry there is going to be no change and, second, as far as I know nobody has died by getting a grip on sight loss.

Not being able to see is only a small part of vision loss and blindness, and until it happens to you there is no appreciation of how it affects every single aspect of your life. It is a no-brainer that losing your sight is going to be emotional, psychologically wearing, and possibly there will be a curtailment of life opportunities. But there seems to be no comprehension of the sometimes frightening physical affects, social implications, or psychological events.

In this chapter I look at the various aspects of sight loss as I found it. As losing your sight is a highly personal experience, it is possible that people do not have (or will not have) all the effects as described. It is also true that there are other aspects that have been endured by others and not by me.

What we do have in common is the need to engage with all these different aspects of the condition. We may not want to do this, but ignoring it will not cut it. Information is power, and the more we learn about and get to grips with our sight loss the greater the chance of managing it. Knowing about, managing and engaging with sight loss are the keys to regaining our lives. This is not only possible, it is perfectly doable. Therefore what follows is a non-exhaustive list of what may accompany the onset of losing your sight, followed by a summary.

6.1 Physical dimension

6.1.01 Not being able to see

This seems rather obvious but is easily overlooked. Most people appear to have a dread of losing their sight and when they meet someone who cannot see it is almost as if they deny or ignore it. It seems as if it is too horrific to contemplate or admit to its existence. I have found that the idea of total sight loss is something that those with sight, with the best will in the world, cannot comprehend at all.

People will ask me what I can see. I tell them absolutely nothing. They respond that I must be able to distinguish between light and dark. It invariably ends up with me asking what part of blindness they do not get.

I have to fight this particular battle almost on a daily basis. People insist on referring to me as sight impaired. My sight is not impaired, it is totally absent. I am blind. People cannot seem to get this into their heads.

6.1.02 Balance is adversely affected

Again, obvious when you stop to think. We are used to our eyes confirming what our ears are telling us about balance. When we can no longer see we lose confidence in what our ears are telling us.

Fortunately, the majority of balance returns after a few months. However, this is not without taking our courage in both hands to practice hard to get it back.

I feel this is something that has to be worked at actively. Some of the exercises you can do to achieve this are outlined in the next chapter. Like so many other aspects of sight loss, only our efforts will provide a way forward.

6.1.03 Loss of spatial awareness

This will vary according to the severity of the sight loss. Being completely blind, I find that there is some spatial awareness from sound provided there is no other noise masking audio feedback. You very quickly learn to use echoes to help define the space around you. It takes practice to get the basics and years to get good at it. Initially, on the whole, not a great deal of use really, so I apologise about that!

6.1.04 Proprioception is affected

Just to remind you, this is the sense that tells you where each part of the body is in relation to the rest. We lose the use of this sense when we first lose our sight. This, like balance, I feel, is loss of confidence without visual confirmation.

It is still there, though, and it is possible through hard work to recover most of it, particularly in static and familiar situations.

This is such an important aspect of our physical being that I devised exercises for its restoration. Or rather, the restoration of the confidence in the sense. These are in chapter seven, 'Getting it back together again'.

6.1.05 Toll of tiredness

The tiredness is due mainly to the intense concentration needed and anxiety in dealing with unknown factors and conditions. There are other possible causes as well and they are listed below in relation to how tiredness affects me, and they may be how you feel sometimes or all of the time.

- The simplest explanation may be that being of pensionable age, I am slowing down anyway. But whilst that might play a small part, I am sure that is far from the whole story.
- Part of the cause must also lie in the intense concentration required to make sense of what is going on around me. This is in terms both of my immediate physical environment and social interactions. A lapse of concentration can be savagely punished, as I found when once turning, as I thought, into my bedroom.

I suddenly found myself flying through the air, whilst a voice from my distant past yelled: "Tuck yourself in!" Landing at the foot of the stairs all was well, until a picture fell off the wall and hit my head and then there was blood everywhere. Grabbing a towel and wrapping it round my head, I then had to reassure my wife I was OK. This incident only caused superficial injury when the picture hit my head, and the fall itself did no damage... or so I thought. It was noticeable that I was considerably less gung-ho and confident afterwards, to the point of presenting as a bumbling old man. In short, expect setbacks to shatter confidence for a while. (I have since fitted a rail across the top of my stairs!)

- In the absence of sight, learning to substitute other senses is frustrating as it requires hard work and furious mental activity to fill in the gaps. There is the belief that other senses become more acute to compensate for sight loss. If you think about it, there is no reason why they should, however. I feel it is much more likely that we pay more attention to the information they give us, and we become more in tune and aware of our surroundings. In many ways we are perceptually lazy when we can see and we ignore other information. It seems that one effective way of coping is to use the information from the other senses to visualise what is in front of us. For example, for me, sound and other information is translated into pictures in my head. We no longer have the ability to visually scan our world and thereby reassure ourselves there is no immediate danger, so we must rely on the other senses to give us clues. The effort involved is considerable, which perhaps offers an explanation for the tiredness.

- In addition to the mental effort, there is also the psychological toll of being in a constant state of anxiety. We are anxious about tripping and falling, about what is beyond our very limited horizon – in my case, my horizon is defined by my feet, hands and cane.
- It is very difficult to adopt new behaviours and not revert to previous habits that might mean we screw up and have yet another avoidable accident.
- We are also aware of the future and how we will cope as our sight fades. In the absence of actual information about what may happen, there is fear of the unknown, and the nagging thought that we will run out of courage and give up the fight, which is also very tiring.
- Yet another part of the explanation for the extreme tiredness might lie in the disruption of our daily, or diurnal, cycle. I have certainly found that my internal alarm clock seems to have disappeared, possibly because it was

dependant on the intensity of daylight to work. When you lose your sight, you no longer perceive the changes in daylight intensity and this also affects your ability to keep track of time. Sometimes this can develop into circadian rhythm disorder. One explanation for this might be that in the absence of variation in levels of light as a consequence of sight loss, the brain is fooled into thinking it is night-time, all the time. Or it may be that when we are inactive we are simply triggered into sleep. Whether this is the case or not, I have found that when inactive I close my eyes as a respite from trying to make sense of everything, and often fall fast asleep within seconds.

- Perhaps one of the more insidious sources of tiredness is the level of physical fitness. As my sight diminished, the slower I moved. This had two effects. Firstly, everything took so much longer to do. Secondly, this left less time for proper exercise. Thus my level of fitness deteriorated and this, in turn, made me feel less inclined to do anything anyway, particularly keeping fit. It therefore became a priority to achieve a balance between doing chores and maintaining fitness.

Having outlined a number of what I feel are reasonable explanations for the tiredness, I have no idea which is most likely. I suspect that there will always be a combination of factors, and that these will differ both between and within each individual.

There will be times when the situation really gets you down and you take refuge in avoidance by sleeping. Bearing in mind the enormity of sight loss, I feel this is both understandable and forgivable. The danger here, however, is that this could slide into self-indulgence – an easy route to giving up the battle to regain a normal and fulfilling life.

Interestingly, now that I have no sight at all I do not experience the same level of tiredness. I put this down to a combination of factors:

- I have become used to using other senses.
- I feel more confident in operating as a person without sight.
- There is no longer conflict between my sight and other senses.
- I have a much greater understanding of sight loss and its limitations.

In short, the tiredness eases as time passes.

6.1.06 Charles Bonnet Syndrome (CBS)

CBS is the name given to the hallucinations that can accompany sight loss. Nobody is sure about how common it is and estimates vary from seventeen to forty percent, which tells me that no one has a clue. The hallucinations occur because the part of the brain that deals with sight, the visual cortex, is no longer being stimulated to the same extent. In the absence of stimulation it will make stuff up – hallucinations.

I would surmise that people who lose their sight through brain damage will not suffer from CBS. If your sight loss is due to the malfunctioning of the eyes themselves or the optic nerve then you may experience CBS. If you do start to see things there are two important things to remember. First, you are not going mad. Second, it is harmless provided you know about it.

My own personal take on it is that as I am totally blind it is quite nice to be able to enjoy the occasional hallucination! And for those of us who have served in the forces and may have had the joy of being on sentry duty at night, you may recall seeing quite vivid images in the dark. I now know that to be CBS.

If you find CBS disconcerting or uncomfortable deploy a distraction technique. There are a number you can choose:

- Get up and make a cup of tea
- Concentrate on doing something, anything

- Rapidly move your eyes to left and right and up and down
- Get up and walk about

One word of warning. In spite of being discovered in the seventeenth century in Switzerland, CBS only became known in this country in 1984. Very few people know about it and until recently it was treated with anti-hallucinatory drugs.

I find CBS quite fascinating and could rabbit on about it quite happily. I will spare you that, though! If you want to find out more, Wikipedia has quite a good article on the subject.

6.1.07 Danger of falling and collision

This might seem obvious, but must be considered. If you venture out, there are a number of scenarios which can make life interesting, and pavement hazards can include:

- Advertising boards
- Traffic signs and cones
- Vehicles parked on the pavement
- Ladders
- Pushchairs and prams
- Kids on bikes
- Steps and kerbs
- Potholes and loose paving slabs
- Post boxes and lamp posts

- Waste bins and other rubbish
- Not forgetting the ubiquitous obeseycles which often have a tendency to charge up and down pavements with little or no regard for others

All these need to be anticipated and tackled with care. There is certainly no point in getting upset about any of them.

The greater the unfamiliarity of the environment, the greater the chance of a mishap. Firstly, consider how to learn not to fall, and secondly, how to fall safely. Learn, also, how to move defensively. This is covered later on in the book.

6.1.08 Torpor and lack of motivation

Sight loss is depressing. That is a no-brainer. It is what you do about it that is important. Try not to be overwhelmed by it, and make a deliberate effort to do something positive every day, something you enjoy doing, instead of giving in to it.

6.1.09 No hand-eye coordination

This is again obvious, but easily overlooked. A consequence of this is that others will most likely try and stop you doing things, thereby denying the opportunity to relearn old skills, let alone new ones.

6.1.10 Difficulty in walking in a straight line

Without being able to see a fixed point to steer by it is almost impossible to make the small and continuous alterations that keep you on a straight line. Learn to use features on the ground that become familiar, and use the sun, when it is out, to help maintain your direction. It might sound strange, but keeping your nose straight and following it can also help to a limited degree. Yet another problem is that there is no way of knowing how far you have deviated off course when turning a corner. Quite literally squaring a corner in your mind can be helpful here.

6.1.11 Having to slow down

Initially there will be a desire to try and do things at normal speed. After a few disasters however you will find that if you slow right down you can start the process of relearning old skills with success. Preparation is everything in this respect, and the time taken to clear the immediate area of non-essentials pays dividends in less collateral damage and having to come up with credible explanations to placate your nearest and dearest.

6.1.12 Frequent minor injuries

Unfortunately, if you are going to be active, this goes with the territory. As your mobility and defensive skills improve, however, the incidents of injuries diminish.

6.2 The social dimension

There are many social implications to consider and, depending on our personality and determination to be reincluded in the pack, these will have an effect to a lesser or greater degree. The main elements are as follows:

6.2.01 Communication skills

Reliance on sound and touch in combination with lack of eye contact and other vital non-verbal communication means that sight loss requires relearning of communication skills. There is an entire chapter devoted to this later on.

6.2.02 Social assessment

Assessing other people, and therefore creating predictable and safe encounters, requires much use of non-verbal communication, or NVC as

I will now refer to it. This process begins the moment we see the person to whom we are going to talk, which disappears with sight loss. Any comparison with the projected image and performance of an individual is impossible, or at least extremely difficult, as we don't know for sure whether their body language matches their language.

6.2.03 Social awkwardness

Not being able to use or respond to NVC in the usual way makes people feel something is not quite right when they talk to us. This can be reduced considerably if we make a deliberate effort to maintain eye contact with whoever is talking to us. There is also the problem that people seem to find any impairment embarrassing, almost as if they are afraid they are going to be involved in some dreadful scene which is out of their control.

6.2.04 Overprotection

There appears to be the belief that if you have an impairment you are also helpless, not to say deaf and daft as well. This, to say the least, is annoying but has to be endured to a degree as there are always going to be times when we will need help. It is possible, too, that the overprotectiveness is not only to protect the person with the impairment, but also their own goods and chattels.

6.2.05 Denial of opportunity

Along with overprotectiveness is the attempt by others to prevent us from doing things. In other words, there is little recognition that our world has totally changed and that we need to engage with it, which includes learning by making mistakes. Mistakes are, unfortunately, regarded as justification for both over protectiveness and denial of opportunities.

6.2.06 Expectations of others

Other people will have certain expectations about how those with sight loss should behave. I have lost count of the times someone has said to me that as I am blind I should not be doing whatever it is I am doing. My response is to thank them for reminding me that, although I am blind, I am completely content doing whatever it is. Whilst recognising the concern of others, it is not their business, and sometimes concern spills over into interference and breach of privacy.

6.2.07 Frustration

It is often the case that we cannot do things we could before our loss of sight and, as a consequence, experience almost constant feelings of frustration. Sight loss de-skills us, so we have to relearn to do practically everything. We must be aware of this frustration and not allow it to influence our behaviour towards others. Our frustration is our problem; it is unproductive to try and make it someone else's.

6.2.08 Responses of others

It is quite amazing how dismissive and brusque people can be when you are attempting to relearn an old skill. To begin with, to avoid disaster, everything must be carried out almost in slow motion. This is frustrating for the person with sight loss, and drives onlookers to the point of tearing their hair out!

Insist on working at your own speed. The pressure of others and your own pride may well tempt you to work faster than you can manage. At all costs avoid this, as the resulting shambles will destroy any confidence in your newly re-acquired skill and serve to confirm the view that you are incompetent.

6.2.09 Audience affect

Be aware that the mere presence of others can affect how you perform, which is referred to as 'audience affect'. When we lose our sight we are under constant scrutiny by others who might sadly be looking for us to fail, which in itself can influence our performance. In effect we have to put the audience out of our minds and do our own thing at our own speed.

6.2.10 Requesting and refusing help

This will be covered at length in chapter thirteen, 'Help, the poison chalice'. Requesting and refusing help is a skill that very much involves the use of the 'I' not the 'you' message. We have to accept we are the ones responsible for what we ask not the person we are asking to help, or the person offering to help. This along with assertiveness skills is a major element in any attempt to regain our lives.

6.2.11 Embarrassment

Embarrassment is when we do not know how to behave, or what our role is, which must be overcome. Sight loss makes us stand out in a crowd and therefore can cause feelings of confusion about our role. Examine carefully why you feel this way and you will quickly realise there is nothing to be embarrassed about. It is important that you become the boss of embarrassment as it can prevent you taking up a long cane or even going out at all.

6.2.12 Relationships

We need to renegotiate relationships with peers, partners and family groups. The onset of sight loss will cause the expectations that others have of us to change, as well as our status in the group or pack. It is easy to collude with this, so conscious effort must be made to negotiate a realistic position within the pack and not allow ourselves to be side-lined.

6.2.13 The behaviour of other people

We have to understand and allow for the difficulty sighted people have with sight impairment. Some of the rather strange behaviours that people inflict upon us can be attributed to their simply not knowing how to respond to our affliction. It is down to us to understand this, not be offended, teach them about our sight loss, and generally go out of our way to make them feel comfortable with it.

6.3 Emotional aspects

Sight loss is emotional, and the emotions can be extremely powerful. We have to work hard to ensure that we are not overwhelmed by them. We also have to ensure that we prevent these emotions from influencing our relationships with other people. After all, our emotions are our problem, not theirs. Both self-discipline and self-awareness are vital here.

6.3.01 Feelings of isolation

Without the usual inclusive nods and smiles etc which make up NVC, and not being able to see other peoples' reactions, can make us feel very alone, even within a small group. We need, then, to consciously ensure we remain engaged in any encounter. Working at using eye contact with any speaker will be a great aid in remaining engaged. It is also important to remain in physical contact with the group.

6.3.02 Constant underlying anxiety

This is due to not only having no idea about what is going to happen next with our sight loss, but also due to having little or no idea about our immediate social and physical environment. We are literally perpetually riding headlong into the unknown. It is important we take this ride with some semblance of dignity and control. The trick is to ensure that the anxiety does not develop into full-blown fear. Listening carefully and judging slowly will go a long way to achieve this.

6.3.03 Feelings of rejection

This is all part of feeling incomplete and therefore unattractive, which probably isn't true, but the feeling is still there and needs to be recognised. It is only too easy to overcompensate and present as needy.

6.3.04 Emotions involved in loss and change

These can include anger, fear, confusion and grief, and need to be recognised and worked on in order to achieve acceptance of our sight loss and a subsequent moving on. This also has a significant influence on being accepted and social inclusion. This is addressed in chapter ten, 'Loss, change and relationships'.

6.2.05 Readjustment of relationships

It's easy to collude with our family's or partner's or friends' changed view of us, but this must be resisted. It is important to appreciate that you are not the only person affected by your loss of sight, and that adjustments will be made. Other people have to learn how to cope with new feelings as well as coping with the differences in you.

6.3.06 Possible lack of respect for self

This must be resisted too. Dwell on positives rather than negatives and regularly review your progress. Try and keep notes on your sight loss as this will help with keeping a sense of perspective. With only minimal effort you will be stunned at the progress you can make. This should be used to spur you on to greater efforts and to enhance your self-respect.

6.3.07 Loss of confidence

This goes with the territory, but it does not have to be permanent. Training and practice and realistic goal-setting will restore confidence in time. Initially any skills re-acquisition has to be in baby steps. And don't forget: failure is merely a step on the path to success.

6.3.08 Gratitude burnout

We are in the curious position of being offered assistance constantly, whether we want or need it, and there are times when it is hard to show the acceptable level of gratitude as help crosses the line into interference. The desire to snap at people must be resisted, though, as a moment of churlishness or ill temper could cause all help to evaporate. Sometimes we get to the point where we wish people would not offer to help so we have to express gratitude, which sounds awful but true. It's important to get a grip as it's inappropriate to yell at someone who only wishes to help. I have seen this and it is very ugly indeed.

6.3.09 Resentment

This also goes with the territory, and can be countered by appreciating positives rather than dwelling on negatives. Remember that whilst others can still do what we used to do, none of them can do what we have relearned to do on a daily basis. It is good to look back with pleasure on the things we used to be able to do. It is also important to appreciate and glory in what we have relearned to do.

6.3.10 Self-pity

This must be treated in the same way as resentment. Also appreciate that all of us are unique individuals with a unique set of skills and talents which, if we choose, can add richness and meaning to the new reality of our lives. Losing your sight does not mean you have lost who you are. It just takes a little effort to find yourself again.

6.3.11 Feelings of despair and hopelessness

This is an obvious result of sight loss, but need not be permanent. It is perfectly reasonable to wake up each day in a state of despair because we are blind. It's what happens in the rest of the day that really matters. With the right frame of mind it is not that hard to find positive and joyful things in our lives. It does not have to be earth-shattering or monumental. The company of friends, birds singing in the garden, a cup of tea in your hand, or the sun on your face all have the ability to make life feel good. Remember that a great deal of sight loss is your attitude or state of mind.

6.4 Psychological implications

With vision loss we have a reliance on the goodwill of others and live in a constant state of supplication. This has many implications for how we behave and present ourselves in public. It is a huge and never-ending burden to which we have to become accustomed very quickly.

This implies that we have need to carry out psychological housekeeping tasks. Sometimes these tasks are obvious and sometimes they are not, but they are always hard work and require a high level of internal honesty. The main ones are outlined below.

6.4.01 Redefinition of self

We have to redefine ourselves. The acceptance of ourselves on the basis of what we can do now and not on what we could once do is a very necessary part of acceptance and moving on. Remember that whilst we may have to relearn everything, this does not mean we lose our knowledge and experience.

6.4.02 Maintaining self-confidence

We must attempt to maintain self-confidence. This can be problematic, but increasing competence through training and diligent practice will take you far on the path back to a normal life. It is important to constantly seek opportunities to achieve. It can be an endless battle to counter the feelings of uselessness. One way to address this is to regularly add to your repertoire of skills and review your progress.

6.4.03 Attribution

We will experience difficulty attributing

values and motives etc to others. This is largely due to the limitations imposed by sight loss on the benefits of NVC. Careful listening and considered judgement will address this in some measure.

6.4.04 Maintenance of status

We may have difficulty maintaining our position in our peer group. Being blind or sight impaired does not mean we have to put up with ignorant behaviour by others or accept being treated as deaf or daft. Not being able to see makes no difference to the quality of our contribution in social activities. This is addressed in some measure in chapter twenty-two, 'Disabled or disenabled?'

6.4.05 Acceptance

We have great difficulty in accepting our sight loss. There is no denying the psychological impact of sight loss. Expect this to be a life-long task that requires an inner strength, on high days and low days, that perhaps we didn't realise we had. This is a recurring theme throughout the book.

6.5 Mental health implications

The knowledge that you are going to lose your sight is enough to make anyone feel depressed. Talking to other people will go a long way to preventing the development of full blown depression and help you to accept it. Membership of a support group will be instrumental in helping you establish a sense of perspective. It will also reduce the sense of isolation which can so easily develop into loneliness. The following aspects may have to be considered:

6.5.01 Depression

If you find yourself in a state where you have no motivation to do anything or you cannot account for lost hours in the day, it may be that you have become depressed. It is vital that you talk about this and seek help.

This is as much for the carers as anyone else. After all, if you are depressed you are unlikely to either recognise or do anything about it, which relates to reactive depression. It is also sometimes triggered by chemical changes in the brain caused by your inability to track time by the intensity of light, which can sometimes develop into circadian rhythm disorder.

6.5.02 Stress

As discussed in the chapter 'Stress – the enemy within', stress will not help you meet the everyday challenges of managing and overcoming sight loss. Again, it is important to talk about this and ask for and accept help when you start to feel overwhelmed. As there is evidence that stress can exacerbate or even cause sight loss this is particularly important.

6.5.03 Acceptance

Developing and sustaining an acceptance of your condition is vital. Without this there is no moving on, and without moving on you will end up stuck in the cul-de-sac of sight loss without hope or joy.

6.5.04 Paranoia

There is a possibility of the development of paranoiac tendencies. When you cannot see it is easy to believe others are talking about you. Firstly, if they are you will soon learn about it and realise they were not being derogatory. Secondly, do not assume you are that important anyway!

6.5.05 Social withdrawal

Withdrawal from society may lead to agoraphobia or sociophobia, and is not healthy or helpful to you or those who love you. There is plenty of support and genuine willingness available to share the burden of sight loss. Do not let fear or pride turn you into a hermit. Get a grip and rejoin the human race.

6.6 General decline

General mental, cognitive and physical decline may happen if you let sight loss overwhelm you. The choice is yours to stay physically and mentally fit by engaging in activities like yoga and joining other social groups. It is important to remain as active as you can socially, cognitively and physically. Being blind and fighting to reclaim our life takes an enormous amount of emotional, psychological and physical strength. It is therefore important we take every measure we can to maintain our general health, and this includes a proper diet, regular exercise, regular sleep and mental stimulation which can be achieved by relearning old skills and acquiring new.

Summary

Sight loss profoundly affects us as a whole person, not just our eyes. Not being able to see is often the easiest part of sight loss with which to deal. It is the other bits that make it so challenging. I cannot emphasise enough how important it is to talk about what is happening and how you are being affected. Only then can you receive the help you need to turn sight loss into the adventure it can be.

People are in the habit of telling me I am amazing in the way I cope with my sight loss. There is no secret or trick to coping. Like anything else worthwhile, you have to work for it. I accept that my background and training have been significant factors in my success in getting a grip on sight loss. In the end, however, it comes down to a willingness to do the work after you have identified the way forward.

A consistent theme through the book is the sheer hard work involved. This is mainly in terms of mental work, firstly in getting our heads round the issues involved, and secondly maintaining constant alertness and effort.

Mind and body cannot be separated. What affects the one affects the other. If you are to deal with the mental effort required you have to be physically fit. It is for this reason that the next chapter deals with not only physical fitness but also associated matters such as balance, coordination and proprioception. In short, what you need in order to become the boss of your immediate physical world.

CHAPTER SEVEN

GETTING IT BACK TOGETHER AGAIN

'Take care of your body,
it is the only place you have to live.'

– **Jim Rohn**

The long haul to get your life back has to start somewhere. That place, I believe, is located unambiguously within ourselves. It is the relearning and mastering the simple skills of movement and control of yourself. Initially this will be regaining your sense of balance and the mindful use of your hands.

In an ideal world the role of helping you do this should fall onto the shoulders of a ROVI (Rehabilitation Officer Visually Impaired). Research by Guide Dogs for the Blind indicates that seventy percent of people who are diagnosed with sight loss receive no support for the first year. In my view that is not only appalling but also far too late. By then there could be other serious issues in addition to sight loss.

The other issues that may develop in the absence of any support are mainly psychological in terms of mental health. At the very least, unresolved issues of anger and confusion, problems with relationships, loss of confidence, low self-esteem, poor physical fitness. There could also be reactive depression which could flip over into full-blown clinical depression.

As the University of Magdeburg so grandly observed, 'Sight loss may be accompanied by stress.' Amazing! Who would have thought it!

Chronic stress, as we know, brings its own problems of ill health and vulnerability. This of course does not even address the hidden minority who have the default position of preferring to take a long swim than face sight loss. The prospect of losing your sight is frightening, and the lack of early support may be responsible for numerous concealed tragedies up and down the land which should, but never will, be added to the roll call of those with vision impairment.

All of this gives you an idea as to why you cannot afford to wait to be noticed and subsequently supported in some way. By far the wisest course is to try and help ourselves, and this self-help should, I believe, be a significant part of our life whether we receive external support or not.

Part of self-help is exercise, and the

exercises in this chapter are intended to help you rehabilitate yourself, preferably with the encouragement and support of a loved one. Failing that, there is nothing preventing two people in the same situation from supporting each other. Peer support is not only something I advocate, but is also a widely practised form of intervention in New Zealand. The exercises are split into three basic groups.

Group 1. Basic mobility, confidence-building and balance. This also includes very basic mental mapping techniques.

Group 2. These are mainly designed to restore confidence in the use of your hands, use of tools, and further work on movement and balance. The main emphasis is on recovering proprioception and balance.

Group 3. This last group is to help maintain physical fitness. They will keep you reasonably supple but will not build a huge amount of muscle. They are meant to supplement regular exercise, such as walking, not replace them. Having said that, doing these exercises on a regular basis, at least every other day, is better than doing none at all.

You may decide to work through the exercises in sequence or you may feel that you can start halfway. If you find the exercises too simplistic, just reflect that perfect and seamless performance of any task or operation comes after considerable practice, and as such should reduce the time spent practicing when trying to master a new task. Basically, they will provide you with a very simple, yet vital, toolbox of skills.

Every quest for normalcy has to start with the first step. I am continually surprised and saddened by how often folk do not seem to have the get up and go to make that step.

Before you even think about trying the exercises make sure that the conditions are such that you are almost bound to succeed. At the very minimum you need to take into account time, space, comfort, distractions and preparation.

Time

If you are going to have a helper, make sure that both of you put aside that time. There is little point in starting if your helper has to go to collect her child from school or race to another appointment in twenty minutes!

Space

Make sure that there is enough space to be

able to carry out the exercises. This may vary according to the specific exercise you are doing.

Comfort

If you are hungry and you are standing there with your stomach growling then this is less than ideal. Likewise if you want to go to the toilet. Also make sure the space you are using is neither too hot nor cold. Finally, make sure that your clothes are comfortable and your feet feel okay too, so don't wear tight shoes or socks that keep coming off!

Distractions

Two major distractions are noise and people. The telephone combines both, and it is a good idea to put your phone on silent when trying to exercise. It is also important that the space you use is not a thoroughfare and you do not have people barging in and out or passing through.

Preparation

This includes making sure all the above points are addressed. It is also important that whatever equipment you use is to hand. And finally, of course, there is the mental preparation. Talk to those around you so they know what you are doing and neither interrupt you nor discourage you. You may have to have a conversation about why you are doing these exercises. This is touched upon in chapter ten, 'Loss, change and relationships'. If appropriate, enlist their support so that they not only provide a degree of safety but also encouragement. To achieve this you will have to explain what you are doing, why you are doing it, and what you would like their role to be. On this note, it is important to establish what you mean by support.

Support

In an ideal world, support is both physical and emotional. Physical support should be where someone is there for your safety; to stop you falling but not to prop you up. And any physical help should only be given at an agreed signal. The aim should be to reduce physical intervention to the minimum. This, however, will only work if stubbornness is put aside and you ask for help in a timely manner. If you fail to do this they will not trust you and they will intervene whether you want it or not. There has to be trust.

Emotional support should be in the form of encouragement and honest feedback about how you are doing. It should also include a willingness to talk over problems and be an active part of finding solutions.

Agreeing signals for when you want someone to intervene is important as this will be vital in maintaining the line between help and interference. Having a good laugh and a joke is one thing; mockery is quite another. Make them understand that they are there to support you, not to take the mickey or knock you down with sarcastic comments. You can do enough of that on your own account; you do not need it coming from elsewhere.

It is important to note that when you move, particularly in a confined space, that you defend yourself. I have found that the basic Tai Chi warding movement is quite good for this. When you move, ideally you should have a free hand. Push the free arm out in front of you at the level of your lower ribs and bend the forearm at right angles to your elbow. Turn your palm to face you. This forms a barrier about a foot in front of you. When you move about this basic warding position prevents you from crashing into things, creating the inevitable trail of wreckage we are otherwise liable to leave behind us in the early days.

With that, let's now talk about the exercises themselves. It is important to read through them several times before commencing so that they are clear in your mind. For those caring for people with total sight loss, performing the exercises whilst blindfolded will provide some insight into our world.

7.1 Group 1 – Mobility and balance exercises

In order to carry out the first set of exercises you will need a dining chair. The chair can be with or without arms, it's your choice. The chair needs to be placed in the middle of the floor so that you can move round it. As with any endeavour, it is important you are in the right frame of mind and that you have freedom to concentrate on what you are doing.

The first step is to prepare yourself mentally for what follows. I have found that by sitting upright in the chair with my hands on my knees and taking steady breaths is very calming, so start by taking notice of the breath. Notice it is cold coming in, and warm going out. Get your breathing regular and even. At the same time clear your mind of distractions. Run over in your mind what it is you are about to do and rehearse it in your head.

This preparation applies to anything you try that is new, and ever afterwards if you are to do things mindfully. This will help you to carry out movements in a considered and careful way rather than just diving in without thought.

7.1.01 Exercise #1.1

Prepare yourself as outlined. Then:

- Sit upright in the chair.
- Stand up.
- Move slightly away from the chair so you can no longer feel it on the back of your legs.
- Stand there for a count of twenty.
- Move back so you can feel the chair.
- Carefully lower yourself back onto the chair again.
- Think about how that felt.
- Think about the problems, if any.
- Consider whether they are real and what steps you need to take to overcome them.
- When you feel ready repeat the exercise.
- This time stand for a count of thirty.
- Seat yourself again.
- Reflect and when you are ready stand up again.
- This time try and stand for a count of sixty.

For someone who has been completely deskilled and become an invalid this exercise may be the first time they have moved independently. If this is the case, this exercise needs to be repeated as many times as necessary until it is executed with ease and confidence.

You may wish to consider whether you need

assistance for the first couple of attempts. This assistance should be discarded as soon as possible.

7.1.02 Exercise #1.2

Prepare yourself as before. Then:

- Stand up and move slightly away from the chair as before.
- Stand for a couple of seconds with your feet hip width apart.
- Once this position feels comfortable and balanced, start to twist a little to each side from the waist, pivoting left and right with your arms swinging freely. This is just a small twist not a full twist.
- Continue for twenty seconds, gradually slowing down and then stopping.
- Take a few seconds to let everything settle.
- Sit down.
- Reflect on the exercise. This is the first step in countering the sense of imbalance that often accompanies sight loss.
- When ready repeat the exercise.

As before, this exercise should be repeated until you are at ease and confident with it.

7.1.03 Exercise #1.3

Start with the preparation as described above. Run through exercise #1.2 to warm up. Then:

- Stand up, touching the chair with your left hand, and walk anti-clockwise around the chair. Complete one circuit and sit down.
- Reflect on what you have just done and when ready stand up.
- Walk round the chair for two circuits.
- At the completion of the second circuit, sit down.
- Reflect again, and when ready stand up.
- This time only brush the chair gently with your fingers.
- Take your time and concentrate on walking upright and complete one circuit.
- Sit and reflect, and when ready stand up.
- Repeat the exercise, this time trying three circuits.
- At the end of three circuits rest.

Repeat the exercise until you feel completely at ease and confident with it.

7.1.04 Exercise #1.4

Prepare as before, and run through exercise #1.2 to warm up. Then:

- Stand up and walk around to the back of the chair.
- Turn so that you are facing away from the chair.
- Stand up straight and let go of the chair.
- Pause for ten seconds.
- Walk forward two paces and stop.
- Pause for ten seconds.
- Carefully turn around so you're facing the chair and walk back to it.
- Walk around the chair and sit down.

Repeat the exercise until you are at ease and confident with it.

7.1.05 Exercise #1.5

This time we are going to extend the previous exercise by walking from the back of the chair to an object or obstacle. Prepare as before and run through exercise #1.2 to warm up. Then:

- Stand up and identify an object, like a footstool or coffee table, that will act as a marker.
- Explore the obstacle, noting the angle and point at which you reached it, for instance how many steps it took to reach it. You will need this information to turn around and find the chair again.
- Return to the chair.
- Sit down and think about what you have done.
- Repeat the exercise for all four sides of the chair, locating an object or obstacle on that side and noting the angle and point where you reached it.
- This will give you four recognisable points within the room from which you can find the chair.

Repeat until you are at ease and confident with the exercise.

7.1.06 Exercise #1.6

Prepare as before and run through exercise #1.2 to warm up. Then:

- Stand up and walk from the front of the chair until you can go no further.
- Move along the wall to the right.
- Carefully find every piece of furniture, plug socket, wall hanging or other feature which will contribute to a mental map of the room.
- When you reach the corner return to the chair.
- Rest and reflect.
- When ready return to the point from which you came.
- Continue your mental mapping exercise until you find the next corner from which you can find the chair.
- Return to the chair and reflect.
- When ready continue the exercise.

After you have done a complete circuit of the room you should have a good idea of the layout and the main features within it.

This exercise, if done properly, should take at least an hour, and should be practised for many days. The point of the exercise is to get you moving confidently around the room, able to find and identify important features at will and create a map of where everything is.

In many ways these first few exercises are the first real steps towards independence and lessening the burden on your loved ones. As such the relationships will begin to change in very subtle ways. Chapter ten, 'Loss, change and relationships', covers this in more detail.

The next step is to extend this confidence of movement to the rest of the house, and this newfound freedom is addressed in chapter sixteen, 'Establishing your base'. Extending that freedom and confidence to the outside world is covered in chapter eighteen, 'Spreading your wings'.

The next set of exercises will help you regain confidence in the sense of proprioception, or knowing where your body parts, like arms and legs, are at any given time. This is crucial when it comes to relearning old skills in a new way. As before, for those caring for people with total sight loss, doing the exercises whilst blindfolded will provide some insight into our world.

7.2 Group 2 – Proprioception and balance exercises

Having talked about the difficulty we have in controlling our limbs and their activities, it seems appropriate to share some of the techniques that can be used to get things back together again in this regard.

For me, the hardest aspect of controlling my hands was to stop them flailing around like a pair of demented paddles – to the cry of "Why don't you look what you're doing!" at the time from my wife, who would then feel awful for uttering such a thing! Even after a number of years it still takes a great deal of self-discipline to move my hands gently and slowly when I am searching for something.

Normally we know exactly where we're placing our hands, even when we cannot see them. This is the sense of proprioception. There is nothing mysterious about it. We have lived with it all our lives and not really noticed it. It allows us to eat, drive a vehicle, dress ourselves and put things away without really looking at what we are doing. In order to get this sense working effectively again, I have created a series of simple exercises that do not require anything but ordinary household objects. By working on these exercises on a daily basis, if only for twenty minutes, you will be surprised how quickly your skill level will grow.

As before, before even thinking about trying to do any of the exercises it is important to feel calm and relaxed. We spend much of our time flapping about, certainly to begin with, so it's important to calm everything down to a manageable level. So before starting any exercise, sit in a comfortable but upright chair and focus on your breath, as before. Then spend some time moving your limbs and body, starting with the feet and legs and finishing with the neck and head. This is an opportunity to really get to know your body and spend focussed time on yourself. Let nothing distract you. This is your time.

As a warm-up exercise you might find it helpful to touch your index finger to your nose. Do this a few times with each hand. Then, before moving onto the exercises, spend a couple of minutes thinking about how you were able to do that. It is so important that we stop taking things for granted and start to do things mindfully. Sight loss and going into automatic pilot are poor bedfellows indeed. Once you feel calm and in touch with your body, start the exercises.

7.2.01 Exercise #2.1

- Sit comfortably in an armchair or at a table.
- Rest elbows on the arms of the chair or the table, with the forearms vertical and the fingertips of each hand pointing toward each other.
- Keeping the hands horizontal, move them toward each other until the tips of the index fingers meet. (You may find this surprisingly hard to do, so take your time until you can make them meet every time.)
- Once you have brought the index fingertips together five times in a row rest for a few minutes and think about what you have just done. When you are ready move onto the next stage.
- Adopt the same position.
- Keeping the left hand still bring the right index fingertip to the left index fingertip. Once you have managed five successful repetitions in a row stop for a minute or so.
- Repeat, but this time bring the left index finger to the right one. After five successful repetitions stop.

When you have completed the exercise successfully then you can safely conclude that your sense of proprioception is still alive and well, and it just needs a prod to restore your confidence in it. The important thing to remember is that you must work at the speed at which you are comfortable and not feel pressure to move onto the next exercise.

7.2.02 Exercise #2.2

This exercise is to build on the work carried out in exercise #2.1. You will need two coasters, or small mats, and one eggcup.

- Seat yourself comfortably at a table or work surface.
- Place the small mats or coasters on the table within easy reach in front of you, roughly half a metre or eighteen inches apart.
- Place the eggcup on the table in front of you.
- Touch the left-hand mat with your left hand, then place the eggcup on the left-hand mat with your right hand without touching your left hand.
- Remove your right hand and place in your lap.
- Pause for a count of five.
- Collect and return the eggcup to the original position in front of you with your right hand.
- Repeat this exercise five times.
- Once happy with placing and removing the eggcup on the left-hand mat, keep your left hand in place as a marker and place the

eggcup on the right-hand mat.

- Do this for five successful repetitions.
- When satisfied you can do the exercise successfully, repeat using your left hand to move the eggcup to the right-hand mat using your right hand as a marker.
- Complete five successful repetitions.
- Repeat the exercise with your left hand to the left-hand mat.
- Complete five successful repetitions.
- Seated in the same position, then place the eggcup in front of you.
- Repeat the exercise for each hand, but this time do not use the non-active hand as a marker but place it in your lap.

Before moving onto the next exercise take a moment to think about what you have achieved. Consider how those simple movements can be used in your daily life.

7.2.03 Exercise #2.3

For this exercise you need four mats or coasters, an eggcup and a table or work surface.

- Seat yourself comfortably at the table or work surface, spread the coasters in front of you in a shallow curve, with a hand's breadth between them, and number them one to four left to right in your head.

- To start, rest your left hand to the left of #1 mat. Keep your left hand where it is throughout this part of the exercise.
- Place the eggcup in the start position just in front of you and inside the curve of mats.
- With your right hand place the eggcup on #1 mat.
- Leaving the eggcup where it is bring your right hand back to the start position.
- Pause for a count of five.
- Collect the eggcup with your right hand and return it to the start position.
- Pause for a count of five.
- Repeat the exercise for #2 mat, then #3 mat, then #4 mat.
- Take a couple of minutes to think about the exercise, then repeat it.
- Using the same hands do exactly as you did before, but this time place the eggcup on the mats in the opposite order: #4, #3, #2, then #1.

When you have completed this part of the exercise repeat it, but with an important difference: the right hand rests to the right of #4 mat and the left hand is doing the work.

When you have completed the whole exercise, you may wish to try it without a hand being used as a marker. But do not consider attempting this until you are satisfied with your performance on this exercise.

So far we have worked at one level, that is horizontally. It is also important to develop skills up and down, or vertically.

7.2.04 Exercise #2.4

This is a simple and practical exercise, but should be attempted only if you can walk easily. Simply walk round your home and locate the light switches. You should find that they are at a uniform height, and that many, if not all of them, will be in a consistent position with relation to the door frame. Then practice by finding and using just one light switch at a time. Once you are satisfied you can find this one switch first time every time, move on to the others. Continue the exercise until you are satisfied that you can find all the light switches first time every time.

If you have some sight, close your eyes as you locate the switches. Despite not making much difference whether a light is on or off, if suffering from sight loss this exercise is a lesson in mapping both your house in general, and light switches specifically, thus aiding memory and coordination skills.

7.2.05 Exercise #2.5

- Go into the kitchen and stand in front of the cupboards.
- Open one of the upper level cupboard doors and remove some items from one of the shelves and put them on the work surface.
- Pause for a count of twenty.
- Put the items back on the same shelf in the same cupboard.
- Repeat for the next shelf.
- Repeat for any other shelves in the cupboard.
- As before, work at this until you are happy you can find any shelf in any cupboard with ease.

7.2.06 Exercise #2.6

This exercise involves getting things organised, as well as using your hands to identify different objects.

- Take the cutlery out of its drawer and place it in a large bowl or container.
- Return the cutlery to the drawer piece by piece.
- Ensure each piece goes into the right compartment.
- If the cutlery drawer is not compartmentalised, then this might be a good time to do it.

The idea of scrabbling around in a drawer full of knives when you cannot see has little appeal. This is why I have my cutlery drawer compartmentalised.

So far only the hands have been used. However, one of the things that makes us stand out from nearly all other species is the use of tools. The following exercises are designed to help you appreciate that tool-use is possible without sight. For example, this very account was written on a PC without a screen or sight, which demonstrates the possibility of achieving all sorts of things.

7.2.07 Exercise #2.7

You will need a thick piece of wood, nails and a hammer for this exercise – and ensure the nails are short enough so they will not go right through the wood. I suggest a ten-centimetre or four-inch thick piece of wood, with seven-centimetre or three-inch nails.

- Start by holding the point of the nail against the wood with the left hand (the right hand if you are left-handed).
- Gently hit the nail with the hammer.
- Continue hitting the nail gently until you feel confident you can hit it every time.
- Once the nail is lodged firmly in the wood

remove the left hand from the nail to hold the wood firmly and start to hit the nail harder.
- Repeat the exercise until you have either had enough or you feel you have mastered using a hammer without sight.

Another similar exercise is to use a screwdriver. This requires slightly different skills and is quite useful for adding to your repertoire.

7.2.08 Exercise #2.8

For this exercise you will need some string or wool and a pair of scissors.

- Seat yourself comfortably at a table or work surface.
- Spread a newspaper or cloth in front of you to contain the mess.
- Cut short lengths off the string or wool onto the cloth or newspaper.
- This is harder than it sounds. You will need to think about how to do it.

If you can master this it will be a useful skill for gardening, amongst other activities.

7.2.09 Exercise #2.9

For this you will require some dried pasta such as fusilli or macaroni, a pair of kitchen tongs and two bowls.

- Seat yourself comfortably at the table with two bowls in front of you.
- Put the dried pasta in one of the bowls.
- Using the tongs transfer the pasta from the one bowl to the other.
- Altering the distance and angle between the bowls, then transfer the pasta back.

All the above exercises help to develop both your skill and confidence in your proprioceptive sense. The last exercises also help with balance.

7.2.10 Exercise 2.10

- Take a plastic jug and fill it with water to within an inch of the top.
- Find somewhere suitable and practice walking up and down with the jug of water. The objective, obviously, is not to spill any!
- Once you feel confident doing that, try going around sharp corners and up and down steps or stairs.
- Once you have mastered carrying something

with one hand without spilling it, try the same exercise with a bowl of water held with both hands.

You will find this surprisingly difficult, but still achievable.

7.2.11 Exercise 2.11

This exercise is to help both balance and proprioception. Ideally it should be carried out whilst standing; but having seen people put their backs out just picking up a pencil, be sure to bend your knees and not your back when practising this exercise.

- Place some objects on the floor.
- Locate an item with your foot.
- Move the foot away and bend down to pick the object up.
- Repeat for all the objects.

Miscellaneous exercises

There are, of course, many exercises you can try to help relearn old taken-for-granted skills. One such skill could be putting a plug in a socket. This is a lot harder than you think, and the more you practice the easier it will become. The same applies to putting a key in a lock or an electric bulb in a lamp. Basically, when you come across something with which you have difficulty, put time aside to practice until it is no longer a problem.

Another skill you might find useful is to learn how to use an electronic keypad. This is made easier by the number five having a little bump on it. The bump is hard to find sometimes, but it is always there. This is essential for entering numbers like PIN numbers at cash points, for example.

As you become more confident in using your hands, it may be useful to consider simple activities that still cause difficulties. As an example, after two years of sight loss I experience no difficulty in picking up a pint glass but found door handles problematic. If you smoke, you may wish to practice lighting your cigarettes in private, on your own, before trying in public. Setting your nose on fire is not cool!

It may seem that many of the exercises are tedious, trivial and dumbed down versions of real life. All I can say is that they have helped me.

An example of this is the simple operation of making a cup of tea and carrying it upstairs. To begin with it was a struggle to find a cup, put a teabag in it, fill it from the kettle, remove the teabag and locate and add milk. There would be a huge amount of thrashing about and fumbling to complete this task. Now, using my hip as a marker against the worktop, the whole operation is carried out seamlessly. But it did not just happen, it was the product of hard work and not a little grief! And I now use a one-cup kettle, because I feel it is far safer as there is minimal risk of coming into contact with boiling water. Whilst passing through the living-room to the stairs is not without its dramas, the act of going upstairs with no sight or balance is, surprisingly, not.

There is an exercise you might like to try just for fun. It was suggested by my daughter Jaelith, so I have called it the JAE or Jae's Awful Exercise. Try laying out the standard patience card game. The hard bit is to get the columns not only straight but also evenly spaced.

Another exercise which is useful when you start cooking again is to slice an onion. Obviously peel the onion, then cut it in half and slice the halves as finely as you can manage. Use a sharp knife and use your finger as a marker. Build speed slowly otherwise you will have bits of finger in with your onion!

I once read that a skill can be defined as a collection of separate operations which come together in a single smooth performance. And in daily life, one of the operations we absolutely need to get right is the accurate use of our hands as they are the basis for so many skills. These exercises help to re-establish confidence in their use and is both enabling and empowering.

7.3 Group 3 – Maintaining fitness

Doing exercises to restore functionality is one thing. Doing them to remain fit is quite another. Just because we cannot see should not mean that we ignore other aspects of our health. Being blind is no excuse to let everything else go. As with everything else we have a choice. We can choose to do it or we can choose not to. If we decide to be fat and slovenly then that is our choice, no one else is responsible for that. Equally, it is our responsibility to not be fat and slovenly but instead to work on keeping a level of physical fitness. So how can we keep fit when blind?

We can walk regularly. Being blind is not an obstacle to that. It does take a little bit of nerve to start with though, which is covered in chapter eighteen, 'Spreading your wings'.

We can go to a gym. I have done this and it is perfectly feasible. You'll just need a trainer to talk you through the machinery and how to use it.

Or you can carry out regular exercise in the privacy of your home. I try and do this every day, but being a mere mortal I do miss odd days. The routine I use is outlined below. It took three weeks to work up from ten repetitions to sixty for each exercise, which take about half an hour.

One word of caution. If you have a cat and you are a chap do not exercise naked! Or shut the cat out, which is easier said than done when you cannot see the damn thing and they are so good at hiding!

The Geriatric Ten exercises
(rather than the Commando Seven!)

Up until my mid-seventies I used to work out with the military's Commando Seven exercises. Now in my mid-seventies, I'm not up to this, but my Geriatric Ten is a good alternative! I was surprised to find that within five weeks I could not only see the floor (in theory at least!), but I could also touch it with the back of my hands when I bent over. So have a go, and take it slowly, remembering to celebrate each small step towards your goal of physical fitness. It is more important to practice and get the exercises right, and this includes the breathing, rather than rush.

7.3.01 Exercise #3.1

- Start with your feet apart at about hip width with your arms by your side.
- Pivot gently at the hips to each side letting

your arms swing with the pivot.
- Try and relax and let everything do its own thing.

Initially ten pivots to each side will be sufficient and I have worked up to sixty. This is really as much a warm-up exercise as anything else.

7.3.02 Exercise #3.2

- Stand with your feet hip width apart and your arms by your sides. Pivot your hands so they face forwards.
- Raise both arms to the sides and reach up to touch your hands at full stretch above your head. Breathe in on this up stroke.
- Place hands horizontal but slightly apart, the left hand an inch above the right.
- Push hands down under tension to chest height. Breathe out on this down stroke.
- Stretch both arms out to the side as far back as is comfortable. Breathe in on this stretch.
- Drop arms to the side under tension. Breathe out.
- Pause and start again.

Remember to breathe in on the up and breathe out on the down, and breathe in on the stretch and breathe out on the return to the start position.

Start with ten repetitions and work up to however many you want. I usually do sixty reps. The first ten are slow and deliberate, with distinct pauses between each move. The second ten are done more quickly, with only very slight pauses between moves. The third set of ten are done as a single fluid movement with no pauses, not even between each repetition.

This exercise is good for coordination as you have to think quite hard to keep the breathing synchronised.

Do not try the fluid movement until you have got the breathing properly synchronised with the movements.

7.3.03 Exercise #3.3

- Shake both legs and arms out then stand still.
- Stand with your feet apart with your hands by your sides.
- Slowly turn your head to the left as far as it will go.
- Pause.
- Slowly drop your head and pretend you are shaping a smile with your chin across your chest until your head is as far to the right as it will go and lift your chin.
- Pause.
- Repeat the move back to the left.
- Pause.

- Repeat the whole exercise.

Breathe out when your chin is moving down and in when it is coming up.

It is important that you do not force the neck beyond what is comfortable.

To begin with you may have to hold onto something as this can disrupt your balance, but try and get to the point of not having to hold on as soon as possible.

7.3.04 Exercise #3.4

- Stand with your feet hip-width apart.
- Place your hands on your thighs.
- Slowly bend forward as far as you can, sliding your hands down your legs.
- Go as far as your hamstrings will let you.
- Pause.
- Slightly bend your knees and return to an upright position
- Pause.
- Repeat.

In time you should be able to bend further, but do not force anything.

Breathe out on the down and in on the up. Try and go a little further with each repetition.

I find that after about twenty reps I can touch the floor reasonably easily.

This will vary for different people, and some people may never get to that point. That is not important; what is important is that your hamstrings get a good stretch and your stomach, thigh and back muscles get a good working.

If you have lower back problems you can modify this exercise by bending you knees whilst bending down and standing up.

7.3.5 Exercise #3.5

- Stand with your feet hip-width apart with your hands by your side.
- Breathe in.
- Lean as far as you can to the left, allowing your hand to travel down your left leg, breathing out as you lean.
- Pause.
- Return to the vertical, breathing in as you go.
- Pause.
- Repeat as many times as you wish and then do the same exercise to the right.
- Finish off by slowly going left to right alternatively.
- Breathe out on the down and in on the up stroke.

7.3.06 Exercise #3.6

- Stand with your feet hip-width apart.

- Raise your arms to chest height with your fingertips meeting in the middle.
- Breathe in.
- Stretch arms to the side as far back as possible, breathing out as you go.
- Pause.
- Bring hands back to the middle, breathing in as you go.
- Pause.
- Repeat the exercise.

Remember to breathe out on the stretch and in on the return.

7.3.07 Exercise #3.7

- Stand with your feet hip-width apart.
- Put your hands on your thighs.
- Breathe in.
- Slowly lower yourself into the squat position. Go down as far as possible, breathing out as you go.
- Hold the position for a couple of seconds.
- Return to standing position, breathing in as you go.
- Pause.
- Repeat.

It is important that this exercise is done slowly and under control, and remember to breathe out going down and in when coming up. Try and increase the depth of the squat as your practice this. Gently does it. Do not force anything.

7.3.08 Exercise #3.8

- Move to a door or wardrobe and stand in front of it.
- Make contact with it with one hand to maintain balance.
- Standing on your right foot raise the heel of your left foot, being sure to keep the toes on the ground.
- Do this slowly and deliberately a number of times, breathing in on the up stroke and out on the down.
- Standing on your left leg, repeat for the right foot.
- Once both feet have been done stand back on the right leg, and keeping the heel on the ground raise your left toes off the ground. Do this a number of times.
- Put your weight back on your left leg and repeat for the right foot, still supporting your balance by keeping a hand on the door or wardrobe.
- After you have completed the toe lifts, lift your left foot off the ground and rotate the ankle clockwise and then anti-clockwise. Repeat for right foot.

- At the end gently shake each leg for a little while.

Apart from what you can feel in terms of stretching your calf muscles, this simple exercise pumps any fluid from the ankles back into the calves where it belongs.

7.3.09 Exercise #3.9

- Stand with your feet hip-width apart.
- Pivot your body to the left and then to the right. This is the same exercise with which we started, with one difference.
- As you pivot to the left raise your left arm bent at the elbow so that your forearm forms a guard or block in front of you at chest height. At the same time bend your right arm so that it forms a guard at the level of your stomach.
- Pause.
- As you start to return from the pivot to the middle position move your left arm level with your stomach, and raise your right arm in the guard or block position at chest height.
- Pause.
- Return to the middle and rest.
- Try to breathe in as you move from the middle to the pivot and breathe out on the return to the middle.

This is an exercise for mindfulness and coordination as much as anything else, but it takes practise to get it right. It is essential it is done very slowly, otherwise you may hyperventilate! Repeat the exercise as often as you wish.

7.3.10 Exercise #3.10

- Walk on the spot for a minute or so, swinging your arms to chest height.
- Slow down and come to a gentle stop.
- Pause for a few seconds.
- Stand with your feet apart.
- Shake out each leg.
- Shake out each arm.
- Gently roll your shoulders.
- Stand and listen to your breathing for a minute or so, and then stop.

These exercises work every part of your body. They need to be done mindfully, slowly, and if possible gracefully. Pay particular attention to your breathing. This routine is good for not only exercising your body but also your brain and mind. As your breathing becomes more controlled your mind calms down.

It does not matter how many repetitions you do so long as you do the same number of reps for each exercise. The goal should be to increase the reps over time.

With the walking on the spot exercise, you can build this up from maybe ten repetitions to up to sixty, which is a good workout. All of the exercises strengthen your core and improve your balance and coordination.

Before leaving this chapter on exercise there is one activity which is both very helpful and accessible. I was invited to a yoga in the dark session as part of raising awareness of sight loss. Contrary to my preconception, this did not revolve around sweat and contortion but proved to be a relatively gentle event, and was extremely useful for enhancing general proprioception. It was also very good for balance. This event demonstrated that it is possible to enjoy a yoga practice with others even when blind. Yoga is not only helpful and influential in dealing with my blindness, it has also become a part of my life. The benefits are quite astonishing, particularly for proprioception and feeling calmer in myself.

It should be noted, however, that yoga instructors are a little like spuds or carrots – they come in many shapes, sizes and varieties! Therefore, you need to choose your yoga class with care, as there is no point in going to a 'body beautiful' class when what you need is a session of gentle, restorative yoga. It is also important that the teacher really appreciates the extra level of description needed for those of us with sight loss or blindness.

Since my first yoga class there have been successful armchair yoga sessions carried out with groups of blind veterans. Blind Veterans UK works with present and past members of the armed forces who are severely sight impaired or blind. The feedback indicated that they all felt the same benefits as I did.

I also had the opportunity to try Tai Chi, which is a very gentle form of martial art. In many ways it is similar to yoga as the emphasis is on breathing and mindful movements. Any gathering of energy is done on the in breath and its expenditure is on the out. (Called the yin and the yang.) The Argentinian rugby team consciously use this practice to maximise power. As the movements in this form of martial art are incredibly slow, I found them very good for balance, proprioception and spatial awareness. I also found the basic warding move very good for protecting myself in confined spaces. (This move is described at the beginning of the chapter if you want to remind yourself.)

Mind and body are inextricably linked in the management of sight loss. Living with it is not a heroic endeavour, but rather a controlled and planned approach where the restoration of movement can be helped with the use of regular, daily if possible, exercise.

LEVEL TWO

MANAGEMENT AND ADAPTATION

Building castles of sand
Management of the descent into darkness
Loss, change and relationships
Adaptation, the key to recovery

CHAPTER EIGHT

BUILDING CASTLES OF SAND

'Sight loss support is upside down.'

– Author, 2019

The path from the cradle to the grave, for most of us, is neither simple nor easy. The way is strewn with rocks, pitfalls and other obstacles. Most of us live our lives within the context of a maelstrom of cultural and normative values combined with the emotional firestorms of ourselves and others. That many people seem to be oblivious to social conflict and the covert violence latent to most encounters only serves to add to the chaos.

For us as sight impaired or blind, the bar to doing things is set much higher, the road to success much rockier, and the margin for failure much greater. In addition to this there is a general suspension of the belief we are capable of making decisions. This may or may not be meant unkindly. The result, however, is the same: the domination, subjugation and restricting of us as people.

We work, play and live in highly complex settings, the most important factor in all these aspects of our lives being other people. Every encounter has the potential for either threat or opportunity. As such, the agenda for many encounters will revolve round issues of power, status, pecking orders and the imposition of will.

In the disciplined services these issues are made crystal-clear by badges and emblems; but even in an apparently obvious environment these emblems are unlikely to tell the whole story. Respect and subsequent obedience are not automatic, they must be earned. Away from these environments we do not have the luxury of clear signposting for interpersonal issues. In addition to that, unlike the services, there is no general conscious recognition that these issues even exist.

People may consider that to be a somewhat jaundiced and harsh view of our social environment. However, a little observation will reveal one inescapable fact: activities, values, opinions and group norms are dictated by the strongest, not by those with the best ideas. Our vaunted democracy requires that there is at least a nod towards persuasion rather than the naked imposition by brute force. This is so at both a national and an individual level.

I feel that everyone, regardless of whether they want it, needs a refuge from this torrid environment. The refuge could be a wooded glade, a haven of some kind, or in the mind. Its form is irrelevant. It has to be a place where wounds can be licked, thoughts gathered and skills and attributes such as patience and fortitude be nurtured. What matters is that it is away from the burl and hurl of life, the attacks of the insidious, and the clamour of the uncouth.

For those of us who acquire any kind of impediment, handicap or disability alongside the burl and hurl of life, things can become rather grim. We have to endure a brutal transition from an 'everyday Joe' into a 'disabled person' (in common parlance). In the course of this metamorphosis all the previous certainties are stripped away – and this includes any previous refuge we may have created. We are literally born again, ignorant, helpless and very vulnerable. We are immediately side-lined, put on a shelf, out of the way...for our own safety. We are considered to be helpless, maybe even a waste of space and a burden.

Many people are sadly fated to remain such. They end up colluding with the popular belief that they are entirely disabled, with no prospects of a fulfilling life from then on and resigned to isolation and eventual decline. And the way in which others relate to us starkly reinforces our new position. Certain words used to describe any perceived flaw are themselves part of the imposition of an inferior status; words like 'disabled' and 'impaired', for instance.

As individuals with disenabled functions, such as sight loss, deafness or mental health issues, we find ourselves in a world where we are expected to be grateful to others for looking after or assisting us. The price for this help is to conform to the expectations of others rather than our own. We are often only helped provided we sit quietly, behave ourselves and stay out of the way.

Individuals such as us with disabilities are generally regarded as an inconvenience or an opportunity to be seen to be doing good. We are rarely considered as individuals in our own right with aspirations, goals and hopes of our own. We, therefore, more than others, are subjected to the domination of those around us.

The processes can be very subtle. It can be something as simple as hiding things so we cannot function. Hide a white cane or a wallet and any foray out into the real world will be stopped in its tracks. That is a very crude though simple example.

Another example is the simple act of being

helped to cross the road. This is a useful way to show some of the dynamics involved in such encounters. With or without sight, crossing a busy road is a hazardous activity, and if someone offers help we would be mad to refuse it. However, we have to be aware of the unconscious search for dominance by the person offering that help.

It can start in one of two basic ways. "Do you want help?" implies that they have recognised your inferiority and are reluctantly, even though they are busy, offering help in a way that makes it very hard to refuse. They are imposing their will upon you because there is an assumption of a higher status. If on the other hand they say, "Can I help you?" then they are leaving the decision to you. They are assuming you are capable of making choices. It is far less dominant.

When we move into the actual helping, the manner in which it is done is also very revealing. Often the helper will grab hold of your arm. When they do this a number of things are going on:

- They are taking control
- They are inferring superiority of status by disregarding your personal space.
- They are removing all choices from you.

In this manner, in the past I have been frog-marched across roads that I had no desire to cross!

My approach is to thank them for their offer and ask If I can take their arm. This achieves a number of things:

- It puts control into your hands. By taking their arm you can disengage at any point.
- You are taking responsibility for what happens.
- You level the status gap by penetrating their personal space rather than them invading yours.
- You ignore their implied higher status as a helper.

It cannot be stressed too much how important it is to be alert for these subtle dominance activities by other people. People dominate us by refusing to allow us opportunities in the following ways:

- By taking charge whether we want it or not.
- By constantly reminding us of the sacrifices they are making, whether we want them or not.
- By constantly doing things for us so we feel a permanent sense of obligation.

It seems to me that our lives can easily boil down

to a stark choice: accepting the inferred higher status of those who are doing things for us, or recognising we are also people in our own right and as such we choose the type and manner of being helped. (Which means we refuse to accept the inferred disparity in status.)

In order to achieve a normal life we have to be aware of the subtle dynamics that are shifting constantly around us. Listening, analysing, being aware and assertive all help us to deal with this, which is where interpersonal skills training comes in.

But first we must understand ourselves. Only when we understand ourselves can we understand others and begin to appreciate the power games that certain people use. People accuse me of constantly analysing what is going on around me. Too right! But the same people have also told me they do not believe in psychology! We all practice psychology at some level. You might as well say you do not believe in breathing if you think you are not.

The work in helping people to be mobile, acquire living skills, IT skills and other practical skills is outstanding. I do have the sense, however, that one important aspect is generally overlooked. It is all very well teaching people skills, but if they do not have the confidence or self-worth required they will not use them. Skills training therefore has to start with the idea that the recipient feels worthy, confident and socially strong enough to be able to use those skills. I feel the current system of skills acquisition is upside down. In other words, it should start with the person and their personal confidence and sense of self-worth before the practical training is even considered. To put it another way, it seems pretty pointless to teach someone to use a long cane if they do not have the confidence to leave their own home and venture into the world outside.

We also have to add to the mix the probable emotional state of the person with sight loss. Neither can we afford to ignore the impact on their significant others. The enforced changes are likely to have a profound effect not only on interpersonal functioning, but also on the receptivity of the potential trainee. To put it crudely, when a man's house is on fire he is unlikely to want to learn how to ride a bike!

Sight loss is experienced as a bereavement, not just for the one with the sight loss but also for their significant others. All the emotions associated with loss and change – like denial, confusion, anger and grief – are present for both parties. Sight loss can also make you feel helpless, hopeless and useless. On top of that, you no longer have access to your physical or mental 'refuge', the place you go to when all around is chaos.

It seems to me that the enabling agencies should have one overarching goal: to enable beneficiaries to rebuild the refuge or haven that will shelter and support them into their future – a future that includes training and eventual re-assimilation back into the real world.

For this to be effective I feel three broad aspects need to be addressed. The first is stability. The second is awareness and interpersonal skills training. And the third is practical skills acquisition. It is my experience that current models of service delivery revolve round practical skills and the other aspects are, at best, given a nod in passing. There is no denying that the work that is done is excellent. I cannot, however, shake off the impression that it is a case of the wrong things being done well; almost a sense that the various agencies are taking a knife to a gunfight.

Stability

By stability I mean the emotional firestorm is dowsed; that the individual is enabled to rebuild their refuge or haven; that they are helped to come to a real understanding of their situation. This involves dealing with the emotional aspects of loss and change, and includes not only the individual but also their significant others. Both group discussions and counselling would be possible routes to achieve this. Once the person has achieved some level of stability this creates a good foundation for the reconstruction of their refuge or haven, whether literal or in their mind.

Awareness and interpersonal skills

Awareness and interpersonal skills training includes listening, and communication and assertiveness skills in combination with other elements of interpersonal skills training. Such training should be a seamless follow on from the process of stabilisation. This will form the walls and roof of the refuge or haven.

Practical skills acquisition

Practical skills acquisition is liable to be far more effective when carried out within the safety of a refuge, and once good listening and communication has been established.

If we use the analogy of the structure of a building one thing becomes clear. The current service delivery model is attempting to place the chimneypot before digging the foundations. It is therefore to the everlasting credit of the many skilled and enthusiastic sight loss support practitioners that any training takes root at all.

Before writing this chapter I contacted a

number of people within different organisations supporting those with sight loss. I asked them a simple question: As a non-attributable ballpark figure, what proportion of people do you think are trained but do not use the training when they get home through lack of confidence, motivation or encouragement?

It was interesting that no one denied the possibility, and at management level the response was to declare uncertainty. On the ground floor, from people actually doing the work, there was a consensus that between thirty to forty percent of people used the training. To put it another way, the organisations are less than fifty percent effective. This I believe is a function of the service model, not the staff as such.

I feel very strongly that current practice is creating sandcastles rather than solid structures, sandcastles that can quickly be eroded by the wind of self-doubt and scoured by the tide of the expectations of others, not forgetting the big bad wolf of society who could huff and puff and blow the whole thing down. So let's first discuss managing the initial descent into darkness.

CHAPTER NINE

MANAGING THE DESCENT INTO DARKNESS

'Sight loss is what you make it.
No more. No less.'

– Author, 2019

The prime objective when managing your sight loss is devastatingly simple: we must not allow sight loss to dominate our lives. If we allow ourselves to be defined by sight loss we will exile ourselves from life for ever more. The major role of managing sight loss then is to achieve a recognition and acceptance that sight loss is only one part of you, that there is so much more to be experienced and enjoyed.

Coming to terms and living with sight loss has been described as a battle. It is far more than that. It is an endless series of battles within a campaign which will continue for the rest of your life. Yet this does not need to be either terrifying or daunting. What you need is faith or belief that you can do it. As the US Marine Corps would say, 'Semper Fie', or 'Always faithful'.

It is also important to point out that it is not all bad. The battles, as you become used to your sight loss, change in nature. They are not quite so full on, in your face or brutal as time passes. They become more subtle and less alarming. But there is no place for complacency. We must stay alert to the changes.

The ultimate objective in the management of your descent into darkness is to remain yourself. It is far too easy to find yourself agreeing to things that, in the end, take away opportunities to learn and regain your independence. When things are suggested you have to ask one simple question: How does this help my goal of being independent? Sometimes the answer to that question is quite shocking, which will be covered in the next chapter.

Knowing about the various aspects of sight loss as outlined in the first part of the book is both useful and, I believe, necessary. Learning how to do things again, to reacquire skills, is also important if we are to make the best of life, and this is where a management strategy or plan comes in. A coherent plan will determine how we cope in the long term. Everyone is different, however, and this means that each of us has to develop our own management plan.

You may be thinking at this point that I'm barking mad talking about management strategies and plans. Maybe I am. Maybe I'm not. But just as with business, we must take the business of sight loss seriously. And that means making a plan. If you think this is unnecessary, try managing sight loss without one. I did. It was chaos.

My personal approach to managing the new reality of my sight loss may not be completely suitable for you, but it will give you some pointers to get you started. Therefore we have a number of elements to consider:

- The mental dimension
- Relearning old skills and developing new ones
- Sustaining social links and connections
- Maintaining physical fitness

9.1 The mental dimension

9.1.01 Rules

This includes accepting the new reality. One way I managed was to develop the set of rules at the beginning of this book – the rules of engagement –which were covered in more detail in chapter five, 'Rules of engagement – Prop or weapon'. These rules kept me on track when things became tough.

9.1.02 Knowledge

Another way of working at accepting your sight loss is to find out everything you can about it. Throwing your hands in the air as a way of acceptance of your lot does not contribute to sustainable long-term acceptance, it merely ensures that everything that happens next is a horrible surprise, which does little to promote peace of mind! Ask questions, demand answers, and under no circumstances accept uninformative answers.

If you do find yourself being fobbed off, you will find the question 'Why?' and its variations very powerful. Medics don't like being challenged, but it is not too difficult to get proper answers if you ask politely but firmly. Once they realise you mean business, they will not mess you about. "But the doctors are so busy! I don't like to bother them!" I hear people say. Just appreciate that without us as patients, doctors would not have a job!

9.1.03 Diversions

Having made my sight loss a major part of my conscious mental activity, it was also necessary to provide some diversion from it. You will have all sorts of things you are interested in, and being blind does not mean you instantly disconnect from those interests. In fact you need them more than ever, so do not give them up. If some of them are truly impossible – like playing golf or riding a motorbike! – find a way to stay engaged with the interests that are possible. And develop new interests. We never stop learning when we have sight. There is no reason to stop when we lose it. My interests will no doubt be very different to yours, but here are some of the things I did to distract myself from my initial descent into blindness.

I found sailing, attending a power boat course and walking gave me everyday activities which took my mind off my situation for a while. Attending the batch reunion of YO 32-33 RM – the Royal Marines – was very much in the same vein.

Planning for the walk along Hadrian's Wall to raise funds for Help For Heroes, the actual walk itself and the aftermath, also occupied much of my mind and time for a good few months. Similarly, planning and doing the walk from Ashbourne to Sheffield to raise money for Blind Veterans UK had much the same affect.

I planned some very useful one-off experiences, such as having a flying lesson in a Microlight and a Tiger Moth. The latter was particularly valuable. As my rapidly worsening sight steadily deteriorated into blindness I found more and more that I needed to take my mind off it. Each year I do the Family Santa Run. This entails visiting my children and grandchildren with Christmas presents and involves travelling from Ashbourne to Market Harborough to Bedford to Bristol to Ludlow and back to Ashbourne. This is all done on local buses using my bus pass! An interesting challenge and great fun!

I also became a volunteer with Blind Veterans UK, and for about two years was a beneficiary recruitment ambassador, which basically meant I spent quite a bit of time going to various venues in the East Midlands talking about blindness in general and Blind Veterans UK in particular. When the 'No one alone' section was closed down I was out of a job, but I'd had an unparalleled opportunity to talk to people with sight loss and the professionals providing support. This gave me enough material to start writing about sight loss from the inside.

The first effort was an article called 'Descent into Darkness' which is on the Blind Veterans UK website. The next endeavour was to write a book, called *A Descent into Darkness* (or blindness in hindsight), and is available from myself or Amazon. I found that writing about my sight loss allowed me to embrace it in a thoughtful way which was also structured. In this way my sight loss has literally become part of me. But a note here. Not all of me. Whilst I cannot deny that I experienced the anger and bitterness associated with sight loss, I did not let it define me. If anything I used the anger and bitterness to help drive my quest for accepting it. The writing proved to be so cathartic that I now contribute regularly to an international health magazine. I also wrote a survival manual for cooking when blind called *First Catch Your Rabbit* which is available through Amazon or myself.

Currently I am volunteering with Blind Veterans by supporting isolated members of the charity by telephone. Volunteering serves a number of purposes. First, it is a chance to share what I have learned. Secondly, it is a very positive way of paying off a little of the enormous debt I owe to the charity. Thirdly, we all need to feel needed. When we become impaired this can be stolen from us, but volunteering is a very giving way of meeting that need.

I still sail with Sailability, am learning Tai Chi and wall climbing, and I'm hoping to have another go at skiing! I'm outlining all this not to brag, but to point out that having an impairment is not the end of life as we know it.

9.1.04 The choice

The choice for me was simple: Deny my sight loss and let it overwhelm me, leaving me a pitiful figure in a corner basically waiting to die, or I could face it square on and dare it to do its worst. It has done its worst. I am totally blind, and I am unimpressed. But it is certainly not the remorseless horror I thought it might be.

We cannot allow negative thinking about our situation to dominate us. When working we seek a life-work balance; similarly, we should strive for an impairment-to-life balance of hard work balanced with periods of rest and distraction.

9.2 Relearning old skills and developing new ones

When we develop any serious impairment we can lose our confidence across the board. This is particularly so in the case of sight loss and is a reflection of its all-pervading nature. It includes being unable to do things which we could previously.

9.2.01 Confidence

You will perhaps find that each time you try to do something in the old way you will leave a trail of wreckage and outraged carers behind you, which in itself further destroys your confidence.

The solution to this problem is not to run round in a blind panic causing more chaos. Neither is it to give up and retire to a corner whilst you endure the wrath of your other half. The solution is to sit down quietly, look at what went wrong, identify the cause, and look for answers. By doing this you will re-awaken an awareness of this vital pre-existing skill of problem-solving. If we struggle with a thing and it goes wrong, most likely this analysis would create the solution which increases confidence. It is no different with sight loss.

9.2.02 Problem-solving

As with any problem, do not overthink it. The old tag KISS, or Keep It Simple Stupid, has much to offer in this respect. Life is complicated enough without making it more so! I will demonstrate this problem-solving skill by showing how the once-simple task of making a cup of tea can be achieved when blind. First break the operation down into its component parts, as follows:

- Find a safe place in your kitchen to stand or sit where everything is in reach.
- Make sure there is nothing on the worktop which will impede or interfere with the operation.
- Locate all the component elements – the kettle, a mug, a teaspoon, a teabag, some milk (and sugar if required), something to put the used teabag in, and kitchen paper to

mop up if you make a mess (which you most likely will to begin with). Have a few practice runs with the mug by taking it. from the cupboard and putting it on the worktop, and then putting it back in the cupboard. (This is where the previous exercises and practicing them comes in useful!) Make sure you don't bang it too hard, so maybe put your other hand underneath it to guide it to the work surface; and test where it is in relation to the edge of the worktop so that it doesn't fall off the edge. Trust me, you will never hide the evidence of a smashed mug from your other half no matter how hard you try. Believe me, I've been there, so get practising!

- Make sure the route is clear between where you are going to make the cup of tea and where you are going to drink it.

It may sound a bit dramatic, but by doing all of the above first you maximise your chance of success. Preparation is key to problem-solving. And success, as we all know, is the best way to regain confidence. Next comes the execution of actually making the cup of tea as follows (which I will cover again later on in the book as a reminder):

- Fill the kettle with enough water for one mug of tea, or use a one-cup kettle, and switch it on. (Empty the kettle if it has water in from previous use and fill the mug you will be using with cold water and tip it into the kettle. This will ensure you have exactly the right amount and you won't overfill the mug with boiling water, risking a mess and a possible nasty burn.)

- Put the teabag in the mug and fill with the boiled water from the kettle. Let it steep.
- Remove the teabag and place it in the receptacle you chose for this purpose.
- Pour in the milk. You will have to find your own method to do this. I tend to do one of two things. Either I slowly pour the milk over a finger (obviously clean!) to gauge how much has gone into the mug, or I use sound, both of which take practise.
- Add sugar if you require it and stir the tea.
- Put the spoon in the sink and use the kitchen paper to mop up any mess.
- Carefully carry the mug of tea through to where you will be drinking it. (Again, the exercises in chapter seven are invaluable in learning to do this without spillage and the subsequent wrath of the other half.)

It may seem terribly longwinded and tortuous, but breaking a task like this into its component elements and rehearsing any parts you find difficult is the key to success – and is vital if you wish to avoid demoralising failure and chastisement.

9.3 Maintaining social relationships

We are pack animals. There are very few people who choose to live, or thrive, in isolation. It is therefore important that we do not allow the acquisition of an impairment to cut us off from other people as this can be demoralising, unhelpful and ultimately have a devastating effect on our mental health.

9.3.01 Isolation

The need for companionship is hardwired into our DNA. Indeed, this dependency on others was graphically illustrated during the Covid-19 pandemic. In spite of the clear advice to isolate, by the third week of the national lockdown Greater Manchester police had to break up more than 650 house parties. It seems that even the threat of catching a nasty disease could not overcome the basic herding instinct of some people. The so-called great and the good also provided many examples of lack of discipline, and a good few broke ranks and ignored their own advice. Having said that, it may well have been sheer hubris and arrogance that informed their actions. Something on the lines of Imelda

Marcos when she said that only the little people paid tax.

Isolation is a clear and present danger for anyone with any form of impairment. Even when people are not isolated, the nature of some forms of interaction may well leave them feeling they would be better off on their own. Many people find relating to someone with an obvious difference very difficult and responses can range from hostility to patronisation. The worst are those who consider it 'their Christian duty' to associate with the impaired. In my view, if people do not want to relate to me because it is their preferred choice, then I'm happy for them to leave me alone. I would rather be on my own than patronised.

9.3.02 Side-lining

So often I have seen people with impairments left out of the cut and thrust of daily life. There are at least three possible reasons for this.

The first reason is that people are embarrassed by impairment. They do not know how to interact with us. Somebody once actually asked how they should talk to me. The answer of course is, 'like anyone else'.

The second reason, I believe, is that people unconsciously attribute imbecility and deafness to anyone who has an impairment. (But if you challenged them over it they would be horrified, even mortally offended.)

Thirdly, I believe that sight loss is a subject that is so horrific it is almost taboo. People really do not wish to be reminded of what many regard as the ultimate nightmare.

In terms of the social transaction theory, people perceive that the cost of interacting with us is unlikely to result in a reward equal to or greater than the cost involved. Therefore we are in a position where we have to use every opportunity to show that talking to us can be rewarding. It feels very unfair, but if you believe that life is fair then you have not been paying attention.

9.3.03 Some ways forward socially

It is down to us to be socially proactive. If we wait for others to take the initiative then we could have a very long wait indeed. But this is often the most significant area where support groups and mainstream society part company. The simple device of asking how someone is can be a very effective way into a conversation. Subsequent careful listening and responding will reinforce this.

There are a number of tested ways of communication in a social group.

First, it is important to speak in your normal

voice, at a reasonable pace, and make attempts to find something interesting to discuss. For most people it is themselves. You cannot go far wrong by asking how they are. This surprises them as they will assume you are the one who needs asking, and it gives you the opportunity to pick up and run with any leads they give you in their reply.

Second, when you are in a group setting do not allow yourself to be separated from the rest. So often someone will say "Would you like to sit over there and we will bring your drink across?" Notice they don't say, "And someone will join you." My response is usually, "Thanks. However, I'm happy chatting here for now." This way you remain with the action.

Thirdly, develop the skills that will enable you to engage with other people on a level playing field. Foremost amongst these are listening skills and assertiveness, which we will cover in chapter twelve.

Perhaps, most important of all, is the ability to adopt a positive attitude and cheerful face, even when all you want to do is just curl up and cry. It is essential that you remain positive in public. Do your curling up and crying at home. Once you get the reputation of being miserable and full of self-pity no one will want to know you.

By using these methods I have found that I

have not been reduced to a lonely figure creeping around town, ignoring and ignored by others. In fact sometimes it will take an insane amount of time to get down the street as so many people want to stop and chat. The great thing about being totally blind is that when people stop you know that this is an active choice. After all, it would be only too easy for them to slide past without being seen!

This level of social engagement is not an accident, it is the product of hard work. Always being seen out and about my impairment is largely forgotten, and the innate good nature of the people in my town asserts itself. It has actually been the case that people have told others, "He's not an effing imbecile! Talk to him properly!" Others have become so comfortable with me that they make jokes. Only the other day someone bade me goodbye, and told me to be sure to look both ways when crossing the road! Some may view that comment as callous mickey-taking, but I see it as a very positive thing that people feel comfortable enough to say a thing like that!

9.3.04 Assuming roles

Many people assume that anyone with an impairment is unable to perform any of the social roles within a group. There are two ways

I have got around this.

The first is to talk to as many groups about my impairment as possible. In this way I demonstrate that I can take a lead role. The second is to become a good listener. Everybody loves to have someone to listen to them. If you take pains to develop listening as a skill, rather than something you just do, then you will never be short of a role. In this way you can begin the long haul back to full social inclusion if you have found yourself isolated.

Perhaps most important of all, if you treat your impairment as a matter of little consequence, others will eventually follow your lead. It is particularly effective if you can treat the whole situation with humour and positivity.

9.4 Maintaining physical fitness

I have talked about the crushing tiredness that can accompany sight loss. I have met people who deny this, and I have concluded that maybe this is because they are doing nothing to accept their impairment. Meeting your change of circumstances takes a lot of work, and furious mental activity. It follows then that we need to be as physically fit as possible. We also need to be fit so we can cope with inevitable minor injuries we will sustain if we are to be truly active.

It is far better if you bounce back from a

fall under your own steam. The alternative of just staying there whilst a chattering crowd gathers is both humiliating and bad for your confidence. Apart from this, news of the mishap is more likely to get back to the other half if you needed a huge amount of assistance to get back on your feet.

In my mid-seventies now, I consider that realistic physical challenges are vital not only for maintaining physical fitness but also mental agility and a positive sense of self. In short, they make me feel alive, and put my sight loss in its proper place: an infuriating inconvenience, but not the end of my life. Keep practising the exercises in chapter seven.

In addition to staying as active as possible, diet and regular sleep are also important. It follows that if your body is physically fit, rested and properly fuelled then you will be in good shape to meet any mental or emotional challenge. Similarly, if you manage to be at peace with your situation then this will contribute to your physical health. Mind and body are so intertwined that to ignore the one is to imperil the other.

Summary

It is clear that just enduring a major crisis and hoping for the best is not the answer. Yet it is amazing how often we do exactly that. The very idea of having a planned, coherent and proactive approach to managing sight loss is totally alien. It is hard enough when you have a plan to work to. It is nigh impossible if you do not.

We also need to learn to forgive ourselves for being impaired and resolve to reskill ourselves in order to lessen any dependency. It is essential that we are brutally honest with ourselves, foster patience, a sense of humour and fortitude within ourselves.

Those qualities lie within every single one of us. Perhaps the most important characteristic we can harness is bloody-minded determination to dig those qualities out. It is here that the anger inherent to any impairment can be harnessed to kick start the whole process. Everything is grist for the mill, and the most powerful resource we have is ourselves.

CHAPTER TEN

LOSS, CHANGE AND RELATIONSHIPS

'The quality of our lives is
the quality of our relationships.'
– Tony Robbins

Change is one of the few things in life upon which we can rely. As we pass from the cradle to the grave our personal circumstances, relationships, possessions, priorities and health will all undergo change. Whenever change occurs there is also loss, and significant loss and change are accompanied by a recognisable sequence of emotions, often referred to as an 'emotional rollercoaster'.

If you do not know about the emotional stages it can be a chaotic experience, and you will feel as if you're in danger of losing your mind. What follows is a description of the stages of the rollercoaster, so you can identify them.

Denial

Denial is the disbelief that what is happening is real. There can also be a refusal to even consider the possibility. Responses such as "That can't be right" or "No way, you're having me on" are quite commonplace. It is also not unusual for people to refuse to seek medical help. People bury their heads in the sand and are then surprised when the reality cannot be ignored.

Confusion

Confusion follows on from denial and occurs as we try to understand what has happened, and when we might ask, "Why me?" or "What have I done to deserve this?" It is during this phase that we begin to feel helpless, utterly useless, and start to question our sanity. Confusion is quickly replaced by anger.

Anger

Anger is triggered by the perceived unfairness and unkindness of fate and is fuelled by a strong sense of injustice, hurt and adrenalin. Anger can manifest as verbal or physical violence, and is often directed at those close to us. In my own case it made life very tedious and difficult for me and those around me. Yet anger can be extremely seductive, as lashing out can be seen as doing something active to address the changed circumstances. It is natural to feel angry, and it does spur us to action; but it is also highly negative if allowed to continue and results in a downward spiral with no happy outcome.

Understanding

After the anger is the beginning of understanding and acceptance. In many ways this is one of the most difficult and painful stages of them all. With understanding and acceptance comes real grief as the extent of what has been lost and the reality of the new situation strikes home. Attaining acceptance is one thing; doing something with that acceptance is quite another. It is a double-edged sword. It is the point where the crucial choice has to be made: Do I accept what has happened and allow events to overwhelm me, or do I face events square-on and not allow them to beat me?

Sadly, it is much easier to decide that you cannot do something and give up than to make the choice to relearn old skills and live an inclusive life. This is particularly so when others around you are attempting to exclude or de-skill you.

The outcomes could not be more different.

One choice leads to inevitable decline, exclusion and dependency within a drab and unstimulating world: the life of an invalid. The other involves continual battling, constant learning, endless tricky social choices, and establishing the right to make your own mistakes. In short, a normal life!

Moving on

In spite of the rollercoaster of emotions, it is essential that we learn to understand and accept our sight loss. Only then will we be able to move on. Moving on happens when we focus on what we have now and not what we had before. What we have now is the new reality however much we might wish for it to be otherwise and involves the following:

- An honest recognition of what we can do now so those abilities help us rebuild our skills.
- Facing up to and finding solutions to the challenges presented by sight loss.
- Working towards positive outcomes, and being prepared to fail and persist until we succeed.
- The patience of a saint when the eager help of others crosses the line into unwelcome interference.
- Being comfortable with our new selves and

recognising the challenges of sight loss and being ready to meet them.

- Putting the current situation into perspective. All of our lives we grow, develop, adapt and overcome challenges. Acquisition of sight loss is no different in kind, although it may feel much harsher than the changes we normally come to accept.

All of this requires reserves of strength, fortitude and patience which few of us are aware we have. It would be difficult to comprehend how anyone could even attempt to do this work without the help of others, either from a friend who is prepared to listen to full-blown counselling. Either way, it is not a task that can be undertaken single-handed.

People will only face the work involved when they are ready. This is why it is so important to talk to people rather than bottling it up. There is no doubt in my mind that the more you talk about an issue the quicker you will be willing to face it.

It is sad but true that some people cannot face this emotional rollercoaster. They get stuck in anger or even denial – what one of my tutors was pleased to call a state of 'stuckness'. It does not take a great deal of effort to spot such people. Unfortunately, many of them are quite unable to understand the need for help, let alone accept it willingly. In the past I have tried to work with people in this situation, and sometimes you get savaged for your pains. Other times you may not. It is always a personal choice whether we reach out or allow others to reach out to us.

Changing relationships

The one part of acceptance and moving on that is unrecognised, and therefore rarely discussed, is how the impact on one person affects the people around them. I know that it has been very hard for my friends and family to come to an acceptance of my sight loss. My wife in particular found it harder than even I did myself. The implications of this are that whilst we are struggling with our own battle towards acceptance, we also have to be mindful of the struggles of our loved ones.

Their experience will be, in many ways, similar to that of the person who had the change forced upon them because of the following reasons:

- They have to accept that their expectations for the future have altered radically.
- They have to live and take on additional burdens in order to accommodate their partner's comparative helplessness, at least

at the outset.
- They have to take on roles they did not anticipate, such as carer, chief cook and bottle-washer, with very little help to begin with.
- They may have to negotiate a subtle shift in the power relationships within the partnership.
- They will feel put upon, despite the grudging gratitude of their partner.
- They may feel lost and abandoned by their partner.

The subtle approval of others may be some compensation, but this is a lot to take on and involves a huge amount of work on both sides if there are not to be frequent tears before bedtime. Most people manage this to a lesser or greater degree as the partnership settles into the new parameters. Nothing stays the same for very long. But where there is an inability or refusal to accept the new normal and move on, by either parties, daily life can become intolerable, a living hell for them both. Bottling up frustration doesn't work either, as it can easily flip over into violence.

The carer may switch between being dismissive, unkind and aggressive, and make it quite clear that the partner with sight loss should just stay out of the way and not get underfoot. This can lead to fierce resistance on the carer's part to our attempts to regain old skills or begin to take an interest in life. I have seen this in action and it has a particularly bad effect on relationships. This, of course, is rarely manifested in public, although the signs are there if you care to look.

The great tragedy is that the parties involved invariably have little insight into what is going on in the other person's head. It is often when the relationship goes horribly wrong that there is any recognition of what is happening and how the other party feels. Even then there can be little or no understanding of this, or both parties are still locked in denial.

When a person with an impairment takes their courage in both hands and elects for acceptance and moving on, a whole host of other factors kick in, because that choice has a profound effect on both parties. The day you choose to say, "You sit down, I'll make the tea," everything changes again. The initial helplessness and lack of hope has passed, and there is the possibility of a whole new tranche of situations; with the possibility of improvement also comes the opportunity of failure and crushing disappointment.

At this point the carer has to adjust again, and there is the possibility they may think their new role has become redundant in some respects, which could lead to a new kind of resentment as offers of help are now being rejected. It could also give rise to feelings of frustration and anger as they watch the awakened independence leave a trail of wreckage behind it as normal skills, like making a cup of tea, are relearned and performance is heartbreakingly, infuriatingly slow. Add to this the growing confidence and competence of the person with the incapacity, and the possibility that they subtly reduce their dependence on the carer, and the situation may get hostile, particularly if those outside the relationship assume the person with the disability has been held back by their partner.

If the partner appears passive, don't think that nothing is going on under the surface. These deep, unsettling feeling are often denied and never spoken about. The fact remains, however, that the dynamics within a relationship have been profoundly influenced, and the associated emotions will surface. In my own case, the transitional period from initial helplessness to a level of competence was hard for both my wife and me. It was a period of unparalleled frustration and misunderstanding for both of us.

She refers to this in chapter nineteen, 'The other side of the coin'. We both accepted that we had, both singly and as a couple, been to the gates of hell and back. But we were lucky in that it made our relationship stronger. It therefore has to be worth any couple's time to take a good hard look within themselves, and into their partner, to try and see what is really going on. This may not be easy, and you may have to drag out whatever you find into the open, kicking and screaming, so that you can deal with it. On the other hand, you may want to leave well alone. As always, the choice is yours. If you opt to bring it all out in the open, you will need the patience of Job, the strength of Samson, and the wisdom of Solomon. But it is worth it, and will bring you closer together.

CHAPTER ELEVEN

ADAPTATION - A KEY TO RECOVERY

'Change is the only reliable constant.'
– Heraclitus of Ephesus, 500 BCE

It is perhaps one of the great ironies of life that few things remain constant and change is coming no matter how much we cling to certainty. When we encounter extraordinary situations, such as sight loss, mental health problems, the loss of a limb or any other life-changing event, then adaptation is brought into sharp focus.

In the armed forces, where continually training for or meeting emergencies is par for the course, there is the mantra of 'Improvise, adapt and overcome.' Blind Veterans stress a slight variation on this: 'Accept, adapt and achieve.' Adaptation, without doubt, is considered to be an essential element in facing any challenging situation. The questions remain, however: What does adaptation mean? What does it involve? There is no easy answer and adaptation varies for each set of new circumstances and the individual involved.

Sometimes the task of adapting can be focussed and minor, such as buying and learning to drive a new car, or highly complex and all-encompassing, such as learning to live with sight loss.

The mental aspect of adaptation is simply that of reflecting on what you can do, rather than upon what you cannot. It also involves developing the habit of putting a positive spin on things. An example of this is believing that there are no such things as problems, only opportunities to find solutions. In addition it is important to identify both the practical and personal attributes with which you can address the challenges of adaptation. These would typically include resources such as a sense of humour, determination, a willingness to engage, internal honesty, fortitude and previous knowledge. Perhaps the greatest, and least common, resource we have to call upon is patience. The need for patience dominates every aspect of our lives when we are facing challenging circumstances. But there is more to the practical aspect than first appears.

If you carry out an audit of how much we actually do without looking it is quite surprising.

Seatbelts, putting on shoes, brushing our teeth and moving objects about are but a tip of the iceberg. We do these things confidently and with ease, without a thought, sure in the knowledge that we have Plan B to fall back upon if it goes wrong. Plan B is sight. If the seatbelt locks we can turn in our seat and investigate why; if our shoelaces get themselves into a knot we can look down and see why they got tangled. It is amazing how this ability, this ease, vanishes when Plan B no longer exists. No longer can we do things automatically and with little thought, but must carefully consider every single step of the job in hand, illustrated by the aforementioned concentration and planning required to make a simple cup of tea.

Another aspect of adaptation is social, and probably the hardest to understand. Having any impairment is of itself a cause of stress and this will affect our general attitude and the face we present to the world. Imparting an air of cheerfulness and positivity is difficult enough without the reactions of others.

These reactions can take many forms. They can manifest themselves as overt sympathy, or over-cheerfulness, or attempts to do absolutely everything for you. It is necessary therefore to remain positive and cheerful, even if you feel like screaming inside and/or screaming at the person. You have to learn to be patient and super tolerant of the inability of others to understand, let alone empathise. You have to learn to insist on doing things for yourself without offending other people.

Perhaps one of the hardest behavioural adaptations is the need to constantly inform people what you are doing and explaining why. Without this people become alarmed when you do something, and try to stop you. They may move things without telling you and generally make an already difficult life impossible. Calmly saying, "I'm going to put my shoes on and sit in the garden for a bit of air," rather than alarming your partner by suddenly getting up and fumbling around for shoes, making them wonder where on earth you're going, works wonders – and drives home the importance of not moving your things, like your shoes!

Another and more subtle adaptation we must make concerns personal space. It is noticeable that many people ignore the idea of personal space when dealing with those they perceive to be inferior. There appears to be a general desire to touch people with impairments, and this is particularly noticeable when communicating with them. In the case of sight loss I put this down to touching being a substitute for eye contact. There is also, I believe, a more unconscious cause. Those of us with impairment may be viewed as somewhat less than others, therefore less likely to judge and less threatening. This seems to give individuals carte blanche to invade our personal space.

As someone with sight loss I welcome this on most occasions as it improves my ability to communicate. Having said that, I fully understand that being touched by strangers is not everyone's cup of tea. Either way, how you deal with this has to be a personal matter. It may be that you have to bite the bullet and learn to accept it. Perhaps the best way to control the touching is to initiate it, so the person feels relaxed with you.

Adaptation is not only multi-layered but also complex. So what is the point of adaptation? In our case it is the means by which we move from being overwhelmed and helpless in the face of a change of circumstances to being an effective individual living our life like everybody else. This adaptation has to take place in the face of both overt and covert opposition, however. There is now no doubt in my mind that if you have any impairment people feel compelled to patronise, albeit unwittingly, and deny you opportunities on the grounds of safety, thereby blocking your personal choice to adapt. The other reason, which is never admitted let alone discussed, is protection of their goods and chattels.

It is clear that adaptation is part of the battle to live with the same dignity and independence as anyone else. Unfortunately the debate tends to be one-sided. The politically correct seem to want to collude with the relatively powerless in making unrealistic claims. I can only conclude that they, in reality, pay no heed to those claims. I frequently listen to people with disabilities or impairments banging on about their rights. Curiously I rarely, if ever, hear any discussion about the obligations, responsibilities and duties that might accompany those rights. It is almost as if impairment or disability is regarded as a ticket for a free ride. The failure of the advocates of those with disabilities to pick up on this is, in my view, not doing anybody any favours and is indeed bordering on criminal negligence.

In many ways the active deployment of the 'disability trump card' can be very seductive. It is, however, something that should be deployed with caution and preferably not at all. I believe that if we wish to be taken seriously again, then use of this card must be resisted. If we do use the card and treat disability as a free ride, we can hardly expect to be regarded with respect and the accompanying social inclusion. I feel that it is the clear duty of any advocate to point this out. At the very least it should be a part of any ongoing conversation.

Surely a major part of becoming an effective individual after a life-changing event must be the reassumption of responsibility for all our actions. Indeed, this has to be a major route back to self-worth and a fulfilling life as an optimally functioning individual.

I have described adaptation within the context of sight loss, but I feel the main points are relevant to any situation. All of us who are trying to get back on a level keel after a life-changing event need to adjust and adapt to the changed circumstances. Recently we have been bombarded with exhortations to adapt to our 'new normal'. The next time someone says this to you, ask them a simple question: What exactly do you mean by adaptation? This should prompt an interesting conversation!

'Improvise, adapt and overcome,
young gentlemen.'

– Sgt French RM, 1967

LEVEL THREE

ENGAGEMENT WITH THE REAL WORLD

Communication skills and assertion
Help, the poison chalice
Labelling, the thief of independence

CHAPTER TWELVE

COMMUNICATION SKILLS AND ASSERTION

'Listen carefully, judge slowly,
condemn rarely.'
– Author, 2019

One of the major outcomes of sight loss is an appreciation of how the majority of people find accurate verbal communication quite difficult. This becomes apparent when people are trying to guide you to do something without the usual accompaniment of frantic hand-flapping. Indeed, there have been many occasions when I've been directed by the phrase "Over there." My usual response is to ask them, as per the cartoon at the beginning of this book, if they are pointing. I feel it is important that we all challenge unhelpful directions like this. No need to be rude or savage, just quietly educate people, firmly but with good humour.

On one occasion a man in the street was

giving me directions. This was in full view of my local pub. The staff and customers were cracking up as the man, in spite of my white cane, was using vigorous arm-waving to reinforce what he was saying.

These examples give a rough idea how bad it can be when communicating with individuals who cannot see. This applies to most people, it has to be said, and we have to be extremely patient with their impatience, frustration and embarrassment when they make a complete hash of communicating with us. I often counter the resulting embarrassment by telling them not to worry as lots of people do it.

Closer to home, it required a huge amount of patience for my wife and me to communicate. When I write I generally tap away on the keyboard in total darkness as I do not bother with a screen or lights. Many times my wife would forget herself and ask if I wanted the light on. This demonstrates that even when living with blindness it is difficult for sighted people to get their heads around not being able to see, which actively affects the way they communicate with us.

As in all other aspects of sight loss, we cannot expect other people to alter their behaviour. Not being able to see is our problem, not theirs, so it is down to us to bridge the gap.

Being able to communicate clearly is probably

one of the most essential skills when we lose our sight. We have to learn to communicate without being able to read body language. At the same time we have to gently guide the other person so that what they are saying is meaningful for us.

It is also important that we quickly learn to hold our own in the hurl and burl of life. Aggression is unenforceable and passive behaviour leaves us isolated. We have to develop the rational and unemotional approach that is embodied in assertive behaviour.

It is worth noting here that the prime requisite of assertion is that you love yourself enough to believe you have as much right to the good things in life as anyone else. It is vital that you appreciate your worth as a person and come to understand you are a unique individual who has an enormous amount to contribute. So many of us can feel guilty about being impaired. If we are to achieve acceptance by others then we have to shake off any such notions. There is no place for feelings like guilt when there are so many issues on which to get a grip. We have nothing of which to be ashamed. Sight loss is our burden, but not our sin.

It is for this reason that a section outlining the basics of communication and assertiveness skills has been included. I have drawn on a course that I wrote and taught, sometimes with profound affects, for twenty years. Using these pointers it should be possible to start the process of developing cutting-edge communication skills. Just as important, success will feed into the sense of self-worth. In this way, when we have encounters with others, at least one of the parties will be a skilled communicator! There is nothing profound here, but it will highlight a great deal of the taken-for-granted knowledge that we tend to ignore.

It should be noted that in general people are dreadful at communication. There is very little appreciation that if it is to be effective it has to be treated and exercised as a highly skilled activity. Even the great and the good can get it hopelessly wrong on occasion. I recall very vividly the wonderful gaff by John F Kennedy in Berlin after the wall had gone up. He told the packed German crowd, "Ich bin ein Berliner!" His intention was to declare his solidarity with the inhabitants of that city by saying that he was one of them – "I am a Berliner!" Unfortunately a Berliner is a popular doughnut-type teacake. Instead of declaring his solidarity he declared himself to be a doughnut, and could not understand why the audience was convulsed with laughter.

Another example was the commandant of the famous prisoner-of-war camp Colditz Castle. He informed the assembled prisoners that he was onto them, that he knew what they were planning, and that it was futile as he would catch them. The prisoners were moderately impressed until he uttered the immortal words, "You damned British think I know nothing. Be warned, all of you, I know damn all!" The poor man probably spent the rest of the war trying to work out why the audience was helpless with laughter.

Nearer to home I daily endure examples of people just not listening. Often I will say to someone, "Terribly sorry, can't do that, I am totally blind," and they will say, "Oh, that's alright." Actually it is not. I would prefer not to be blind. Whilst I do not expect sympathy, it would be nice to have an acknowledgement of what I have said.

It seems to me this indicates that such a response is automatic, with no relevance to the context. I frequently listen to conversations, an activity my wife called earwigging, and it is remarkable how many of them are automatic with no reference to any mutual context.

Another example is when I talk to companies on the phone. A classic was when I rang Amazon KDP to try and find a way of accessing my sales account on Kindle. I prefaced my enquiry with, "Please bear with me, I am totally blind," and went on to explain to the advisor that I was unable to access my account as I could not find the links. "What is the nature of your error?" was the response. Gritting my teeth and being as restrained as possible I replied, "I can't see what I am doing." This was followed by total confusion as the advisor realised they had not listened to a word I had said.

It is here, in the field of listening, that we can make major progress in levelling the playing field. If we can develop listening as a skill rather than something we do automatically, poorly and ineffectively, then we have a major advantage over possibly ninety percent of the people we encounter. So let's start at the very beginning.

12.1 Communication skills

In order to really understand how we communicate it is necessary to go back to the very basics. Much of it you already know without even being aware of it. Consequently it may seem insultingly simplistic, but stay with it. I believe all of it is valuable.

12.1.01 Basic communication

At the very simplest level, basic communication can be defined as the passing of a message from point A to point B. So far, so good. But think about what happens to the message from its inception at point A to its final reception at point B.

- The message starts as a thought or idea.
- It then has to be translated into language that can be understood.
- It must then be transmitted over a channel which may or may not be subject to interference.
- It is received at the other end as language.
- Lastly it is translated from language to an idea.

Remember, this is only A to B. In normal conversation there is usually a response that has to go through the same process. Thus we have point A to point B to point A. But this time, instead of the five stages highlighted above there are ten stages, because the communication process is now two-way. Mistakes can occur at any stage:

- The initial idea may be poorly formed.
- The translation into language may be inept.
- The transmission of the idea may be disrupted. (Try having a conversation on the platform of a busy railway station, for example.)
- Not all of the message may be heard or understood.

If the message is incomplete or not understood,

it is anybody's guess how the original idea will end up in the receiver's mind!

Bearing in mind what can go wrong, it seems that effective communication is nothing short of a miracle. I used to drive this point home by getting the students to play Chinese Whispers or to guide a blindfolded person through a maze. They would then see how and why the results of both exercises related to the lesson. The points to make here are:

- The message can be scrambled or suffer deletions in transmission.
- Not all people think in the same way.
- Not all people have the same ability to either think or use language.

The ability to think and use language is influenced by a large number of factors, such as:

- **Education.** This will have a huge influence on the ability to analyse and understand abstract ideas. It will also determine the complexity of the language you can use and comprehend.
- **Age difference.** Age-different generations will have experienced different forms of the same world. They will have varying experiences which inform their view of the world.
- **Upbringing.** The way we are brought up influences our beliefs, attitudes and values.

It will also give us varying amounts of emotional scarring, which will in turn affect our willingness to listen.

- **Interests**. These will give us specialist knowledge and motivation.
- **Social background**. Being herd animals we tend to take on the views and attitudes of our immediate peers. These views will affect the weight we give to individual messages, and this weight influences our attention level.
- **Work environment**. This is another peer group which will influence how we think, and again it will give us specialist knowledge.
- **General life experience.** How life has treated us will influence the way in which we interact with people in general. This in turn affects how we listen, for example whether we are either receptive or closed to the message.
- **Familiarity.** This will influence the way in which jargon or shortcuts can be used in communicating.
- **Complexity of the topic.** Complexity will clearly influence the degree to which the message is understood.
- **New ideas.** How familiar we are with thinking or dealing with new ideas will affect our ability to listen.

There are, of course, many other factors, such as English not being a person's first language, for example.

The task of communication is to enable a common understanding between unique units, or people, and we are all unique. Just looking at this very basic model of communication it becomes clear why it is that people cannot understand each other. Indeed, as Churchill once remarked: 'We and the Americans are two nations divided by a single language.'

I often marvel that we can communicate at all. Having lost my sight I listen very closely to what is going on around me. Sometimes the lack of comprehension between people is truly staggering, and yet they seem to be oblivious to any problem!

12.1.02 The role of communication

One of the facts about communication that always amazes me is that there are only three roles for messages:

- Messages can give information.
- Messages can give orders.
- Messages can ask questions.

This might seem to be an extraordinary claim, but I challenge anyone to refute it. Indeed it could be said that there is only one true role for communication and that is information-giving.

Why do I say that?

If you look at asking questions, you will see that a question is information about what the questioner wants to know. Questions themselves can influence the course of an encounter. For example, a closed question can kill a conversation. If for we ask, "Is it raining?" the person, if they choose, can answer only yes or no. If on the other hand we ask, "What is the weather doing?" this is an open question which could lead to a conversation. The other way in which we use questions is to seek confirmation of our own viewpoint. For example, "It is a lovely day, isn't it?" is seeking agreement. This is called a question tag as it is tagged onto the end of a statement.

And if we look at giving orders we can see that an order provides a lot of information. It tells us about the status of the people involved and it also tells us whatever the person wants to happen. So this too can be regarded as information-giving.

Having looked very briefly at some of the factors that influence even very simple communication, we can now move on to listening.

12.2 Listening

Before looking at listening in more detail it is

also important to draw attention to the basics. We use our ears to hear noise. It is therefore important that they work. Before doing anything else have your hearing checked. As we get older our hearing can fade, so if we have to wear a hearing aid then we do so without diffidence or embarrassment.

12.2.01 Listening as a skill

Listening is probably the most skilful yet least practised aspect of communication. It is far more than just registering a person's words. Proper listening should involve the whole person, which means paying proper attention.

In some respects there are two types of listening. The first is conversational, where there is no outcome hanging on the result. The second is when someone is unburdening themselves. Under these circumstances it is important to suspend judgement and run with the other person's agenda.

The importance of actually being listened to cannot be over emphasised. Erickson, one of the early child psychologists, commented that being attended to, observed and looked upon are 'potent reinforcements for self-worth', and that the moment a person glances or turns away, then begins a sense of rejection.

Whether you agree with that or not, it does

seem that when someone pays full attention to us it does make us feel worthwhile enough to warrant that regard. The extraordinary thing is that although we have two ears and one mouth, we often seem to behave as if we have one ear and two mouths. Real listening is rare and generally can only be achieved after training. It requires self-discipline, knowledge, and suspension of prejudice and patience. It also requires you to put your ego on the backburner. For some this is an almost impossible requirement to meet.

True listening is, therefore, mentally demanding, but it will act as a very powerful affirmation of the speaker. As such true listening can make you a highly valued member of the pack and help with the process of re-inclusion within it. So often those of us with a disability are denied opportunities to be needed. Learning to listen will provide many chances to meet this need.

12.2.02 Attention and hearing

How often have we been with someone who has protested that we haven't been listening to a word they've been saying. We will protest that we have, and then repeat every word back! But so can a tape recorder. What people are picking up on when they accuse us of this is our lack of attention.

Managing our attention levels is one of the skills with which we must become comfortable if we are to be effective listeners. To listen effectively, there are three basic sub-skills that have to be mastered:

- The maintenance of attention levels.
- Getting the NVC, or body language, right – and this is possible, even with sight loss.
- Picking out and registering the core of what is being said.

Just to add to the fun, these three skills have to be practised simultaneously to be an effective listener. It sounds impossible, but it's not. And it's amazing how quickly proper listening can become almost second nature.

Studies have shown that maintaining attention levels throughout the time someone is talking is far from straightforward, however, because the following can happen to the attention levels of the listener:

- Attention starts very high to find out the subject matter.
- Attention drops quite low as you make encouraging noises.
- Attention rises to moderate level as you check they are still talking about the same thing.
- Attention will fall as you think about what is

being said.

- Attention rises to a moderate level again as you consider this.
- Attention will fall again as you wonder what you'll be having for dinner or whether you locked the front door etc.
- Attention rises briefly as you check again what is being said.
- Attention drops to rock-bottom as you work out what you are going to say in response.
- Attention rises to the maximum as you wait for a chance to reply.

Basically, we listen hard at the beginning and end of someone talking, but not particularly well in the middle. So, as most people introduce a topic, talk about it and then wrap up, it is clear that they are not generally being heard for most of the time.

This has two important implications. First, we can use this to inform how *we* present our own topics. Either we have to hit the listener hard, with enough information, so that they do not turn off – literally grab their attention; or, alternatively, we can positively encourage a response, so they do not have to go looking for the chance to reply.

The second implication is that if we can control our levels of attention when someone else is talking then we will be good listeners. And as listening is one of the best ways of making someone feel worthwhile, then in terms of being a pack member we will enjoy high value.

We must accept, however, that it is difficult to maintain a high level of attention throughout an entire conversation. There are a number of factors that will influence attention levels:

- Your own comfort, such as hunger or cold.
- The amount of distraction.
- Your relationship with the talker, including status.
- Your interests and sense of security.

These are just some of the factors. Also, do not forget our old friend the social transaction model. In other words, whether we think that listening will be worthwhile or not will have a significant influence on our attention levels. This is why the suspension of prejudice is so important. It also follows that trying to listen to someone in the middle of a noisy and dangerous street before lunch is far from optimum conditions!

As a social work team leader my job involved supervising staff who were doing a difficult and sometimes dangerous job. Highly focussed listening was thus a vital part of the job. I would make sure there were no interruptions, make sure we sat at the same level, ensure I had my back to the window, that we both had a cup of coffee, and I fed back my understanding of what was being said as we went along. In addition to this I would deploy the sub-skills outlined below.

Taking these sub-skills into consideration, we can try to structure listening by actively managing our attention levels.

Managing attention levels

Sampling

- Pay high attention for a quarter of a minute or so.
- Deliberately stop listening and log the keywords in your mind. This should take a second or two.
- Return to a high level of attention for ten seconds or so.
- Deliberately stop listening and log the keywords and link with previous keywords.
- Return to high-attention listening for ten seconds.

Continue this process of high attention and not listening until it is clear some response is needed. Why? Because this sampling technique is a good way of pacing and achieving consistently high attention levels. When you deliberately drop your attention level you are unlikely to miss anything, because speech is normally full of redundancies such as repetitions, errs and ums. By using this method, you will pick up and lodge the essentials in your head and therefore make an informed and relevant response.

Do not expect to be able to do this straight away, however, as it takes practise.

Using body language or NVC

The second sub-skill of effective listening is the use of non-verbal communication or NVC. This can be demonstrated by:

- Standing or sitting with your body orientated towards the person to whom you are listening. This indicates you are listening to them and no one else. (People indicate this to me as a blind person by touching me.)
- Keep an open posture without crossed arms. This indicates you are open to whatever they want to tell you.
- Lean slightly towards the person. This indicates you are drawn by what they are telling you and you are eager to hear more.
- Eye contact is important to maintain the link. As a blind person, aiming just above where the voice is coming from works pretty well.

By now you probably feel you have tied

yourself in knots to get into the right position to listen and apply the 'method' of listening. It is, therefore, ironic that the last part is to relax, and is probably the most important part of NVC when listening. To help remember the different elements of NVC, here is the mnemonic **S O L E R**:

- **S** for sit or stand.
- **O** is for open posture.
- **L** for lean towards.
- **E** for eye contact.
- **R** for relax.

The third skill is wrapped up in the first. Having registered the core of what people are saying we have to make a response. Sometimes a nod, or encouraging noise is enough. Other times a response is definitely needed.

Reflective listening

This is the sub-skill of reflecting back the very core of what the person is saying. This does two basic things:

1. It tells the speaker whether you have heard them properly.
2. Hearing their own words allows them to consider if that is what they really meant.

If you intend to reflect back from the outset of listening then you are straying into one of the core skills of counselling. It can be incredibly helpful, and it keeps you firmly on the speaker's agenda.

To the speaker this can be extremely positive. In this high-speed world one of the great fears we all have is whether we are actually being heard. A demonstration that we are is rather refreshingly positive.

Suspending judgement

One of the hardest things is to suspend judgement. You are there to listen, not criticise. Nonetheless, if you are listening properly people will sometimes tell you appalling or incredible things. Whilst it may be tempting to inquire if they are effing barking, this is not really helpful. Far better to repeat it back as said so they can hear for themselves how it sounds. This will either result in confirmation of the original statement, which is unusual, or a modification or retraction of it.

Responding is something that has to be done with great care. It has to be not only non-judgemental but also non-directional. The minute you stray into giving direct advice you assume responsibility for the outcome of following that advice. As far as possible help the speaker identify and explore options for themselves.

As can be seen, responding is complex and challenging and needs careful thought. If you feel you are getting out of your depth it might be appropriate to signpost the speaker to a professional. Having said that, it can be incredibly rewarding. If you wish to know more, a very good starting point is *A Still Small Voice* by Michael Jacobs.

Before moving on to look a little more at NVC, let me stress again that skilled listening is probably the best route back to inclusion in the pack as a blind person. And with our minds uncluttered and distracted by vision, we have the opportunity to become very skilled listeners indeed – but only if we want to and are prepared to put the work in.

Not everyone is cut out to be a counsellor; but there is nothing stopping us all from becoming more effective listeners, and patience and suspension of judgement are vital.

12.3 Non-verbal communication

We pride ourselves on being able to use complex sounds to communicate with others. This verbal communication is a relative latecomer, however, and it is clear that long before verbalisation there was a rich system of gestures, signs and body language.

The non-verbal side of communication stems from our earliest times. As such it is rich in meaning, and has its own grammar and structure. Its current role is to give added meaning to the spoken word, and to provide emphasis and meaning to the social world around us. It includes features such as:

- **The way we speak.** This will demonstrate to others who we think we are, or in some cases what we want others to think of us. As non-sighted individuals this is one of the few aspects of NVC available to us.
- **What we wear.** Clothes tell us much about a person's desired status and to some extent their current mood. We cannot be influenced by what others wear, but can still influence others by how we are dressed ourselves.
- **How we stand or sit.** At a very crude level this will inform you whether that person has been in the forces or not. We can project a number of things, already discussed above, although we may not be able to observe it in others.
- **Our orientation to others.** We can achieve this for ourselves even if we cannot see others.
- **The way we move.** We can pick up on this up to a limited degree. We can tell whether the footsteps are sharp and crisp or dragging and shuffling. This too is an important part of

how we present ourselves to others.

- **The gestures we use.** Again, this is important in how we present ourselves to others. Sometimes people will make gestures by touching us.
- **How we use eye contact or shake hands.** How people shake hands can give you a wealth of information. You might get a handful of wet fish or a firm grip. Both will tell you much.

When we meet someone for the first time we make an instant judgement of who or what they think they are. This is based on all of the above. NVC provides a way for us to make predictions within a complex and shifting social world. We do this so that we get some idea as to how we are expected to behave. If we do not know how to behave, we have no role. When we are barred from playing a role we are embarrassed.

Those of us who cannot see are denied much, but not all, of this information. This is why the rule of listening carefully and judging slowly is so important. It is also important to not lose sight of the fact that others have all that information to judge you.

As far as projecting body language to others is concerned, nothing has changed. Other people will judge us by how we present ourselves initially, and then by what we say. It is therefore necessary that we are careful about how we present and project ourselves. The problem we have is that we cannot see how others are responding to us and modify our behaviour accordingly.

The two major aspects of NVC that we can receive and use, however, are the type of speech used and touch. Even without sight there are many hidden clues about the speaker and how they would like to be perceived through these two aspects. For instance:

- The complexity or simplicity of the language used will give an indication of the level of education enjoyed (or endured!) by the speaker.
- Fluency and content will give indications of their intelligence within the context of what they are talking about.
- Speed of delivery may be an indicator of their emotional makeup.
- Volume of delivery may indicate their current mood.

Of course, the better you know a person the more easily you will be able to read them through their voice alone. This does not come naturally with strangers, however, and requires application and work for it to become a reliable tool. This is particularly so when people choose to talk to us slowly and loudly as if we were deaf or imbeciles.

Our second tool, that of touch, can be a substitute for eye contact, and can tell you a fair amount about the person who is touching you. For instance:

- It can tell you whether the person is relaxed or tense.
- The pressure of a touch will increase when they are emphasising something.
- A tentative touch might indicate that a person is not naturally tactile, or they may be nervous.
- A touch can project a threat, an opportunity, or is just neutral.

My experience has been that people use touch to reassure me that it is me and no one else to whom they are talking. In that respect it seems to be an alternative gesture of inclusion when eye contact is no longer viable. As such it should be welcomed as a valuable source of information and a potent message of inclusion.

A further aspect of NVC that we can use is smell. As we routinely take note of how people smell, whether we are sighted or not, there seems little point in going into too much detail. Just remember, though, that the sense of smell will become increasingly important as sight fades, and indeed you will notice many things that perhaps you missed when sighted. With respect to communication, it is possible to smell nervousness on a person purely because they tend to sweat more, for example!

12.4 Basic assertion skills

There is a general misunderstanding that assertion is about being tough and always getting your own way. This is not true. If we look at assertion in the continuum of behaviour, then behaviour can range from passive to aggressive behaviour with assertiveness in between, or neither passive nor aggressive just assertive.

To put it another way, assertiveness is when you take clear responsibility for your own actions and you uphold your own needs and rights without impinging on those of others. For those of us with no sight this is a skill that we have to learn and learn quickly if we have any chance of not being side-lined.

Although assertion is classed as a skill it is far more than that. It can become a way of life. As such it contributes considerably towards reducing the level of stress.

It cannot be denied that the bar is set so much higher for anyone with sight loss and that there is continuous opposition to our being independent. Assertion, being firmly as it is in the rational dimension of behaviour, is an essential tool in keeping us focussed. The moment we become emotional we have lost any argument and any progress towards independence will be stalled. Both passive and aggressive behaviours are irrational and emotional. Neither one nor the other impresses anybody.

Before looking at assertion we need to understand why passivity and aggression are such poor options.

12.4.01 Passive behaviour

Passive behaviour can be defined as allowing others to have what they want regardless of your own needs, wants and feelings. It is a deeply irrational behaviour and involves the abject surrender of self to others. Being passive is an active choice made by many for a number of reasons, one of which is that doing the bidding of others is easier because there is no requirement to think or take responsibility. It also excludes any element of choice. Another reason is that by making themselves a martyr people hope they will be appreciated and praised; but generally they are used and otherwise ignored. Being passive is also used as a tactic to avoid being bullied. Unfortunately this does not work, however, as the passive are viewed as easy pickings by the aggressive. Being passive can easily lead to frustration, illness and stress.

You may choose to be passive. Sadly, the result will be that you will find yourself shunted to one side and the only way your needs will be met is if someone happens to notice and can be bothered to do something about it.

In the end, passivity can cause resentment which could flash over into aggression (the worm turns!), or it could be buried deeply and cause long-term stress or even psychiatric problems.

To sum up, passivity is both an irrational and unhealthy option. More importantly, it does not work.

12.4.02 Aggressive behaviour

Aggressive behaviour is also deeply irrational and takes a great deal of energy to maintain. In fishing terms, you could call it a 'coarse feeder'. Aggressive behaviour is used as it is seen, as a sure-fire way of getting what you want without having to consider the needs, wants and feelings of others. There are numerous disadvantages of being aggressive.

Firstly, an aggressive person is in constant fear of coming across someone who is tougher, meaner and more aggressive than they are. Therefore they will constantly be worrying about what their equally aggressive rivals are up to.

Secondly, there will always be the chance

that the people they have trampled on will one day get their own back.

With respect to this, there is the story of the farmer who obtained five thousand gallons of petrol early in the war when rationing was in force. Calling his farmhand, who he treated abominably, he told him to dig a hole to hide the petrol. Five hours later he saw the farmhand and asked if the job was done. The answer was yes, and the farmer demanded to see the hole. The farmhand showed him a metre-square hole about half a metre deep. Asking where the effing petrol was, he received the reply that it had been 'poured down the effing hole'.

At the time, the story was told to demonstrate the stupidity of the farmhand. I have always felt that it demonstrated exactly the opposite. As mentioned above, maintaining aggression is hard work as it uses a lot of energy. It too can lead to stress and long-term health problems.

No one is invincible. The fall from the top of the pile is inevitable and complete.

12.4.03 Assertive behaviour

Assertive behaviour is neither passive nor aggressive. Rather it enables someone to claim whatever they have a right to without trampling on the needs of others. It is behaviour where you take responsibility for your own actions, where you are in control without being controlling. Unlike passivity or aggression, which are emotional and irrational, assertive behaviour is rational and unemotional. This allows for much clearer and objective thinking, and enables you to remain cool and logical when others are losing it.

Those of us who are sight impaired or are blind are faced with an immediate necessity to work out how we are to conduct ourselves in the seeing world. We might choose to be aggressive; but being blind we have no ability to enforce our aggression. If you meet an aggressive blind person, walking away and leaving them to rant and shout is highly effective. This provides evidence of the fact that if you are aggressive, people will choose to be elsewhere.

Assertive behaviour, where you take responsibility for yourself and take matters into your own hands, is a far more positive way forward than either passivity or aggression. This is also the way to take on the responsibilities that must go with any rights you may claim.

There are basic techniques that are used in assertion.

The first general technique is to think very carefully about whether what you are about to ask for is actually reasonable and possible. If it is, then move to the next step, which is to rehearse what you are going to say in your head.

Ensure it is polite, clear and unambiguous.

Perhaps the most important aspect of assertion is establishing ownership of the problem. In a world where the tendency is to blame everybody else, (Donald Trump springs to mind), the idea of claiming ownership of a problem is somewhat alien if not completely counterintuitive.

The 'you' versus the 'I' message

If someone tells me, "You have to help me!" my instinct is to think *No I don't; how dare you dump your problem on me*. Alternatively, if someone says, "I have a problem, can I have some help please?" my instinct is to say, "How can I help?" The difference is that in the first example the person is using a 'you' message, and in the second an 'I' message.

'You' messages are generally unhelpful. They remind us of getting into trouble, and the immediate reaction is to start putting up defences and stop listening. Messages like "Where have you been?", "Oh, you think that do you?", "What time do you call this?" and "What have you done now?" all have associations of guilt and some form of wrongdoing. They imply you may have to do something against your will, or that you will be required to take remedial action to solve a problem that belongs to someone else. The problem has been firmly dumped on your shoulders.

Take the message, "Oh you think that do you?" The person who has the problem is the person asking the question. But by using a 'you' message they are trying to make it your problem, to which you have to find a solution. You on the other hand are quite happy to think what you do, and then someone comes along and wants you to do something about it. If you think about it, we have been subjected to this unsubtle pressure all our lives. Above all, 'you' messages are unhelpful as they rarely work without some emotional and irrational encounter, which is unpleasant for everybody.

The 'I' message, on the other hand, squarely takes ownership of the problem. People will listen because the lack of the word 'you' does not provoke them into putting up defences. It is also a much more accurate rendering of the situation in that it states to whom the problem belongs. Above all, 'I' messages actually work without the need for some ghastly scene.

The use of 'I' messages will be illustrated as we go through the various techniques, and consequent ownership of the problem or issue is of course the most important technique of them all. Before moving on to look at specifics, there are a number of things of which you need to be aware.

12.4.04 Things to avoid

There are certain things that should be avoided when framing an assertive message. One of the most important is to avoid absolutes. Words like 'never' and 'always' are good examples of absolutes. They do not work because they are untrue and give the person you are talking to a chance to argue and disrupt your message. For example, "You are always late!" can be met with "I was on time the other night." When that happens the encounter is lost at the outset. You are forced to give ground.

Another thing to avoid is bad language as that immediately surrenders the moral high ground, and instead of delivering your message you will end up apologising. It's also important to avoid swapping personal remarks or getting into some irrelevant competition. This is a common way to move the encounter away from your intended outcome. Just ignore it and persist with your message.

Avoiding debate or arguments is also vital. You are there to state your case not to listen to irrelevant nonsense. I remember a time when one of the chaps at the warehouse I was working at was asked why he was not doing much work. He began some long story, which was cut short by my colleague: "I do not want a life story. I want some work to be done." Absolutely brilliant response. It was an 'I' message. The problem and the solution were clearly stated and, above all, it was polite and left nowhere to go but to do the job.

Do not allow yourself to be drawn away from the core of your message; but do not get so locked into your message that you are unable to review it if necessary.

In addition to the things to avoid, you must always remain calm and rational. Once you get emotional you are working to the other person's agenda and not your own.

Additional points

- Take responsibility for the message by using 'I' messages like, "I would like...'. "Mr Smith has told me that he would like..." is not taking responsibility.
- Do not show doubt or hesitation.
- Use a basic technique known as the 'broken record', which we will discuss now.

12.4.05 Broken record technique

Those of us who have or work with children will know all about this technique. Basically a broken-record request is a request repeated until you lose the will to live and agree. If it works for kids there is no reason it can't for adults. Obviously you have to be a little more sophisticated about it. An adult repeatedly whining "Mum, I want..." would do little to display your credentials as a rational and assertive person!

Assertion is a skill, and like any skill it has to be broken down into its component parts and then put together as a single, smooth performance. Therefore:

- Work out exactly what it is you want to happen.
- Check it for reasonableness.
- Check that what you are asking is actually possible.
- Work out exactly what it is you are going to say.
- Rehearse the message in your head.
- Greet the other person and engage in a little small talk. This will warm your voice up. There is nothing worse than having the perfect assertive message and it comes out as a squeak!
- Communicate your message.
- Meet any response with a repetition.
- If you are greeted with silence tell the person that you assume silence implies assent. (That usually gets them thinking!)
- Repeat the message.
- If after a few repetitions there is still resistance, reconsider what it is you are asking for.

- If still reasonable, repeat.
- If possibly unreasonable adjust your position and start again.
- Throughout remain calm, rational, clear and unwavering.
- Above all own the message by using I.

This does work. It takes patience and practice. As time goes on you will find that if you are assertive people will know it is quicker and much easier to comply. Note that being assertive involves being reasonable. The moment you start to use it for dominance then it flips over into aggression.

The broken record technique is a useful tool when trying to get something done or a problem solved. The overriding technique is, of course, the I message. You also use this when fielding criticism.

12.4.06 Dealing with criticism

It seems that some individuals like to spend much of their time criticising, shouting and generally being unpleasant to others. If someone starts raising their voice at you, you know that you are on the edge of an irrational encounter. The best way to calm things down is to use a basic de-escalation technique. Simply lower your voice and speak slowly and calmly. At heart, everybody is a conformist, and you will find the other person will eventually match your volume and speed of delivery. If you do the opposite and start shouting back, this will only feed the anger and the encounter will quickly escalate out of control.

On one occasion my wife and I parked in front of someone's house. This was perfectly legal as all parking was on the public road. But the householder came out screaming and raving. My wife wanted to move to another spot, and I disagreed. The chap raved for a few minutes more, and then I quietly asked him to stop shouting. His response was to shout that he would shout if he wanted to. By this time we had an interested crowd of bystanders. I continued my quiet assertive message to stop shouting. After a few minutes the volume dropped, he realised he was making an idiot of himself, and he retired to his house.

It does work. I use it all the time. Once things have calmed down the other person may still try and provoke you by criticising. But there are a couple of techniques you can use here. The first is to agree.

An example of this is when I was walking with my dog on one of the local trails and someone snarled at me, "Your dog is not on a lead!" I calmly replied, "Yes, I agree, my dog is not on a lead." This simple tactic of agreeing is often enough to confound people as they have no idea where to go next.

On another occasion I was standing at the pharmacy and some woman snapped, "Your dog is too fat." Resisting the urge to ask her if she had looked in the mirror recently I replied, "Yes, just like her master. Do I hear an offer to help me walk her?" There is nothing quite as gratifying as the sound of spluttering and retiring at speed!

If you meet someone who is persistent, you can use the second tactic of exhausting the criticism. So, if after commenting about the lead they then go on to criticising you as an individual, you could say, "I am sorry about that. Is there anything else?" And continue like this until they get bored, at which you can move on. Whatever you do, however, do not lose your cool, only use I messages, and do not get into swapping insults. This sounds very unnatural, particularly when you are itching to tell the other person's fortune. Rest assured, though, that this approach works and the other person will end up far more frustrated than you.

Sometimes you have to use assertion with little or no warning. Such an occasion was when someone, out of the blue, commented, "You don't look blind." A remark like that can be taken in a number of ways. Keeping my cool I merely replied, "We cannot tell the taste of a sweet by its wrapper." He became quite cross and barked at me, "What I meant by that is that you do not behave as if you are blind!" I answered, "When I could see, I never could tell who was stupid by just looking." I am pretty sure he is still trying to work out whether I was being rude or not. The use of I messages and avoiding you messages took the sting right out of his comments.

All of the above might sound a little strange, but using some or all of the points you will find your ability to communicate will improve beyond all recognition. With assertion, rehearsal and thinking it through beforehand are important. In the early days, however, choose battles you can win and build the skills carefully. Do not expect these skills to just appear, however. They take hard work, and one of the hardest parts is to resist the temptation to go round on autopilot.

Another of the major problems we meet is that other people do not tend to be naturally assertive. They often act within the irrational dimension that is either aggressive or passive. It is very hard to resist the habit of conforming, and it is important we remain rational whilst those around us are losing it. This is probably the hardest aspect of assertive behaviour, resisting being drawn into other people's emotional firestorms.

Summary

Everything in this chapter is stuff we all know; but life tends to make us forget it. Once you start to communicate mindfully with your environment, physical and social, you will find life less stressful and less out of control.

The information is there. Whether you use it or not is down to you.

CHAPTER THIRTEEN

HELP, THE POISON CHALICE

'No one is useless in this life if they ease the burden of others.'

– Charles Dickens

It's clear that provision for people with sight loss needed improving, and I'm pleased to say it is now improving all the time. The work carried out by the many charities on mobility, living skills, IT skills, support for the workplace is, in some cases, exceptional. The training does however seem to focus on the basic practical aspects of living with sight loss. This is not to fault such training; on the contrary, the training and emotional support I have received from Blind Veterans UK has been superb. But there are still many areas in which training for people with sight loss is either lacking or lamentable. Of these perhaps the most important topics are the management of sight loss, regaining a foothold in society, communication, assertion, interpersonal skills and asking for and refusing help.

Those of us with severe or total sight loss are, whether we like it or not, in a constant state of supplication. We need the help of people around us, including casual strangers. For many of us who have been used to being fiercely independent, this can sometimes prove to be difficult if not almost impossible. Recognising that we need help and accepting it with good grace is probably one of the most important parts of acceptance. It is almost certainly one of the most difficult, least understood and poorly executed.

We have to learn very quickly how to ask for help, to be a supplicant. We have to learn to do this with humour, patience and gratitude, but without losing our sense of self-worth. Sometimes it seems an impossible balance to achieve. If we are unpleasant and angry, or sarcastic and grovelling, then it will not be a pleasant task to help us. Casual helpers will be noticeable for their absence, and regular helpers will be reluctant, tardy and resistant.

As asking for and refusing help is such an important aspect of our new lives I will cover it in some depth. I make no apology for this, even though a lot of what I write about might seem very simple and obvious. But then it seems to me that people are so busy looking under rocks that they often fail to notice what is in plain view.

Both refusing and asking for help are highly skilled activities, and both have to be carried out seamlessly so that the right outcome is achieved and nobody ends up feeling offended, used or dissatisfied. It is also the most common and obvious point of contact between those with apparent disabilities and those without. But it is fraught with issues of power, control, status and pride and the chances of misunderstanding are enormous.

The matter of help is a clear example of where assertion skills can play an important role, which falls into parts. First, having the basic belief that you are worthy of receiving help. This notion of self-worth is so central to everything we do that without it we will not even try let alone succeed at new things. Second, those who have been paying attention will recognise that there is one vital element here: use of the I message rather than the you message. If you compare "You have to help me" with "Can I have some help, please?" the differences are clear. It is much harder to ignore the second than the first. The I message has a curious power of its own. On the one hand it assumes responsibility, and on the other absolves the potential helper from having to take charge or assume any other burden. On occasion I have received abuse when doing this. As you can imagine, this is a little off-putting. I have then received the help from the same person, which is staggering. None so queer as folk, I guess.

Asking for help is wrapped in issues of power, control, status and pride. It involves admitting vulnerability and putting your welfare in the hands of others. This is why it is so important to be assertive. It is also important to remember that you are asking for the temporary access to someone's time and abilities, not demanding they lay their life down for you, yet the opportunities for causing unintentional offence are endless.

Conversely, refusing help is an extremely complex and also an emotionally loaded activity involving issues of power, control, status and pride. When you refuse help you are in effect doing any number of the following:

- Rejecting the helper as a person.
- Denying the helper the chance to feel good about themselves.
- Imposing your will upon the helper by stopping them from doing something they had chosen to do.
- Creating potential negativity around a positive experience.
- Creating a disconnect from the helper's

expectations.

But you are also taking responsibility for what happens next. Before dismissing this as fanciful, consider how you feel when you have an offer of help rejected.

There seem to be two clear options when refusing assistance. A soft option and a hard option.

The soft option

The soft option is where you accept the offer of help and keep strict control. This can be achieved by telling the person exactly what they can do to help. You can also insist that you take their arm, rather than them taking yours. I explain this by saying that I can let go if I fall, and when they have stopped laughing they will be able to help me up. In this way you are controlling their actions and can put a stop to it at any point.

It is also making a clear statement that you are choosing to accept help rather than having it imposed upon you. This makes a subtle alteration to the balance of power and status within the encounter. Most people do not recognise this, however, and thus you are able to avoid overt struggles and causing offence.

In the early days of my sight loss I would

allow people to take my arm. But having been frogmarched across roads I had no desire to cross I soon learned not to permit this. In a situation where we are asking for help we are vulnerable, but we must be so without surrendering what control we do have. This is not paranoia; it is trying to maintain a power balance.

There is one thing that helpful bystanders sometimes do that really tries my patience. Some people will grab the end of my cane and try and pull me along by it. Depending on how I am feeling at the time I will do one of two things. Either I will say, "I wouldn't do that, mate, I've just passed through a big patch of dog mess" – which usually has the desired effect! – or I will simply let go of my cane so they end up looking foolish and not me. When they ask why I then explain, politely, why I simply cannot keep up with being led by a cane that is designed to help me sense the ground and where my feet are treading...whilst itching to respond in a way that is neither fair nor printable!

If you wish you can limit their help to advice or information only. When crossing the road, for example, you could simply ask them to just let you know when it is safe to cross.

The hard option

The hard option is to refuse any help at all.

Pragmatism and courtesy dictate that this should be done with politeness and consideration. My usual response is something on the lines of "That is very kind of you. However I really need to do this for myself. Thank you anyway." This upsets nobody and states exactly what you intend to do. It is also an assertive I message. Those on the end of a brusque refusal can get upset if they feel so moved.

Many of the people who help me have stories of being savagely rebuffed by people with sight loss. Whilst this may be understandable it is not helpful to those of us who are trying to deal with the matter of being helped or not with some semblance of grace and courtesy.

Being gracious

Even under the most favourable of circumstances, crossing the road is hazardous. I liken it to playing Russian Roulette: you may choose to play it, but it is a hazard, and there is no point whingeing when you traumatise someone by stepping in front of their moving vehicle. Indeed, when the wind is blowing, when it is raining, or when there is a lot of other background noise, it is like playing Roulette with an automatic pistol.

The hazard will only increase as electric and hybrid vehicles become more common, which is a major concern. Unless something is done to make them as noisy as conventional vehicles I have visions of those with severe or total sight loss being culled at an alarming rate. Apparently after fifteen years of discussions the motor manufacturers still have to agree to not make noiseless vehicles.

I used to be quite independent crossing roads, and I still do it with relative ease in the town where I live. I am fortunate in that I live in a small market town where most people seem to either know of me, or are acquaintances, and the traffic will stop both ways if I stand as if I am waiting to cross. I do not rely on this entirely, however. I make sure to listen very, very carefully.

I have known people stop their car, get out and escort me across the road. This is both heart-warming and a little embarrassing. There are others of course who slam to a halt in front of you and yell at me asking if I know where I am, do I know what I am doing, and should I be out on my own. It is sometimes difficult to remain calm under these circumstances. My responses will vary depending on how wicked I feel.

Sometimes, in response to whether I should be out on my own, I reply, "Probably not!" and start roaring with laughter. Other times I will be better behaved and reply that I am trying to cross the road and they are blocking the way. I suppose that what I am saying is that whilst we may be supplicants that does not give anybody the right to treat us as imbeciles. In short, supplication does not deny us the basic right to stand up for ourselves.

Crossing the road in my hometown, however, is a far cry from a big town or city, where if someone offers help in crossing the road I accept it. I usually remark that I would be grateful as it can be a little tricky sometimes.

There are some situations where I not only accept help, but also actively seek it. The two main examples that spring to mind are supermarket shopping and travelling. I make a distinction about supermarkets, though, as we still have many small shops in my town where the old model of actually serving customers still exists, but most larger supermarkets will happily provide a member of staff to help you shop. On the surface this assisted shop could not be simpler. Merely walk into the store, find customer services and ask them for an assisted shop. However, if we drill down into this, if you want a totally positive experience the matter has to be given serious consideration. (This of course is true for any activity which we attempt.)

Assistance when shopping

There are two ways of asking for assistance with

shopping. You can charge in and demand an assisted shop if you wish, but if you do it rudely or at a busy time you will discover it takes a long time to find someone to help you. And if you do not make a point of engaging with and being pleasant to the member of staff helping you then you will find the whole experience pretty hideous. Apart from that, the next time you go into that shop there will be no staff available.

I have found that introducing myself by my given name is a good ice breaker. They will invariably respond by giving me theirs, so I follow this up by asking if they have escorted a person with sight loss before. If the answer is in the negative I will spend a few seconds covering the main points, which are:

- They need to give warning of any change of direction.
- They must make sure to allow space for you.
- They need to warn of a narrowing of the aisle so you can walk behind them.
- They must check that each item that goes in the basket is what you want.

Before you start shopping tell the member of staff everything you are looking for or give them your list. In this way they can plan the best route around the store. This will not only reduce the time it will also reduce the distance, and chance of accident, to the minimum. At the end thank them and comment honestly on their performance. If there are issues, point out what was right and useful before offering advice on the issue in question. Finally, be sure to thank them again. This is very simple stuff but it makes the whole experience more seamless. It also gives the helper training that they can take anywhere.

If you take pains to find out when the least busy time is, you will find that the wait is negligible, there are less people to barge into, the member of staff is going to be less hassled, and the experience can be quite pleasant. By engaging and being pleasant when teaching the staff the best way to help you, you not only make it easier for yourself, you are also adding to their skills set.

The above points revolve around matters of ease and courtesy. There is, however, another highly important reason for behaving like a reasonable human being. Whether we like it or not, all of us are ambassadors for all blind people. The better we behave, the more pleasant and accommodating we are, the better the impression on the people we meet, the consequence being the next time they are in contact with a blind person the better they will treat them.

You may decide that you do not need staff

to help with your shopping. If so, a couple of things need to happen.

First, make sure that you pull and not push your trolley. The damage and destruction to both people and property if you are charging around with a trolley when you have no sight is beyond description.

Second, you will have to have your free hand in a warding position to avoid ramming people and shelving with force. The warding position is quite simple. Place your free arm in a curve in front of your body at just below chest height. This will give advance warning of any obstacles.

Having solved the problem of moving around a crowded store without injuring people or knocking over shelves, the issue of locating the items you wish to buy still remains.

There are three options you can pursue here.

The first, and simplest option, is to ask fellow customers. This involves firstly asking where a particular item is located, and then asking whether they have what you want. I have found that fellow customers are, on the whole, more than willing to help. The main thing to remember is that you are, by asking for help, requesting the use of someone's eyes and time. If you make it a pleasant experience they will be happy to help you when they see you next. The opposite is also true.

Sometimes it is a little difficult to identify

good quality help. This is where we have to be a little cute. If someone sounds flustered or in a hurry there is a good chance that any assistance is not going to be forthcoming or of poor quality. On the other hand, if someone sounds casual and relaxed then it is probable they have time to spare and will therefore provide good quality assistance. Indeed, it has often been the case that someone has said they have plenty of time and would be happy to come round with me. But we must not presume upon their help for hours. Get the job done, thank them, and part company with a smile.

The second option can only be used if you have a mobile phone with a camera and audio feedback. I understand that many smart phones have audio communication functions now. There are also applications that can be used with the simpler mobile telephones. I have a Samsung Galaxy with the synaptic application. As the phone talks to me I can use the scanner on my phone to identify items. This is, however, pretty laborious and taking independence to a ridiculous degree.

The third option is to use an application called 'Be My Eyes'. This is an application which is free and free to use. All you need is a mobile phone with a camera. Once you activate the app you will immediately be put in touch with one of 1.5 million volunteers who will use the camera on your phone to help you find whatever you need. The same rules of engagement apply to these volunteers as to someone who is physically present.

There is one final option, but one which I am a little hesitant to mention. It is a device made by Oculus. It is a very small camera which fits onto your glasses frame. It can recognise faces, and read print and barcodes. It is still under development and very expensive for what it is. You will need to do the research and decide for yourself.

The best option by far is to swallow our pride and ask for an assisted shop. Apart from being quicker and much easier, it also gives you the opportunity to be an ambassador for sight loss.

Assistance when travelling

Travelling is certainly an area where assistance should be sought. This help can be as little as asking people at a bus stop to tell you when your bus arrives, to the full-blooded support given by the rail networks.

Some years ago I had to travel from Ashbourne in Derbyshire to Westminster Abbey in London. I booked my seat on the London train and on arrival at Derby station asked for assistance. A member of the station staff took me to the platform, waited with me and then helped me onto the train. Having a reserved seat he knew my location and this was telephoned to St. Pancras station. In London a member of staff came onto the train and found me. He took me to the tube station and handed me over to the underground staff. They passed me to Westminster in the same seamless way, even though it involved a change at Victoria. I have had the same help every time I go anywhere by train.

On another occasion somebody put me on the train for Crewe when I was going to Bedford – the opposite direction. Once the railway staff were aware of this they first of all offered to pay for a taxi from Crewe to Bedford, which I politely refused. They finally arranged to stop a nonstop train so I could board it and get to Bedford, which was greatly appreciated.

It is probably best to follow the rules and book assistance twenty-four hours ahead. Having said that, I generally rock up unannounced and have always been treated well. Indeed I was quite excited when they referred to me as a VIP. Sadly, it meant visually impaired person, and not a very important person!

It is quite clear to me that if you have a white stick and a mouth that rail travel is usually seamless. I sometimes feel it is much easier than when I was sighted.

As explained earlier in the book, each year,

with my companion dog Becky, I embark on what I call the Santa Claus Run where I visit my grandchildren and children in Market Harborough, Bedford, Bristol and Ludlow. It takes me about three or four days and is one of the highlights of the year. I have now demonstrated, to my own satisfaction, that the whole trip, roughly five hundred miles, is entirely possible using local buses. The most gruelling leg is Bedford to Bristol, which involves Bedford to Oxford, Oxford to Chippenham, Chippenham to Bath, and finally Bath to Bristol. But I've had a number of great conversations and met some truly lovely people along the way. Above all, I had a ball!

When you are visually impaired or blind it seems that the entire world is trying to cocoon you and prevent you from doing your own thing, whatever that entails. Just to stress the point – normally activities for people with disabilities are highly supervised. To be able to make this trip and to make my own decisions is an important confirmation of my independence. The only real incident was in Bristol. I took my daughter out for a meal and the taxi driver, after my daughter had got out, locked the taxi with me inside and demanded double fare. A poor choice on his part! With my daughter giving it large on the outside, and me giving a vivid description of exactly what I would be doing with my white cane, he had a change of heart and saw the error of his ways. We reported him to both his taxi firm and the police, and hopefully he will not try that one again in a hurry. This is a situation where the normal rules of requesting help do not apply.

Throughout I have stressed the need to request and refuse assistance with grace and courtesy as our behaviour will have influence on how people view all those with the same condition. So there is a kind of ambassadorial responsibility, whether we like it or not.

The other reason is deeply pragmatic and firmly rooted in social transaction theory. To put it as simply as possible, this theory suggests that parties in an interaction will only start and then continue that interaction so long as the perceived reward is equal to or greater than the perceived effort, or cost, involved. In other words, people only stick around if they think it is worth it. We very often say we cannot be bothered to do something. What we actually mean is that we can see no reward. It is the same with interactions. It sounds quite calculating, cynical and brutal, so consider a normal daily situation, such as going into a pub.

The first calculation is into which bar you will go. Any choice will be based on the sort of people you might expect to meet in one bar or the other. So, anticipating a reward, you enter the bar of your choice. But where you sit will be determined by a number of factors. If someone is there you like, you may choose to sit with them as you can be sure of a good time. If they are engrossed in conversation, however, you will not get the reward you anticipate and you will choose another place. You will also avoid bores, people with whom you may have had a dispute, and total strangers. Every choice will be determined by the reward you anticipate from that choice. Having made your choice, if you fail to receive the anticipated reward you will terminate any interaction and look elsewhere. Next time you go into a social situation, stand back and observe. You will be amazed at what you discover about your choices.

So how does this apply to the social minefield of seeking, accepting and refusing assistance? The answer is very simple. If you go out of your way to be courteous and pleasant then the rewards for helping you are very high. Basically people get the feel-good reward with little or no cost. As a consequence, people will not only be willing to help you again, they will actively look for the opportunity. If on the other hand you are unpleasant and rude, then the cost of helping you will outweigh any reward to the helper and they will not help you again.

As has been made clear, accepting or refusing assistance is very complex. If we wish to be accepted as regular members of society then it has to be done correctly. We must also be aware that by taking charge of the situation we are taking responsibility and that there is no point whining if it goes horribly wrong.

Before moving on there is one aspect of helping which has not been addressed yet, and that is the issue of offering to help others.

As we are in an almost permanent state of supplication, the notion of us offering help may seem a little strange, but just because society will tend to write us off as helpers it does not mean we have to collude with that idea. Whether we have a disability or not we are still, first and foremost, people. As such we have something to offer.

The major difference is that we have to push harder to offer that help. Initially there will be incredulity and resistance. Do not be offended by this. Indeed, as usual, it is down to us to behave like an adult when everybody else is having a hissy fit.

It is important therefore that we persist if we wish to help. Helping others is what fully paid up members of society do. Do I really need to say more on this?

Summary

This chapter has, I hope, given you some

pointers on how to survive as a supplicant with something approaching good humour and grace. I have also attempted to outline some of the interpersonal dynamics involved. This will enable you to operate more mindfully instead of just blundering around demanding or refusing help with little or no consideration of the helper.

One final word of caution. Most of the people you will encounter are only too happy to help; but it cannot be denied there are many miserable sods who are so wrapped in themselves that they fail to notice or care, and certainly do not want to get involved. Do not let people like this upset you. They are outnumbered by so many who do want to help.

Note: Any entity providing goods and services must make reasonable steps to make their services available to all regardless of disability. Assisted shopping is therefore mandated by law.

CHAPTER FOURTEEN

LABELLING - THE THIEF OF INDEPENDENCE

'If you want to change the world,
start with yourself.'

– Gandhi

Every one of us is constantly bombarded with information about our physical and social environment. It also appears that for many of us the default position is to either ignore this information or deal with it in the laziest way possible. This is particularly so in the case of our extremely complex social world. It's very complexity seems to force us to take shortcuts. This could be referred to as proactive perceptual parsimony, if you wish, but however you dress it up it is still laziness.

A clear outcome of this laziness is the common use of stereotypes when relating to others. A stereotype can be defined as 'the best possible rational guess in the absence of information'. Further to this, laziness will generally cause us to accept any information which appears to support the stereotype and ignore any which does not. This rejoices under the name of 'confirmation bias'.

Typical stereotypes would be that Welshman can sing and Scots are tight fisted. Clearly these may apply to some, but certainly not all. Neither do they advance our knowledge of specific individuals. In addition to this, if a person fails to conform to the stereotype then we claim they are the exception that proves the rule!

Applying labels to people is a very common version of stereotyping. As soon as we decide that a label fits someone we drag out a photofit kit of stereotypes and assumed behaviours to fit our picture of the person concerned. For example, if someone is sight impaired or blind then the people around will have preconceptions of what to expect from that individual in terms of intellectual capacity, behaviours and capabilities. The same applies to any person with an obvious impairment. There is an automatic presumption of incapacity and witlessness.

The question "Does he take sugar?" should be burned into the consciousness of any socially aware person, representing as it does the negative influence of labelling. If someone is labelled as handicapped or disabled then it is likely that those around them will assume:

- They can do nothing for themselves.
- They are not very intelligent and have nothing to say.
- They are deaf and it is acceptable to shout at them.
- They are faceless cyphers and their needs and wants can be largely ignored.
- That in every important respect they are a non-person.

In effect the list is endless. As manager of the day centre I used to carry out disability awareness sessions with the local schools and societies. Some of the assumptions were positively medieval. Further to this, the idea that people with disabilities have the same desires, drives and needs as everybody else was considered to be highly offensive in some quarters.

Labelling can create a box where the expectations of others form the walls. It seems that as much as we try to climb out of the box we encounter those who cheerfully try to stuff us back in. It is bad enough that people with apparent impairments are treated in this way. What is truly appalling is that laziness seems to compel those with disabilities to accept the labels about themselves with no resistance. On the one hand, therefore, we have society applying labels to people, and on the other those very people collude with the label. Labels limit life opportunities even when they are offered.

There is, of course, another reason why people choose to use stereotypes. My old mentor used to say, "Everybody is afraid of everybody else, which means everybody is afraid of you." Whether you agree with that or not, it is often the case that when we enter into a social situation we feel a little uncertainty, if not trepidation. I know I present as a confident individual who will engage with anyone in any situation, but this does not mean that I am not frantically assessing the people around me in order to make my world predictable and therefore safe. We all do this to a greater or lesser degree. Part of the assessment is to use stereotypes as a base from which to develop our picture of the dynamics within a social encounter. Sometimes we are able to move away from the comfort of the stereotype, sometimes we are not.

The main reason for not looking beyond the stereotype is that it requires effort on our part. We have to look outside the box and exhaustively search for who other people really are. This requires a recognition that we should do this and a willingness to make the effort. To do this we have first to establish whether the effort is worthwhile. Laziness will invariably prevent any such effort. The other reason is that social situations can be so dynamic and fast moving that sometimes the only way to make sense of them is to use stereotypes.

When this is applied to people with impairments, disabilities, handicaps, or whatever you want to call it, it can have unfortunate results. The outcome for those individuals is the very strong possibility of a singularly drab existence living a very limited and unfulfilling life.

In my own case, being newly blind, the fight to retain my independence was not too bad as I had the support of both my wife and Blind Veterans. I still had to work out my baseline capabilities and fight for the space to build upon them, however, as people were so willing to do things for me because I was considered helpless. One of the first skills that had to be acquired was to refuse help without offending people. My life then became dominated by the need to assess whether I needed assistance or not. There is nothing quite as humiliating as refusing help and then making a complete nonsense of the task and causing damage in the process!

But there is a fine line between permitting someone to help and the need to learn to do something. Everywhere I go I have to ask the question "Why not?" when faced with people who try to limit my opportunities in case I might hurt myself. The bad thing about this is that I am denied the opportunity to learn through failure. People cannot understand that failure is a catalyst for success and not an unmitigated disaster. Unfortunately when failure is turned into a disaster by others, then we become reluctant to try anything. It's a case of assessing the potential for disaster and deciding whether to accept help on that occasion.

In *A Descent into Darkness*, my first book, I gave the example of re-sculpting my finger with a chisel when replacing my conservatory floor. The admonishment to not do that sort of thing when blind by the nurse I saw totally overlooked the fact that I could quite possibly have injured myself whether I was blind or not!

Another example of this is when I changed my Sky box. I made the decision to invest in a Sky Q box because it would make it easier for me to flick from one channel to the other. The Sky engineer called at my home as arranged. I apologised for being slow to answer the door as I was blind. He responded by telling me that was OK, which told me he had not really listened. He then asked me to clear away the dog mess in the garden so he could use his ladder. I did as requested, and asked him to check I had cleared it all. When he asked why he had to check I told him, again, that I was blind. He then informed me, as quick as you like, that he could not fit the box unless there was someone else in the house. I asked him why. His reply was interesting: "I cannot come into the house because I am unable to take responsibility for you." I told him that I wanted him to fit the Q box, not babysit, feed or toilet me. He insisted that if he came into the house he would be responsible for anything that happened to me whilst he was there. In the end I took him by the shoulders and solemnly intoned, "I absolve thee of all responsibility." Three times. At that point he relented.

This raises an interesting point. It seems that the expectations of others due to the adherence to a stereotype can result in the denial of services. This is inappropriate, humiliating, and quite frankly not to be tolerated. Basically this man assumed I was totally helpless, and was prepared to leave me on my own but not prepared to enter the house to do his job. It does make you wonder exactly what companies like Sky consider to be appropriate training for their staff. It may be, of course, that this is a classic example of the influence of stereotypes operating at a corporate or institutional level. When we consider that these bodies are made up of ordinary men and women then this should not be too much of a shock. There are a number of studies that highlight the mechanism and consequences of stereotyping and labelling.

The first is the Rosenthal and Jacobson study carried out on a group of New York primary school children in 1956. The study was called 'Expectations in the classroom'. They tested the IQ of the primary school children. Whilst the true scores were recorded, the teachers were given scores that had been allocated at random. Thus some bright children were allocated low scores, and other children who were behind were allocated high scores.

A couple of months later the children were retested. It was found that bright children who had been allocated low scores either scored the same or less on retesting, but the children who had been allocated high scores achieved much higher scores on retesting. The investigators concluded that the performance of the children had been significantly influenced by the expectations of their teachers – expectations generated by the false IQ scores. In other words, the teachers expected more of the children who had been labelled as bright because of the higher score and this label influenced the behaviour of the teachers.

Another study was the 'Stamford Prison Experiment'. Here a group of volunteers were randomly split into groups. One group was to play the role of prisoners, and the other that of the guards. They were then placed in a mock-up prison. The experiment was to run for six weeks, but it was stopped after three. Why? Both groups behaved in the manner dictated by the stereotype they held of their role. Guards became brutal, officious and inhumane, whilst the prisoners became increasingly downtrodden and hopeless. In the end, so much damage was being done to the participants that they had to stop it. In spite of this a television channel tried to repeat the experiment in the UK as a reality show. I remember watching it with absolute horror as the inevitable tragedies unfolded. It was stopped before its time. Interestingly, in this one it was the prisoners who had the whip hand. This was a clear example of where adherence to a stereotype produced the behaviour located within it. Presumably confirmation bias would have mediated against any behaviour that was not stereotypical.

Yet another study was the 'Sane in an Insane Place' study. As far as I can recall, the volunteers were medical students. They presented themselves at a number of mental institutions as having schizophrenia and were subsequently admitted and treated for the condition. After a short and predetermined time they announced that they were in fact perfectly well and it was all part of an experiment. Without exception they had the devil's own job to gain their freedom. In some cases it took weeks. This was a clear case of confirmation bias blinding the staff to the fact the volunteers were only pretending.

The power and influence of labelling on lives cannot be underestimated. It can be both life opportunity limiting and a denial of many basic rights. A major outcome of labelling can be that it takes away a person's right to be needed. In effect, if someone is regarded as helpless then there is nothing they can do and are therefore not needed. We all need to be needed in order to provide meaning, structure, a sense of self-worth and motivation within our lives. Above all, being needed gives a sense of belonging to the herd. Once we perceive we are no longer needed, then we lose some of the sense of who we are and life can become featureless and pointless.

A current twist on stereotyping is the insistence on the use of the word 'community'. This I feel both legitimises and gives focus to the use of labels and stereotypes. That its use is promoted by the politically correct, the self-appointed guardians of sensitivity, only makes it more hideous. To my mind the word almost forces us to reach for the stereotype photofit kit to regard people, and works against the idea of seeing people as individuals in their own right. This is covered in much greater length in a later chapter, 'Community – the new C word'.

There are so many ways in which stereotypes and labelling can skew our social world. It has to be something for which we must be alert. Not only that, we must actively challenge it wherever we find it. One of the major ways we can address this issue is to be careful how we describe ourselves to others. When I ran the day centre I insisted that disability was put in context. They were people first, with disabilities second.

I could describe myself as a blind writer, but all that people would hear would be the word 'blind', and the word would make them stop listening as they got busy summoning stereotypes of blind people.

If I chose to describe myself as a writer who enjoys sailing, walking, music and cooking, who happens to be blind, it would create a totally different impression. I would at least be afforded the chance to have a normal conversation.

It is not always that straight forward, however. I had the opportunity to be on a panel discussing cooking for the World Service Food Chain programme. There were three of us. One was a professional cook from India. The second was a professional cook from America. They were both blind. Then there was me. I am not a cook. I am a blind man who can cook. A very different beast from the two women...! I never said it would be easy, did I?

The language we use when we describe ourselves is so important. It can not only change how others view us, it can also begin to change the world. And it does have to start with us. There is no point in waiting for others. As Ghandi said, 'If you want to change the world, start with yourself.'

LEVEL FOUR

PRACTICAL STEPS TOWARDS INDEPENDENCE

CHAPTER FIFTEEN

RE-INCLUSION INTO THE MAINSTREAM

'Success is not final; failure is not fatal.
It is not giving up that is important.'
– Winston Spencer Churchill

Sight loss is an all-embracing condition. As such it involves never-ending challenge to function as a reasonably competent human being.

There is no doubt in my mind that when you lose your sight you are perceived as somehow less of a person. This has to be resisted with all the means at your disposal. To make the transition from a person who is seen as useless and a burden to one who is a valued and accepted member of society is incredibly difficult. The start of the transition has to begin with ourselves. We cannot allow ourselves to accept, collude with, or buy into the idea that we are less of a person and a burden.

We are pack animals. We live in packs. We

work in packs. And our recreation and social activity is more often than not carried out within or as part of the pack.

We do not, on the whole, thrive in isolation, which is why it is sometimes used as punishment. This can range from being 'sent to Coventry' to being 'slammed in the cooler' or being declared an 'outlaw'. It is pretty clear that, for most of us, having people around with whom we can interact is vitally important to our humanness and sanity. The recent lockdowns demonstrated very clearly the importance of the pack and the real suffering of people when deprived of the proximity of their pack. Indeed, a major concern for many people during the pandemic was the behaviour of others. So many chose to ignore the social distancing guidelines that it became yet another major source of stress. That the concern was justified did little to help matters.

If we look at the basic pack unit, the family, this provides a solid and reasonable base from which people can venture out to engage with various groups or sub-packs to which they are obligated or choose to belong. The family will have signals, routines and rituals which make it special and unique for its members. On the whole, the individuals within the family will be working to the same agenda, though admittedly at times it may well feel very different! Once a member of the family suffers serious sight loss the norms, values and expectations of the family shift, the old certainties are challenged, and in many ways the family with a disabled member becomes itself disabled. And here begins the possible start of isolation for that family member.

No longer are they seen as a functional, let alone useful, member. Instead they become a burden, they have to be looked after, and they become difficult to engage with as the emotional turmoil accompanying the onset of sight loss bites home. The family agenda will alter to accommodate the disabled member, and in turn the agenda will become almost completely dominated by the sight loss. The rest of the family may become frightened and resentful of the person with the disability and they, in their turn, might resent the family member for creating unexpected changes in activities and general family life. In this way the disabled person begins to feel isolated from the basic pack unit.

As far as the wider community is concerned, it may well be that friends and acquaintances will rally round...for a while. After a time, however, the clear suffering of the person with sight loss and their changing moods might drive all but the most determined away. In addition, there is also the underlying horror and the difficulty of confronting your worst fears in the form of your friend's sight loss.

In this early phase of adjusting there will be a natural withdrawal from the wider community, and as you become more dependent on your family, there is less need to venture out. In addition there will be real fear of coping in an unfamiliar environment, apart from the embarrassment that often accompanies the onset of a disability.

As your vision deteriorates there will be increasing pressure to remain in your chair. Initially it will be on the grounds of helping you, then it moves to keeping you safe, and finally to keep you from being underfoot and in the way. In the worst-case scenario your chair you are confined to is in your bedroom, so you do not serve as a constant reminder of what people do not want to think about. And there you have it. Due to having an incapacity that is too awful to contemplate you find yourself isolated, not only from society but also your family.

Another side of this is that being waited on hand and foot, where all your obvious needs are met without having to stir from your chair, can be very alluring. In reality it is abdication from life and there is only one end to that. The question is how do we jolt ourselves out of this stupor and begin the long haul back to something resembling a fulfilling life?

Steps to re-inclusion

The struggle to achieve re-inclusion, in all its forms, is a marathon and not a sprint. It is essential that this is appreciated fully. Do not expect to make a huge effort and bingo! everything is back to what it was. Not only does this not happen, you also have to realise that things will never be as they were before. Having said that, it may well be the case that with hard work and good fortune you achieve something as good, if not better.

There is no doubt that the experience you are going through will be changing you, and these experiences cannot be imagined, let alone shared, by others. This can form a barrier in once were easy, natural relationships.

The first step to re-inclusion is to take a hard and brutally honest look at yourself in terms of what you can do, not what you wish you could do.

The next step is the creation of a set of rules of engagement, which we discussed at the beginning of the book. This task will seem very daunting, and perhaps impossible, and it is not until you begin to break the process into stages that it becomes even remotely comprehensible let alone manageable. The stages then need to be broken down into a series of objectives that will enable you to begin to engage with the process of re-inclusion. In essence you are using a 'management by objectives' approach. This method has worked for the armed forces and within industry since Noah was a lad, and there is no reason it should not work for you. The first stage has to start with your family.

In my case I was aware there were a number of things that upset and annoyed my family, things which made them unwilling to spend time with me. For instance, it became a habit to respond to any criticism with, "It might be that I cannot see!" While I felt this was a perfectly acceptable reason for getting things wrong, it became apparent very quickly that this was not what people wanted to hear. Within a reasonably short time I learned to modify my approach to doing things and apologise for fouling up. There are two aspects to this.

First, identify what you need in order to do something. At the early stage this meant readjusting the way I moved about, practising walking so I learned to counter the lack of balance, and learning to control what my hands were doing. This was done by devising the exercises earlier on in this book which helped me to regain confidence in my balance and proprioceptive sense. In this way I was gradually able to learn to do more for myself, and as success followed success my confidence grew, until I eventually reached a point where

I could do most things for myself. In doing this the disability gradually became less of a burden for the family.

The second part of the initial effort to reintegrate was how I presented myself to the family and the wider world, and it had to start with the family first. I took great pains to present as positive a picture of my sight loss as I could. My wife used to be enormously embarrassed about verbal mistakes (as she saw them) such as, "You haven't got a light on, how can you see what you are doing?" and "Did you see that?" and so on. From the very start of my sight loss I had anticipated these ordinary things would still get said, and as part of my personal rules of engagement was determined to not let it upset or annoy me.

By trying to modify the way in which I presented myself, in combination with reacquiring mobility and handling skills, I was able to reclaim my place in the family group. One important detail that I worked hard at was achieving a good approximation of eye contact when talking to anyone. This became such an important factor that my wife often forgot I was blind, as did some friends. My wife would regularly say, "There are times when I wonder whether you are blind. It's uncanny the way you do so many things."

This did not happen naturally. It took months

of practice and frequently asking whether I had achieved eye contact. The trick is to listen very carefully to locate the source of the sound and look just above. Be aware it is too easy to end up looking over someone's head, so the looking up really is just a couple of inches. It is also important to achieve eye contact without appearing to stare. Blinking and glancing away are therefore also important. With constant rehearsal and constructive criticism, which has to be requested and accepted gracefully, it is possible to achieve a very realistic approximation to appearing to be sighted. I'm not suggesting that you deny your sight loss, but making the effort not to ram it down everyone's throat puts people at ease with you, so they feel comfortable, and thus your re-inclusion is on sure footing.

It is clear that both behaviour and capabilities need to be addressed in this initial phase of becoming acceptable and therefore accepted. As your skills and capabilities improve, either through training, practice or both, the behavioural aspect becomes increasingly important. This is why membership of a support group is so valuable. Having served in the Royal Marines I was able to join Blind Veterans UK, and their contribution to my living with sight loss and achieving acceptability went well beyond any rational reckoning. The advantages of belonging to a support group are numerous:

- You realise in a very real sense that you are no longer alone with your struggle with sight loss.
- You will pick up many tips and hints from the other members of the group, and you come to appreciate that you will always know more about your condition than any sighted person. In short it helps you recognise your own expertise, and recognising this expertise is a significant part of the process of redefining yourself and the much-needed reintegration into family and social life.
- The group will have access to information which might be otherwise unavailable.
- The group may well give you opportunities to help others in a similar situation. As previously discussed, this re-awakens the issue of being needed which is another part of your redefinition of yourself.
- The support group will allow you to regain confidence so that you can consider coping with the real world.
- Your old behaviours, social and communication skills can be re-adjusted in a safe and supportive environment.
- Finally, it will give you a firm footing in the world of sight loss and this will provide a solid foundation to continue your progress towards being a fulfilled human being.

A support group is just a stepping-stone, however. It is not, and can never be, an alternative to the real world. Dealing with mainstream society can be difficult and full of heart-breaking setbacks, but if you wish to achieve the metamorphosis from someone considered an invalid to a fully acceptable and productive member of society, then you have to run the gauntlet of social scrutiny.

My early plans involved getting out and being highly visible in the local community. As people became used to the idea that there was a blind man amongst them they seemed to overcome any diffidence and started to talk to me. This was initially in the form of offers of help, and I was very careful to accept these offers with grace and humour. (For those of you who know me you might find it hard to believe I can do anything with grace! It's amazing what being cornered by a life-changing situation will do for your manners and general demeanour!) From these initial offers of help some valued and friendly relationships have developed.

In a similar vein, I made a point of cultivating a relationship with the local bus drivers. This was not only pragmatic in that they have proved an invaluable source of information about local goings on, but many of them have become good friends and a never-ending source of banter and conversation. I also made it my business to get to know the local shopkeepers. Throughout all of these encounters I have been careful to present a cheerful aspect, be as charming as I can be, and always be ready with a quip or a joke. I am also aware that this can be overdone, so it is important that there is a balance between enjoying a bit of banter and taking up far too much of their time.

As people have come to know me they have asked me about my sight loss, and I have used these opportunities to inform as many people as I can of its extent in the country. Most people are very surprised, and appalled, having had no previous idea of the number of sight impaired or blind in the UK, and it makes them more understanding and happier to help.

Of course the willingness to help is not universal. I still hear people hurriedly scuttling past, for as everyone knows sight loss can be caught by just talking to someone who is blind. Sometimes the refusal to help comes from a surprising quarter. One day I was returning from town laden with heavy bags and without my dog. Just to add to the fun it was raining solidly. I could not find my front gate, and after fruitless searching I called for help. Fortunately a very pregnant lady came out of her house and guided me to my gate. It was only a few yards away, but it might as well have been a mile. This did much to reinforce my faith in human nature. However, I later learned that my next-door neighbour, who I have known for over eight years, had been standing there smoking and grinning like an idiot, watching me struggling. My reinforced faith took a bit of a knock that day. Fortunately, people like this are few and far between and rarely do anything hostile. They're just idiots.

On the whole the campaign to be reaccepted into mainstream society on parity with others has been reasonably successful, but it has taken nearly five years of hard work to move from a situation of pitying tolerance to full acceptance. Perhaps the most valuable tool has been a sense of humour and being as positive as possible.

In an interview on Radio Derby I somewhat surprised the interviewer when she asked me very sympathetically how I was coping with sight loss. My reply that I had had a ball since losing my sight left her almost speechless. On another interview with Radio Connect, the RNIB radio station, it was more matter-of-fact. I was being interviewed on some of my views after the publication of my first book, *A Descent into Darkness*. When I was interviewed by Peter White for the BBC Radio Four In Touch Programme, he, and the rest of his team, obviously set great store by humour. As I walked into the studio I was met by Peter himself. My dog Becky thought he was wonderful and was all over him like a rash. There was a short silence and then I heard Peter say, "Change of plan. We will interview the dog!" Talk about being put at your ease. After that the afternoon was seamless and I had a wonderful time.

Being interviewed by various radio stations after the book's publication touches on the third major aspect of being accepted: being able to contribute something that is valued by society. The book, talks to groups, radio interviews and regular contributions to the work of various organisations can all be seen as contributing to, as opposed to taking from, society. There are two other routes that I have taken as well.

The first one was to hone my listening skills to a very high level. I recall that at my granddaughter's wedding I was allocated an escort to keep me out of trouble. Some people joined us, and for some reason we started debating the relative merits of British and American railway locomotives. Before long we had quite a large group listening to the discussion. My blindness was completely forgotten. Afterwards my daughter said she was surprised I knew so much about trains. I told her I knew absolutely nothing about trains, and what she had heard was the product of good listening!

Another route to being accepted as a valued member of society is to work as a volunteer.

This quickly dispels the myth that people with sight loss are net takers and contribute nothing. There are nearly three million of us with some degree of sight impairment in the UK, with another eighteen hundred plus joining our ranks every week. Surely out of that number there must be a couple of thousand people who would be willing to act as mentors, or buddies, to those newly afflicted with sight loss? This provides a golden opportunity to address the great disconnect between eye care and sight loss support.

The role of a mentor is primarily to share their hard-earned knowledge and to offer comfort, guidance and moral support through the stages of loss and change as described elsewhere in the book. Later, the role might involve helping with finding resources and acting as a buddy when the newly blind take their first tentative steps of operating within the pack.

This has clear and obvious benefits for both parties. For the person new to sight loss, there will not be the isolation so often experienced. There will, instead, be someone who can warn them what to expect, thus removing the underlying fear of the unknown. The importance of this cannot be over-estimated. Fear is irrational and a great driver of irrational behaviour, which can cause huge damage to personal credibility and eventual acceptance. At a more basic level, it has to be better to greet a challenge with "Ah, I was expecting this" rather than "Oh good grief! What the hell is going on now?" A mentor can also help with the intricacies of registration.

As well as the above, the primary outcomes or benefits for mentors are as follows:

- The satisfaction of knowing we are carrying out a vital role.
- Being respected for our skills and knowledge.
- Living a more meaningful and fulfilled life.
- The act of addressing sight loss actively with another person is highly cathartic for us too.
- The mentor feels useful, needed and appreciated.

There is nothing new or original in the idea of peer mentoring. Indeed, the principle of 'Sitting with Nellie' has been a long-established practice in industry and commerce. Similarly, the junior leader and the eight-man section has been part of military organisations from before the Romans.

Given the very large numbers of current and projected people with sight loss, mentoring presents a cost-effective and extremely relevant way of actively supporting a service which can easily be tailored for individual needs. Above all, it provides very early intervention, saving much unnecessary suffering and avoiding automatic and costly dependency. Sadly I feel we are a long way away from the ideal of mentoring, which is something that needs to change if we are to support each other through sight loss.

There are other volunteering roles which are less demanding. You could consider joining a telephone support service for isolated people if there is one in your area. If there is not, contact your local volunteer co-ordinator and suggest the formation of one. Loneliness is the modern epidemic, and when we lose our sight we can experience it in bucketloads. One of the positive aspects of being in lockdown was the growth in telephone support for vulnerable, isolated and lonely people. Time will determine if this is something that continues when the pandemic is just a memory.

We all have some talent or other which we can offer to other people. As discussed, another valued skill is active listening. Becoming a good listener can contribute to being accepted. One of the major elements of becoming acceptable is your ability to communicate, which was covered in chapter twelve on communication skills and assertion. The fact you have a disability cannot, and should not, be hidden. Your disability is now part of what you have to offer. I use this to talk to groups and bring the taboo subject into the open. As one in four eighty-year-olds have or care for someone with sight loss, I consider this important work.

An interesting aspect of a disability like sight loss is that it is never constant. The food we eat, the amount of sleep we have had, the level of ultraviolet radiation and barometric pressure (see Appendix One), amongst other factors, can cause variations in our level of performance. When we are trying to present as acceptable, others find it difficult to understand how it is that our competence fluctuates so widely. It is bad enough when it varies from day to day. When it varies from minute to minute, which can happen, then the confusion of others can go off the scale!

The best way to deal with this is just to say that you are having a bad day. Most people can relate to that. Now that I am stone blind I do not have to put up with these fluctuations in competence. This is covered in chapter eighteen, 'Spreading your wings'.

Returning to something resembling a normal life, whatever that is, is a long process with no certainty of success. Even when you feel that you have achieved some kind of parity with everyone else, there will always be people who delight in trying to stuff you back in the box of disability.

In my previous book I described how a woman once told me that I should not be in a supermarket if I was blind. Very recently I was walking out of the supermarket when I heard a voice say, "Here he comes. Bloody blind bloke. Thinks he owns the effing place." This did not upset me particularly, but I did challenge him to explain, there and then, why he felt that way, and he fell strangely silent.

This remark was interesting for a number of reasons. He clearly felt he could bully someone with a disability with impunity. Wrong. He clearly held the view that anybody with a disability should be eternally grateful for being allowed to mix with decent folk. Wrong. In addition there seemed to be an expectation that I should creep about like a victim anticipating the next kick. Wrong. There are in fact Hate Laws in place you can call upon and quote from if you so desire. But are people like this really worth the effort?

We must be on the alert for behaviour like this. Every time someone makes such a remark and it goes unchallenged the more difficult it will become to get our lives back, and the lives of others like us. As stated previously, the challenges have to be made as much for everyone else as on our own behalf. Rest assured, other people will have heard, and they will be waiting to see what you will do. Your challenge, if executed with firmness but not rage, will receive the unspoken approval of those others.

Summary

I have outlined how I have managed to make the transition back into a functioning and largely accepted individual. The way in which I tackle things may not be the way you choose to do things. But at the very least I hope it has given you some pointers. Above all, please know it is possible. Being aware of the power of reintegration puts the ball firmly in your court. The choice, as always, is yours to make.

CHAPTER SIXTEEN

ESTABLISHING YOUR BASE

'Home is where the heart is.'
– Pliny the Elder, AD 23-90

Establishing your base means taking steps to familiarise yourself with your home environment. You may feel you already know your home. Of course you do. But when your sight goes all the accepted certainties vanish, and that includes knowledge of your home. Here begins the opening of the comprehension gap, and possible conflict, with those with whom you share your home.

Familiarisation, or more appropriately re-familiarisation, is only one part of establishing your base. Another major part of this is reshaping your home to make it blind friendly. This also can be a source of incomprehension and possible conflict. Why? Re-familiarisation and making things blind friendly are just the practical aspects. Any difficulties inherent in those activities pale into insignificance when contrasted with the very complex personal and social negotiations that will accompany any change which might be viewed as an attempt to disrupt the status quo. As most of us are largely unaware of this complex psychological background music of life, life can become a little fraught!

One of the practical aspects of sight loss we have to accept is that everything will take longer. Certainly in the beginning. This is not only because we cannot see what we are doing, but also because of the accompanying loss of confidence and a fear of possible injury. What is frustrating about this is that we could have an accident that could happen to anyone, like cutting your finger on a knife, or tripping over something, but because we have sight loss it is a much bigger deal. The interpersonal consequences can end up far out of proportion to the original event.

Whenever I foul up or injure myself my automatic response is, "What am I like? I shouldn't be allowed out without my mother!" I call this a pre-emptive admonishment technique. In other words, I say what others are probably thinking and, because I have said it, they dare not. It also introduces a bit of humour into the situation, and people can then be so busy trying to reassure you that they quite forget to give you hell for being a twit in the first place. It is vitally important that you take setbacks as an opportunity to examine what went wrong, to use them as a learning opportunity, despite them knocking your confidence. You also need to be prepared to challenge people who try to question your bid for independence.

It is neither appropriate nor fair that standards should be higher for us just because we have an impairment. Nonetheless, life is what it is and we have to be extra vigilant if we are not to attract unwelcome attention. Taking more time and being mindful of safety means only one thing: we must check and double-check everything.

We have to accept, without frustration or irritation, that things will take longer. Allow for this and do not let others push you into moving faster than the speed with which you are comfortable. Going faster than you want to means you will have mishaps and get yourself into a right pickle. When people try and hurry me I find it far better to merely comment, "Since losing my sight I have really learned to appreciate the value of patience," rather than admonishing them for hurrying me. For all sorts of reasons, which I trust are obvious, this usually stops any further criticism and is, in fact, a very useful and assertive response to a number of situations.

One of the factors which causes people to interfere when we are doing something is simple self-interest. Those around us, even with the best of intentions, will always be mindful of the safety of their property and belongings, and this invariably comes into any calculation when deciding to enable us to do things or not. This is one of the continual and sometimes hidden power struggles and complex social negotiations that are an inevitable part of the sight loss landscape.

Having offered something of a Job's comforter as an introduction to this section, we now have to move onto the specifics. These are not complete, as every home is different, but they are points to march on, if you wish. If we take each part of a typical domestic environment in turn then it is clear there are practical tasks peculiar to each as well as common to all.

16.1 Bedroom

The basic operating principle is to reduce things to the minimum. If you share a bedroom this can be applied to your side of the bedroom without impinging on your spouse, partner or roommate.

The first part of the process is to explore the bedroom so you know the location of every feature within it. This includes every plug socket, every lamp switch, every piece of furniture, and even every bump or ruck in the carpet. At the end of this you should be able to fix your location in the room and the direction in which you are facing merely by touching something. This might seem extreme, but it is worth the effort for future ease of movement. This actually takes less time than you might imagine.

I find that if you adopt the 'Rupert Bear' strategy then mapping a room is child's play. The two major features in any room will be the door and windowsill. If you establish those as your reference points then you can work out the bearings and distances from those points. It is always best to establish a frame upon which you can hang everything. The Rupert Bear story strip in the *Daily Express*, by the way, consisted of a picture, strapline or summary, and then a narrative so it could be enjoyed at various levels. You can adopt the same approach with room mapping. The overall picture of the room, the strapline of major features, and the narrative of the detailed features.

The next part is to make your side of the room as blind friendly as you can. Make sure that any plug sockets on your side do not have extension leads attached to them. These can cause unnecessary confusion if you cannot see what you are doing. Cut your electrical appliances to the minimum and remove the others. For example, I only have the plug for the riser-bed and the charger for my Kindle plugged in. Being blind I do not need a lamp!

Once you have simplified your appliances turn your attention to your bedside cabinet or table. Again, cut things down to the minimum. If you keep your teeth in a glass at night they can go in the bathroom. Whilst it might be nice to have your teeth smiling at you in the morning, firstly you will not be able to see them, and secondly they constitute clutter! I suggest you need to have your medication and a glass of water on your bedside cabinet. And possibly your Kindle or telephone if they are in frequent use. Get rid of everything else. This way, if you wake up and need something from your bedside cabinet it is easy to find and you will not be knocking things on the floor. To make doubly sure of this, put the items on a high-sided tray on your bedside cabinet. This will prevent things rolling off the cabinet, which seems simple but it can save a great deal of unnecessary grief.

The final part is to deal with your clothes and shoes. The first task is to identify seasonal clothing. Remove any that are not right for the season you're currently in to another room or under-bed storage. The next step is to identify the clothes you wear regularly. Remove the rest to another room or storage so that they no longer clutter up the wardrobe, then group the remaining clothes into ensembles, like trousers (or a skirt), shirt (or a top/blouse) and a jumper/cardigan, which you can then hang on a single hanger. You can either remember the order of the ensembles or label them in some way. If you have an electronic penfriend audio labelling device this is simple. If you do not you will have to find another way. Different shaped cardboard or plastic cut-outs placed over the hangers may be one way. However you sort your clothes out it is important that you can identify them without having to ask someone else. It is also essential that you are disciplined in maintaining the system. Any moments of sloppiness will negate all the work.

Shoes can be clipped together using strong pegs or shoe hangers. You can usually scrounge these from Asda. Other retailers also display shoes by hanging them and may be happy to let you have a few hangers.

In a similar vein, clip your socks together. You can buy sock locks quite cheaply. They sometimes have them in Morrison's, and they're certainly available on the internet. If you do not have access to the internet you are bound to know someone who does. Just get them to Google sock locks. These not only keep your socks together, which saves pairing them up after a wash, they also seem to stop single socks disappearing into the black hole that is the inside of most washing machines.

The same rigour should be applied to the drawers containing clothes, including the removal of any unseasonal clothes and the thinning out of clothes you wear often and those you do not.

The last task to make your bedroom blind friendly is to identify and rehearse routes out of the room to include:

- To the bathroom.
- To the top of the stairs if you have them.
- The route to the nearest exit in case of fire.

These routes need to be identified and every aspect recognised. You need to rehearse their transit so that you can find and use them even when foggy with sleep. I can clearly recall not being able to find the bathroom in the middle of the night, and I admit to some rather unmanly whimpering at the time. My wife woke up and eventually it all ended happily. We had a good laugh about it later, in fact. At the time, however, it was far from funny as I blundered around, heavy with sleep, knocking into furniture and generally making an unwelcome racket!

Not knowing the location of the top of the stairs can lead to an unwanted adrenalin rush of fear, let alone denting your credibility. And knowing how to leave a burning building really is a no-brainer. Having said that, it is incredible how many people never give it a thought, sighted or not. In addition to this, in conditions of smoke and darkness it may well be that someone with no sight is the best equipped person to lead others to safety.

As a final observation about the bedroom, learning to change the bedding can be done with no sight, and might be an area where you can make a normal, mundane and no-drama contribution to the household routine. Not being able to see is not a reason to avoid most chores. When changing the bed, however, it is much easier to fit a duvet cover without a cat inside. Therefore, first remove the cat. In a similar vein, if you have a riser-bed or drawers, check under the mattress and inside the drawers and remove the cat if present.

16.2 Bathroom

This is an area which has the potential for endless fun in terms of accidents and injuries. As before, learn every nook, cranny and feature of the bathroom. There is nothing quite so annoying as being on the Seat of Ease and not being able to locate the loo paper!

Once you have made yourself thoroughly familiar with the bathroom, and this includes knowing how to open and close the window, locate the loo roll and their replacements, locate the hot and cold taps, and how to work the shower, the aim is to be able to function in there with confidence. The confidence gained in your own bathroom will enable you to be comfortable in public toilets or in bathrooms belonging to other people.

You may find it useful to have a grab rail fitted in the shower cubicle. This is not only to meet the unlikely event of losing your balance, but also a very useful landmark. I have also found it useful to have a rail around the Seat of Ease. This not only helps with locating the loo, but also takes the fear out of lowering yourself backwards when you cannot see. Social Services may provide these if you ask them. If they do not, they are available from outlets who cater for the elderly and disabled. As a final point here, if we fellas abandon the habit of a lifetime and sit on all occasions, it stops the other half becoming really vexed at the wet floor! I appreciate we are attempting to undo a lifetime of conditioning, but forget your pride and do the sensible thing, sit down to pee.

Most washbasins have some kind of shelf over them. Try and leave this as uncluttered as possible. If the other half objects, then store whatever you need to use in a container which is in easy reach and leave the rest of the shelf alone.

One thing I have been asked about often is cleaning teeth. People ask me the best way to put toothpaste on your brush without putting too much, too little, or missing altogether. My reply is always, "Put the toothpaste straight into your mouth." This is such a simple solution that it never occurs to most people. After using the basin be sure to give it a good swirl round and clean. This is not only basic hygiene it also prevents the other half becoming vexed. Again.

One of the chores that many of us fellas have to do is shave. I tend to shave when I have my shower. Provided you check the filter on the shower drain regularly this presents no problems. If you shave over the wash basin it is probable that you will be unable to clean the sink afterwards. One of the early tasks we absolutely have to master quickly is shaving by touch (With sight loss mirrors tend to be a little redundant).

As one of the features of sight loss is a degree of unsteadiness on the feet, it may be useful to consider ways to stop yourself slipping in the bathroom. The best solution is obviously the installation of a non-slip floor. You might be able to get Social Services to do this for you. Do not count on it, however. A much cheaper alternative is to put a towel or bathmat on the floor. This is ideal for dealing with the inevitable drips of water when getting out of the shower.

They will need to be picked up immediately after they have served the purpose of preventing you going base over apex, however, as they then present a trip hazard!

16.3 Stairs

If you have them, these can be absolutely terrifying when you lose your sight. The most important thing is to be absolutely sure you know where they are. Not knowing has a habit of being punished.

If you do find yourself taking a flight of stairs in one, tuck yourself in and try and relax. This is easier said than done, but I have no doubt this is what saved me on a couple of occasions. The best solution is to not fall down the stairs at all!

The installation of a grab rail at the top of the stairs although not essential is very useful. It gives you something to hang on to whilst you locate the first step down. Again, you may be able to persuade Social Services to fit one. This is useful when transiting to the bathroom at night and also prevents you hurtling down the stairs when doing something on the landing, such as hoovering or drying the dogs after their bath.

Once you have located the first step down practice completing the journey to the bottom.

To begin with you will want to grip the bannister like grim death, but it is amazing how quickly you will become proficient and will be running up and down the stairs as if to the manor born. Fear should be regarded as a spur to action and learning, not a barrier.

16.4 Living-room

Originally my living-room had to accommodate both my wife and me, plus four dogs and a cat. As such there was very little that could be done without seriously getting up people's or animal's noses.

Again the first task is to learn every bit of the room and its features. You must be able to go to any part of the room and know exactly where you are and the direction you are facing. I use features like the TV, sofa and cabinets as landmarks. If the room is going to be re-arranged by your spouse, not only must you know about it, you must also be an active part of the process so you know where everything is!

There is a slight issue with using landmarks in a room that sighted people cannot comprehend: they do not understand why we have to touch them. Often I would go into a room, deliberately heading for a known landmark in my transit, only to be warned that I am walking into something. Explaining I need to touch something in order to get an exact fix seemed to fall on deaf ears.

With the absence of sight the hands are invaluable for giving you information. As indicated above, so are the feet. The location of draughts, their force, direction and level for instance also give us valuable clues as to where the doors are. In the process of learning about your immediate environment as an unsighted person you must learn to take notice of sensory information of which you were previously unaware. As you use these other senses more you will find that they not only give you a huge amount of information, you also learn to have confidence in what those other senses are telling you.

If you have a particular part of the room that you inhabit – most people do – remove as much clutter as possible and ensure that the area around your chair is organised to your satisfaction. Keep items down to a minimum, like your Kindle, your phone or the radio, and learn to operate them. You can of course go down the route of having everything on voice control. Devices such as Alexa and Amazon Echo can do this for you. Whilst I am not particularly keen on such devices I have found them useful. Finding my mobile phone, using the timing device, asking for the radio to be played and reading my Kindle are just some of what it does.

16.5 Kitchen

This is arguably the most dangerous room of any home for sighted let alone unsighted people. The combination of electricity, water, extreme heat and sharp objects make this area an accident waiting to happen. This will ensure that any suggestion that you are let loose in the kitchen will be met with laughter, rage and absolute determination to prevent you.

The excuses will range from health and safety concerns, to the complaint you will make such a mess that it will take forever to clear it up. It may be well disguised, believe me, but the warning to stay out of the kitchen will be there. Suffice it to say that after a number of years of sight loss, combined with the increasing infirmity of my wife, I was let loose in the kitchen. I then learned to cook and prepare the dog food, load and unload the dishwasher, load and load the washing machine, and cook meals from scratch. There was no drama. I was just using pre-existing skills which had been reworked after sight loss.

It goes without saying that I now know my kitchen inside out. I know the location of every device, plug socket, sharp object and source of water and heat and can go to any one of them without hesitation from any point in the kitchen. I know what every cupboard contains, its location and which side the doors open. Every feature and device acts as a landmark.

This was hard work, and when my wife was alive it took a long time for her to remember to tell me when she had moved something. She was not being difficult or awkward. Sighted people genuinely cannot, and probably do not want to, put themselves in our shoes. Consequently they find it very difficult to understand that moving things around can cause life to be a nightmare for us. On top of this, of course, is the underlying issues of power concerning who has 'ownership' of the kitchen. The aforementioned patience is required in bucketloads, and a willingness to explain, over and over again, why you need to know precisely where everything is.

There is no shortcut. If you go into a kitchen not knowing where everything is you are walking into a potential disaster. The kitchen is not the place to even think about taking risks.

I have some gadgets to help. I have a speaking microwave oven which I use if I am cheating and having a ready meal. There are also speaking kitchen scales, which are useful but not essential. The main approach to making the kitchen blind friendly has lots to do with choosing the right devices. My hob, oven, washing machine and dishwasher are all operated by buttons and knobs which are easy to locate and use. I have an electric slow cooker, an electric wok, and electric frying pans. All of these are easy to use and relatively safe. They still need a little practice to be entirely user friendly. If in doubt, ask for help the first time you use these appliances.

Apart from obtaining and using usable devices the main route to success in the kitchen is organisation. When attempting any operation in the kitchen there is a set procedure you would be advised to adopt which will make the operation structured, predictable and safe. These are the five basic procedures:

1. Ensure that the area in which you intend to work is clear of any debris.
2. Select the working area so that it is in easy reach of the devices you will be using.
3. Make sure that you have everything you need to carry out the operation.
4. Make sure that what you are about to do is confined within a limited area. Working within the confines of a tray on the worktop can work well.
5. Make sure that whatever receptacle you are going to use is not only available but within easy reach.

This is not rocket science, just common sense, and is explored in far more detail in the next chapter, 'Cooking without fear'.

One of the major hazards in a kitchen is placing and removing objects from cupboards. The high cupboards are fine provided you check that there is room to place objects inside and you take care to know the distance from shelf to worktop when removing stuff.

Cupboards under the worktop can be an endless source of cracked heads. The solution is simple. Get as close to the cupboard as possible and keep your head above the level of the worktop. This will feel strange to begin with, but it is worth persisting as cracked heads can be tedious. At one point I was cracking my head almost every other day. It was so bad that my wife started muttering about getting me a scrum cap to wear. That was the final incentive to work out how to avoid doing it.

I found over time that my wife was quite happy for me to be in the kitchen, her main complaint being the mess that I left behind. I therefore learnt to be scrupulous in checking where I had been working and leaving nothing behind. For instance, I found the best way to chop ingredients was to put the chopping board in a tray. This confined the mess and made it much easier to throw away.

In a more general sense, you have to take every safety measure you can. Whilst injury is painful, it is only temporary. In the immortal words of Sergeant French RM, "It is only pain, gentlemen!" The dent to your credibility and confidence will last considerably longer than the pain of a banged head or a sliced finger. The fundamentals are pretty simple:

- Check and double-check everything is in place before you start.
- Thoroughly prepare mentally and physically for the task.
- Close cupboard doors and drawers immediately after taking something from them.
- Turn off electrical power and appliances when not in use.
- Use sharp knives. Blunt ones are hopeless and are far more likely to cause injury because you have to press so much harder.
- Clear up as you go along.

Follow those very simple guidelines and you will optimise your chances of success.

Summary

Regaining the use of your home, so you're not confined to your chair for the rest of your days, requires thought, planning and application. Above all, you have to want to do it. What appears to be a daunting task is, in the end, a simple matter of adaptation and being prepared to trust yourself. Nearly every task when you are blind is the same in that it requires equal levels of concentration at all times, but there is far less drama involved than you might imagine. Just stay mindful, move slowly, and know where everything is.

Before moving on to talk about regaining the outside world, we will now take a closer look at working in the kitchen, in particular preparing food.

CHAPTER SEVENTEEN

COOKING WITHOUT FEAR

'There is no love sincerer than the love of food.'

– George Bernard Shaw

Call it grub, nosh, scran, or whatever, food is and always will be a fundamental need. It is also yet another area where those of us with impairments can be subject to the subtlest control or abject power of others. We can circumvent this power by doing one simple thing: we can take charge and learn to cook our own food. In addition to that, learning to cook is a massive step towards establishing our independence and taking our lives back.

In this chapter, then, the intention is to outline how someone who is blind and/or has never cooked before can prepare food. More to the point, how to do it with safety and efficiency. Many people with sight impairment refuse to even consider cooking because:

- It's too complicated.
- It's too dangerous.
- You have no idea what you are touching.
- It will upset the other half.

Interestingly I was talking to a sighted person about this, and they were quite clear that if they lost their sight there was no way they would consider continuing to cook. This seems to be a very specific extension of the ill-considered, unthinking public perception of people with sight loss and cooking. In short, we simply shouldn't do it, right?

If we think about the potential for serious injury in the kitchen the very idea of a blind person in such a setting is seen as particularly foolhardy. Certainly it is something not to be encouraged or countenanced at any cost. Given that most people consider sight loss to be characterised by helplessness, then this is not an unreasonable viewpoint. If, however, there is a recognition that people with sight loss are not universally helpless, then it is a matter for focussed training rather than incredulity. It is also a matter for some serious negotiations if there is a sighted cohabitee, carer or spouse to be considered.

I contend that anyone can prepare food and

feed themselves successfully. I am completely blind and do it every day. What is required, above all else, is a belief that you can do it, a willingness to do the work, and common sense.

Let's talk about knives and forks for a minute. For reasons I have yet to fathom I just can't master them. I therefore tend to cook food that can be eaten with just a fork. I also go for quite a lot of finger food. In addition to this, I use a high-sided plate or bowl so I can trap the food against the sides. This is accepting things as they are and certainly nothing to be upset about. It is just one of the many adaptations I have made since becoming blind. I even have one of these bowls at my local watering hole. It is referred to as 'Simon's dog bowl'. This horrifies new members of staff and vexes the hell out of Environmental Health, but we all take great pleasure in this. The manager once had to go to a meeting about serving food on the correct plate and caused utter consternation when he informed those at the meeting that he served food to one of his customers in a dog bowl!

When one part of you does not work this places a strain on the rest. It is therefore important that what we eat is of good quality, and the most cost effective way to achieve this is to cook meals from scratch with fresh ingredients. This involves both frequent shopping for fresh food and the development of a large number of sub-skills, the core of which is the accurate use of your hands. The exercises outlined in chapter seven, 'Getting it together', will come into their own here.

So, let's cover some basics first. The five basic aspects of cooking form the mnemonic **SLOPE**, or:

- **S** for Safety
- **L** for Lazy person principle
- **O** for Organisation
- **P** for Preparation
- **E** for Execution

Each one of these aspects is as important as the others. Miss one out or carry it out poorly and the whole process is put at risk.

Safety

Before you even start to prepare a meal consider the risks and take practical steps to eliminate them:

- If there is stuff on the floor that is a trip hazard, like shoes or a rug or the broom, remove it.
- Make sure that all cupboard doors are closed and check the power points are switched off. In this way you start with a clear and safe

environment.

- Make sure you have full use of your hands and confidence in your proprioceptive sense and sense of balance.

I have created a 3D map of my kitchen in my head, which includes the position of any features on the wall, the position of cupboard handles, the sink, oven and breakfast bar. These form landmarks and datum points – and by datum point I mean any one of the features will flag up in my head as a bearing and distance to any other feature. How ever you choose to map your own kitchen, it is vital that you do so so you can move seamlessly from one point to the next instead of blundering. Blundering is not good for blind people. We don't like it.

Lazy person principle

When you cannot see, any movement has the potential for an accident. To move when pre-occupied with something else is inviting disaster. Think about how you can reduce your movements to a minimum. Therefore, make sure everything is in one place where you can easily reach it before you start, and if you do need to move – to the sink perhaps – move like a lazy person: slowly!

Organisation

Think about the equipment, implements and ingredients you are going to use. This involves reverse engineering the whole process. Reverse engineering is something that everybody does at an unconscious level before they carry out most tasks and involves identifying every single element of a task. In the context of cooking, this includes every ingredient, even down to the liquid you will use. It also means you identify every piece of equipment and implement you will need, to the last teaspoon or can opener. There are two elements to this. First you need to locate each item and check it is working and fit for purpose, which includes cleanliness. The second part is to place everything within easy reach of where you will be working.

This might sound like a lot of faffing around, but it can prevent unnecessary work and mistakes. I will give you an example of what can happen when you fail to approach a task in this organised way, and the little incident happened around the time I was ready to publish my cookbook.

I had been speaking with my editor and she had given me a great deal to think about. I came off the phone after talking to her and started to make a quiche. At this point, I add, I considered I had cracked this cooking lark. After all, was I not about to publish a cookbook? But! If I had reverse engineered the quiche, if I had followed my own rules, if I had stayed focussed...well, what happened would never have happened. It was a mistake so staggeringly stupid I can still hardly credit I did it!

I was at the point where the eggs needed to go into the quiche. I reached for a bowl, but I had not reverse engineered the meal and there was no bowl, so I reached under the counter to get one. Putting it on to the counter, I cracked three eggs into it. I added pepper and salt and herbs. I then picked up the bowl and started to beat the eggs. The ghastly rattling sound told me I was beating the eggs in a colander.

Reverse engineering applies to cooking probably more than anything else we will ever do. I never made the same mistake again.

Preparation

Establish your workstation. I tend to place a large high-sided tray on the worktop within reach of cupboards, the sink and the cooker, with everything I will need laid out around it. The tray serves to contain the mess, which saves a huge amount of work at the end of cooking. It also acts as an unmistakable landmark and point of focus on the worktop. I trialled a number of different sized trays and eventually settled on a silicone pet tray measuring 600mm by 400mm. It is easy to clean and perfectly functional.

Next prepare your workstation by:

- Clearing the worktop of everything except the work tray. Give both the worktop and the tray a clean.
- Placing all equipment you will be using next to the tray.
- Placing all the ingredients you will need on the tray.
- Placing a bowl of warm soapy water in the sink and keeping a clean towel close by.
- Putting a large mixing bowl near the workstation for rubbish. This prevents you having to go to the waste bin during the execution stage.

Execution

This starts with double-checking you have everything you need and then washing and drying your hands thoroughly. I will now demonstrate the five aspects of SLOPE by talking you through making a cup of tea. This is a great introduction to the SLOPE method and very quickly increases confidence to try other things in the kitchen.

We should all be able to make a cup of tea. There is even a video on how to make a

British cup of tea on YouTube. It was made by Americans, however. I ask you. Americans showing us how to make a cup of tea! Oh dear, oh dear, oh dear. Suffice it to say that sticking a teabag in cold water and bringing it to the boil can only produce something unspeakable. To be fair to our cousins across the pond, when the standard is set by tipping tea into Boston Harbour the bar is set pretty low.

Interestingly, most tea comes from India, China and Kenya, but tea is now being grown in the Highlands of Scotland, and successfully I might add! So, using SLOPE, let's make a good old British cup of tea.

Safety

- Clear away anything you will not need.
- Make sure the passage is clear from where you will make the tea to where you will drink it.

Lazy person principle

- Move carefully and mindfully around the kitchen. In other words, slowly!

Organisation

- Check you have the equipment you need:

kettle, a mug or cup, a spoon, and a bowl for the used teabag. (As discussed earlier I am not a fan of lifting heavy kettles and trying to pour boiling water into a mug I cannot see. I use a one-cup kettle. You could also use an urn.
- Check you have the ingredients: a teabag, water, milk and sugar.

Preparation

- Ensure the worktop is clear.
- Check the work tray is clean and empty.
- Put a bowl of warm soapy water in the sink.
- Place a mug or cup on the tray.
- Make sure the kettle has enough water in it.
- Put spoon on tray.
- Put milk near tray.
- Put sugar nearby if you take it.

Execution

- Wash and dry your hands.
- Put teabag in the cup.
- Boil the kettle and pour water into cup or fill the cup from the urn. With practise you can hear when the cup has just the right amount of water in it.
- Allow tea to steep.
- Remove teabag and place in bowl.

- Put milk into cup. I usually pour the milk over my finger to gauge the amount.
- Clear away any mess.
- Carefully carry the tea through to where you will drink it and enjoy your success!

Throughout the operation imagine what you are doing at every stage. This is called visualisation. Visualisation not only makes it easier to carry out the operation, it is also the best way to make a mental record of what you have done. Be aware that after a prolonged period of visualisation it can be a shock when you come out of it and are reminded that you are blind! It happens to me all the time!

It sounds like a lot of fuss. However, follow the basic structure of safety, lazy person principle, organisation, preparation and execution and you have the basis to make any meal. Cooking for yourself is not just doable, it is also good for your physical and mental health. It is also a massive step in the long struggle to regain your independence. Plus, being able to prepare what you would like to eat or drink when you feel like it removes the burden from a carer or spouse, and once the possible power struggle is under control they will be amazed at what you can achieve.

For a much fuller account and clear instructions on how to make a variety of meals

– from very easy to a full roast! – grab a copy of *First Catch Your Rabbit (or cooking without fear)*, which is available from Amazon or via my website www.wingingitblind.com I can also be contacted by email at:

simon@wingingitblind.com

Note: There are further tips for cooking in Appendix Two

CHAPTER EIGHTEEN

SPREADING YOUR WINGS

'Every journey starts with but a single step.'
– **Pin Lin**

Leaving the security of your own home when you have significant sight loss can be frightening. But for anyone who has their wits about them, so is life! If we look at it logically, we are merely doing something we have done thousands of times before. The only difference is that we have to rely on visualisation and sound combined with texture instead of sight.

Visualisation is an extremely valuable tool that can be used in all situations. To demonstrate how it works, instead of trying to work out what is going on by sound alone, use your imagination to build a picture in your mind. The picture can be built up from pre-existing knowledge of a place, listening to locate various objects, like people, and the feel of what is under your feet.

You can practice this in your home so that when you do venture outside it is easier to do.

Before even considering venturing forth there is something to be discussed. It is the elephant in the room. The free, unembarrassed and active use of a long white cane.

I refer to it as the elephant in the room for the simple reason that so many blind people would prefer to ignore it, even though their lives could be improved significantly by its use. I have met so many people who tell me they have a long cane but do not need to use it. What they mean is that they are too embarrassed to be seen with it in public. They clearly regard it as a badge of shame announcing to the world they are disabled. They feel they might as well have a bell and shout, "Unclean, unclean, unclean!" I have news for the people who think that: the world is too wrapped up in their own affairs to give a toss whether you are disabled. Apart from that, with a quarter of the population having some degree of sight loss, what makes you think your blindness would be singled out for attention? I can understand it, though, so I'm not mocking.

The earlier adoption of a signal cane, prior to a long cane, was a huge deal for me. It marked the final transition from sighted to unsighted. It was the crossing of the Rubicon, the point of no return, and it had huge symbolic significance.

Yet only a few months later I realised I would have to use a long cane. Apart from the fact the signal cane, when held correctly, was perfectly placed for poking out the eyes of children, it was not particularly useful as an information giver.

If you're not sure what a signal cane is, it is a short cane about thirty inches long (or seventy-five centimetres) intended to signal the fact that you have limited vision. But because it is held across the body it is just at the right height, as stated, to poke a child in the eye. As such I found it more of a menace than a help. Moving onto a full length roller ball cane was a relief for everyone, including myself!

I attended a course for long cane training, and my attitude to it changed profoundly. Instead of regarding it as a badge of shame I now saw it for what it truly was: an essential tool. But more than that, it was a symbol to the world that I was meeting and overcoming challenges they could never imagine. It also provided a simple and courteous way of informing others that I may need a bit of slack. Above all, the white cane announced to the world that I was adult enough to accept my impairment and was working on adapting to it. This is something that should attract admiration rather than sneers and stupid remarks. They do happen occasionally, sadly, but if you immediately confront the person responsible they soon wind their neck in.

A long cane is designed to be held at midriff level and swept from side to side in front of you. Typically it is white and can be made of aluminium or carbon fibre. The aluminium bends if put under pressure and a carbon fibre one will break. Because of being very active, the very thought of being marooned with a broken and useless cane meant I chose the aluminium version.

The covering of the cane is reflective and therefore affords a degree of protection at night. It is important then that the covering is kept clean. The cane itself pulls apart into four sections joined by elastic and should be kept taut, otherwise the cane can come apart when in use. Not very helpful. The elastic forms a loop at the handle end. I put my wrist through the loop which means we do not become separated from each other.

At the business end of the cane is the tip, and they will typically have a rotating ball, wheel or point on the end. The tips are interchangeable and clip onto the other end of the elastic cord. Care should be taken not to allow the cord to disappear up inside the cane, but there is a little cross piece that prevents this.

Be aware that the tip, when in use, is rolling across the ground in an arc in front of you and you have no idea what it is rolling through. It is therefore not a good idea to touch it until it has been cleaned. After use, stand the tip in a small bowl of disinfectant. Do not take it to a sink to scrub it clean. Flicking unmentionable matter all over the kitchen as you scrub it is not the best way to maintain a cordial relationship with the other half.

To use the cane most effectively there is a prescribed method that has been developed from experience over the years. Fortunately, unlike many other procedures, this method has been developed by unsighted people and as a consequence makes sense. I'll outline a few points here:

- Use an underhand grip on the handle with the cane running from your wrist, across the palm of the hand and through the fingers, which should be gripping it lightly. Make sure the flat side of the handle is by the thumb. Make sure it feels comfortable.
- The handle should be held roughly above the belly button. Practice swinging the cane in an arc on the ground in front of you in order to check there is somewhere to place your feet. The average width of swing is roughly just under the width of a standard doorway. To practice, stand in front of a doorway and gently strike the doorframe at the limit of

each arc. Once you have got the feel of that, practice swinging the cane and stopping just short of the doorframe. What you are doing here is creating and reinforcing muscle memory for the correct swing of the cane. Once this is established it is one less thing to worry about when you are using the cane for real.

- Find a smooth, safe area where it is possible to move at least ten paces. Use this space to get a grip on the basic drill for the cane. It is a drill, and like all drills it feels unnatural and awkward to begin with. With application you will be surprised how quickly it will become a part of you.

The next part is to learn how to walk longer distances with the cane where, essentially, the cane is acting as a minesweeper. When it swings to the left it is checking for a clear place for your left foot to occupy. The same happens with the right swing and the right foot. It is vitally important that you sweep for every step to check there is nothing there. There is nothing quite so foolish as setting off carefully, but then getting a bit complacent and promptly falling over something. The initial sweep is sometimes referred to as the 'sleeping dog sweep'.

Once you know that the space immediately in front of you is clear you can move off with safety like this:

- Place the tip of the cane where your left foot is going to land.
- Step off with the left foot and occupy the space cleared by your cane. At the same time sweep your cane across to where your right foot will go.
- Take the next step with your right foot whilst swinging the cane to your left.
- Continue with the left foot with the cane swinging to the right and so on and so on.

It is important that you remain in step. If you get out of step, stop and reset. Swinging at random is unstructured and dangerous, as the information required for the next safe step will not be feeding up the cane to your brain and consequently your foot.

To begin with this feels horribly awkward, like learning to drive a car, and you think you will never get the hang of it. Start slowly and mindfully. Try half a dozen steps first. Continue this until it begins to feel comfortable. The main thing is to get the feet and cane tip working together as naturally as when you step off with the left foot and your right arm moves. Indeed, this is really only an adaptation of that natural movement.

Once the use of the cane begins to feel like a

co-ordinated movement rather than the antics of a manic marionette, it is time to face the next stage: using the cane on a real stretch of pavement. Begin by walking up and down outside your own home, where there will be at least some sense of familiarity of sounds, like the road. This is the time when you reinforce the separate parts of the operation – the grip, the position of the hand, the length of the swing of the tip – and practice staying in step.

Once you are content that it is all happening with reliability you can begin to use the cane in its real role as a gatherer of information. This information not only keeps you safe but also plays an important part in telling you where you are. The texture of the pavement, for instance, first discovered by the feel and sound of your cane and then confirmed by your feet, is invaluable information. The echo, or not, of your cane is also an important source of information.

In the course of moving about with your cane you will come across different features like lamp posts, bollards, roadside poles, kerbs, bubble pavement at junction crossing, potholes, verges and so on. These are all invaluable landmarks you can check with your cane. As you are walking along with your cane it will suddenly strike something in front of you. At this point you must stop. Carefully move forward until you encounter the obstacle. Explore it and log it in your memory: There is a post box on the left twenty paces from my front gate, for example.

If what you find is a drop, big or small, it may well be a kerb. Kerbs can be so low that they are barely detectable. They can also be quite a long drop. Kerbs can also disappear completely where private driveways cross the pavement. The cane is invaluable here and again the use of the cane must be reduced to a drill.

If you encounter the kerb and you are going to cross the road, move to the edge of the kerb as established by your cane. Use the cane to gauge the drop and if there are any obstructions, like piles of leaves or rubbish, by sweeping the cane along the gutter. When you've established the way is clear, listen carefully for traffic and step into the road when it all goes quiet. Crossing the road, use your cane normally until it encounters the opposite kerb, then allow your cane tip to ride up onto the pavement and follow with your foot, then carry on as normal.

Another thing you might encounter are steps, which on the face of it are terrifying. You have two choices: you can decide that you are not going to attempt them; or you can decide to go for it.

If you decide to go for it, and we will use the example of steps going up, move to the bottom of the steps and ascertain whether there is a rail or not. If there is, grab the rail and hold the cane directly in front of you, feeling for each step until you reach the top. If there is no rail it is perfectly doable to go up the steps using just your cane. Do this carefully, mindfully and aware of your balance, feeling for each step and moving slowly. When you run out of steps stand still and explore what is in front of you with your cane before proceeding.

The same method can be applied going down steps, using the rail and the cane, or just the cane to feel for the edge of each step before stepping down. The cane will let you know when you have reached the bottom.

When moving about in the real world the cane is invaluable. This in combination with your feet and other sources of sensory information will allow you to navigate with relative confidence.

I often walk into town and I split the journey into a number of stages, moving from one visualised point to another, points that I have mapped in my head for each stage of the walk. One of the hardest things to do is to actually walk in a straight line. This is because in the absence of sight you are unable to fix on some point in front and make the constant and minute alterations of direction that keep you on course. I find the best way to manage this is to follow your nose. By that I mean I glance neither to the left nor the right, as that will cause me to veer in the direction of the glance. This is quite hard to do as it is natural to turn towards any noise. My editor, who is also a biker, likened this to riding her motorbike. When training she was taught that the bike will quite literally go in the direction you look, which was demonstrated by nearly riding into a wheelie bin to test the theory! So keep your nose pointing in the direction you wish to go, and this includes corners, and do not get distracted.

Another distraction is when you meet someone who knows you. In the town where I live I am known by many people (who consider it 'awesome' the way I get about!). Consequently many people will stop to exchange greetings or chat. This is one of the aspects I love about where I live, but it is still a distraction as it's easy to forget where I am on my journey and which way I'm facing. I counter this by keeping my cane pointed firmly in the direction of travel. In this way I merely carry on where I left off when I stopped. I also commit to memory my last landmark, like the post box, and reset my journey from there.

It is important you appreciate there is nothing that awesome about the way in which I find my way about. It has been achieved by a number of techniques and factors:

- Excellent training by my ROVI, Liz.
- Learning the route.

- Correct use of the cane.
- Determination and sheer hard work.

The last factor is the necessary accompaniment to everything new that we, as people with severe sight loss or blindness, do. There is no substitute for determination and hard work, and the constant effort does contribute to the chronic tiredness discussed earlier.

I will now demonstrate stage one (of four stages, which I will not list) of how I make the journey from my front gate to the bank. Your journeys will of course be different, but you can apply the principles.

- Walk up the garden path until I encounter the gate.
- Go through the gate and turn to the right.
- Walk along the path to the road. The distance is about seventy paces. The path is concrete and not very smooth, which I can feel with my feet.
- As I walk along I can feel my cane hitting the grass to my left and the wall to my right.
- As I approach the end of the path the wall is replaced by a wooden fence. The path rises slightly and the concrete becomes smooth.
- At the end of the path the wooden fence ends. There is some foliage at the end of the fence. One more step and I am at the kerb to

the road.

- Listening for a lull in the traffic, I use my cane to gauge the height and step off the kerb and cross the road.
- My cane hits the kerb on the far side. I slide the cane onto the pavement in a single smooth movement and step up onto the pavement.
- Once on the pavement I turn left and walk up to the larger road, which is about two hundred paces.
- On my right-hand side there are an assortment of brick walls, wooden fence panels and hedges. These all help chart my progress up to the large road. There are also a couple of lamp posts which are valuable landmarks.
- Underfoot there are numerous dropped kerbs and the path has a tarmac surface.
- Very near the junction there is a dropped kerb with a bubble pavement, which is there to indicate to blind people that it is a place to cross. I know I need to turn right here and start walking alongside the larger road.

This first stage leads to stage two and beyond of my journey, where I apply the same attention to the surfaces under my feet, the walls, fences and hedges, other landmarks like the fire and ambulance station, until I reach the street where the bank is. Although I have stated the approximate number of paces, I do not count them now as it's more a case of knowing roughly how long each stage of the journey is. But then this is a fairly frequent trip for me and most of the time it is accomplished with little problem. In addition to this, as I do the trip so often, people look out for me and offer to help me cross the road if there is more than the usual amount of traffic. And if I meet someone and they are going in my direction I do not hesitate to take their arm if offered.

When blind, the perceived enemies of potholes, lose paving stones and uneven camber are actually our friends as they help us to navigate. Indeed, the pavements in my town are so bad that the day they repair them I shall be totally lost!

It is possible to use the sun as a guide, when it is actually out. For instance, if I start my walk to the bank in the spring about noon, the sun is on my face, and switches sides depending on which way I'm facing. You could also use the wind for the same purpose, which is more likely in the UK! Some people use a talking compass – some mobile phones have them – but it can be distracting when trying to pay attention to so many other things. As with all things, it's what works for you.

Finding your way about with confidence is a vital aspect of regaining the use of your immediate world. When you first venture from home, people will naturally be concerned for your safety. It can be highly disconcerting to see a blind person tottering about, and some will stop and ask if you are OK. Others will scuttle off as if you have the plague.

It is important that at all times and in all situations you present as positive a picture as you can, and you also learn to 'read' enquiries after your health. If someone passes you and says, "Hi, how are you?" it is important to appreciate that on the whole they may not have the least interest and are merely being polite. If you launch into a pitiful diatribe about how awful the world is, and how no one wants to help you, you can guarantee they will not ask again! People often greet me with that question, and my response is always a smile and, "Fine, thank you, how are you?" which works whether the asker has no time or a little time to spend answering the question.

Given the prevalence of sight loss it is often the case that people will stop and ask for my advice on behalf of a friend or relative. Many times such a conversation has ended with me giving the person a contact card for Blind Veterans UK, for which they are very appreciative.

In the final analysis, whether we like it or not, we are ambassadors for everyone else with a sight problem. It is a role we should adopt with enthusiasm and be grateful we can function as well as we do. Every walk and every encounter is an opportunity to be that ambassador.

CHAPTER NINETEEN

THE OTHER SIDE OF THE COIN

'It takes two to tango.'

– Al Hoffman and Dick Manning, 1952

When someone is afflicted with an impairment, it is not only they who are affected. The lives of their friends, family and spouses or partners are also altered. There will be the loss of opportunity, the disruption of expectations, emotional turmoil, the grief and the constant reminders similar to that experienced by the person afflicted. They will feel resentment about the huge additional burden at a time when they were least ready for it. And there will be a whole host of conflicting feelings, combined with the very difficult adjustment of roles and power within the relationship.

There are occasions when families are so locked into the idea of impairment that it has taken on the role of being the reason for the family to exist. In some cases, impairment has become the family meal ticket, and any attempt to reduce the level of dependency and increase independence has been met with furious opposition.

I was reminded of this when talking to a couple at an exhibition. I was chatting to them about Blind Veterans UK and what help it could offer. The wife abruptly said, "I don't think so. I know my husband." That statement made me incredibly sad. It was clear that the husband was not going to be allowed to consider any other option but to decline assistance. In other words, the wife was saying that it was hard enough caring for her husband, without the nonsense of encouraging him to do things and get under her feet. A cruel interpretation of that remark? No, I do not think so. Having received that kind of response many times in another context, I have little room for doubt. In many ways, however, such an approach to something as overwhelming as sight loss or blindness is understandable.

Where married couples are concerned, roles within the marriage will change. The spouse becomes more of a carer and less of a partner, and this is particularly so in the early days. And as carers they bear a huge burden in addition to their own sense of loss and grief over the change of circumstances. For this reason, after a period of huge adjustment for us both, I asked my wife to give her perspective as a wife and carer. (And it brought tears to my eyes to read this again now that she is gone.)

My wife's perspective

I am Kelly, Simon's wife, and would like to share a few additional comments on some of the difficulties that often occur when living with a man who cannot see. There are many pitfalls, some of which can be avoided, some not so easily. Even the act of asking him to pick something up off the floor can result in either an all-out shouting match, or both of us rolling around laughing at the sheer futility of it.

Nothing is easy, but if you can get past the first eighteen months of crying, temper tantrums, clearing up spilt milk/food/toothpaste, and more odious stuff, you will probably be able to weather the storms that are inevitable, and learn to make light of so many incidences that you may have taken for granted all your life. It is difficult for anyone to be comfortable with someone's problems, but we have found that a simple act that turns into a minor adventure becomes more manageable with time.

I have to jokingly tell anyone who comes for a cup of coffee that in this house it's "chips with everything"! Every mug or plate seems to have a chip out of it! And every item of clothing has stains of who-knows-what that won't entirely come out with washing. And letting Simon be as independent as possible – his choice – allows for the mirth of inside-out sweaters, odd socks, and even unmatched shoes. Simon has actually been known to put two left shoes on and not realise until I noticed and told him!

One of the most frustrating things we have encountered has been the fact that everything is now done in what seems to be slow motion. For example, even asking him to hand something to me takes a frustrating amount of time to explain, as I have to itemise every little part of what I would like him to do. And for someone like me, who has never had a great deal of patience, that sometimes seems to take as long as peeling teeth! It goes without saying that the learning involved in allowing Simon to complete even the most simple of tasks takes more time than if I do it myself. And the difficulty is in allowing him the time to do this without springing up and taking over. This sounds fairly obvious just writing it down here, but when one is attempting to sit patiently whilst someone completes that simple task, it often results in agony of almost heart-attack proportions.

For example, a blind person has very little awareness of distance so, as I mentioned before, directing Simon to pick something up from the floor leads to all manner of seemingly unnecessary instructions and actions. This is because "It's six inches to your left and about four inches forward" can result in the object ending up even further away rather than retrieved, or being trodden on, or kicked under a chair!

One of the most difficult obstacles to overcome is when we are out and Simon has gone off to do something on his own. When he arrives back at the car park, it must be quite disconcerting for someone sitting in their own car to have a man tap on the window and say, "Is that you, Kelly?" to a total stranger! Luckily, the majority of people are really helpful once they understand that Simon is not an escapee from a secure place, but simply a person with a difficulty asking for a little help.

I have seen little old ladies protectively herding him across a car park, or road, clucking like a mother hen and making a huge fuss of him! On the downside, though, there are still people who have no idea how hard it can be to have an impediment and actually have to ask for help. And sometimes the hostility Simon encounters is truly awful, though thankfully not too common.

An example of this came in a local supermarket when he asked a person (not one of the staff) to help him find something. The woman asked Simon why he needed help and he told her that he was blind. Her very disgraceful response was, "If you can't see you shouldn't be in here!" This left him feeling he should perhaps admit that being out on his own was not acceptable. Luckily, this was a rare encounter and, after a great deal of discussion with his friends and me, he has put it behind him. But the stain still remains in his mind.

In our house we have several dogs. I have three Shih Tzus, and Simon has his walking companion who goes everywhere with him, even travelling all around the country on buses. His biggest grumble on this point is that although he travels free on his gold card, he once had to pay twenty-five pence for the dog, and he has never stopped moaning about it! The Shih Tzus are wonderful companions, but sadly devilishly difficult to housetrain. Although we have puppy-pads down, quite often they miss the pad and drop a little 'packet' on the floor.

Simon calls these packages 'sticky doggy pudding', amongst other, more colourful descriptions that are not suitable for the public domain, and this provides us with many a session of hilarity – or shouting and raving depending on his mood at any particular time! And as my personal handicaps make my mobility more than a little difficult, I can only sit and instruct him as to where the offending package might be – and it sticking to his foot has still not persuaded him to wear his slippers; instead he has to do a 'hop-along' to the loo to deal with it. At the time it isn't funny, but we very often talk and laugh about these unpleasant times rather than letting them get on top of us.

From my personal point of view, one of the very hardest things has been coming to terms with everyday phrases which are horribly uncomfortable to use around a blind person. "Look at the colour of that sweater," in a clothes shop, or "Have you seen my pen?" are simple sentences that take on a whole new life when dealing with sight problems. And "Can you watch out for the postman," or "Don't step on that dog toy," or "Could you pass me my book, please?" are all fraught with implications that can easily take one on a guilt trip par excellence! Not to mention such phrases as, "Can't you see what's happened?"

Although he shrugs these statements off with rueful acceptance, it is sometimes truly embarrassing for me, or any person talking to him. Having been sighted for most of his life, Simon knows very well, however, that many figures of speech involve referrals to seeing that don't necessarily infer sight.

Another aspect I'd like to address is more of a social one. When watching television, I have to provide a bit of a visual commentary for him. Going to the cinema is now out of the question, as I would have to keep talking him through the whole movie. It would be a very simple thing for a cinema to allocate a small section of the seating and install an audio system that the blind could plug their earphones into so that they could listen to some verbal cues as to what is happening on screen. Why has nobody thought to do that, bearing in mind that cinema-viewing is often a group activity? There are many issues that nobody ever tells you about until they happen. For example, because I am disabled and wheelchair-bound, there are difficulties that nobody could ever dream of.

As Simon can't push me – who would be brave enough to let a blind man wheel you down a busy street? – we were very kindly gifted an electric powered wheelchair by Blind Veterans to enhance both of our qualities of life. This has proved to be an absolute boon, as we can now go out together, which was almost impossible to do before. However, getting ready to actually leave the house is fraught with all manner of difficulties.

Loss of sight makes even simple chores a potential disaster. Simon has to put my shoes or boots on, for example, and in doing so he struggles not to hurt me. But many times I have the right shoe put on the left foot, or the painful situation when a toe gets left behind as he is putting my shoe on and it gets bent!

One might say that this is not really relevant to the main issues of dealing with blindness, but there must be others in our situation too, so my advice to them would be to treat every event as a sort of game. Laugh together, and award points for getting things right first time. Use everyday scenarios as a talking point on how to improve next time, and try hard not to get angry, as this hurts both of you in the long run.

Believe me, we have been through all of this and, after two very difficult years, we are just beginning to emerge from the tunnel and come alive again. It has not been an easy journey, and there will always be pitfalls and setbacks, but the important thing to remember is that this is now your life, and you can either work together with it, and enjoy any small pleasures, or sink into a self-pity that is going to be sad and pointless.

It is difficult for sighted people to adapt their lives too; but since blindness affects more than just the person with the problem, sharing the highs and lows with humour is always a better course. Talking, explaining why something is a problem, sharing good things as well as bad, can all lead to a better way of coping.

Kelly Mahoney

As Kelly rightly points out, a disability in one member of the family affects the rest. What she has not identified is the fact that with blindness it is far harder for the onlookers than the person with the condition. This may sound strange, but a little thought will clarify this comment. Being the one who is blind, I know exactly how bad the experience can be. My wife, bearing in mind the general horror with which blindness is viewed by the sighted, could only imagine what it was like for me. In terms of horror, she was well off the mark, however, as I found the experience quite tolerable. On the other hand, she could possibly imagine the practical difficulties. Our relationship was therefore a constant struggle to give clarity and meaning to the mutually incomprehensible.

As time went on our relationship was sorely tested. We both found my sight loss difficult to manage. I am glad to say we did come to develop a joint acceptance of it, and it had to be joint otherwise it was too easy for the person who had not accepted it to drag the other down. As neither of us had an abundance of patience, it was not the easiest of times.

As a kind of footnote, some cinemas are now providing headphone jacks for audio description of films. Some of the theatres are doing this as well.

Kelly's second account of our life was found

on her computer after she had died, which makes it doubly profound for me. In a relationship of two or more people, it will always be a 'game of two halves'. So this is for and from Kelly, my other half.

Kelly's second account

I am Simon's wife, and we have been married for nearly six years, just around the time when his eyes were deteriorating big-time. He finally became totally blind after five years and I am going to try and tell you what you may have to expect. A great deal is said on the blind person's perspective, but we had very little knowledge of the really difficult and often horrifying times that were to come. Hopefully this will help those who may also be starting this awful journey, and maybe put to rest a few of the fears and frustrations encompassing their partners that will undoubtedly follow.

I feel that I must mention at this stage that I, too, have multiple disabilities needing a lot of careful handling, including helping to dress and bathe. I can no longer walk more than three or four steps, and am totally reliant on my power chair for transport. In short, I cannot do many things an able-bodied person takes for granted.

Just to help you understand, we have four dogs and a kitten who thinks she, too, is a dog.

One of the dogs is a bit 'doolally' and will NOT go out in the rain under any circumstances. This sometimes results in a little gift on the conservatory floor. "All very well," you may say. "Just pick it up and dunk it in the loo." That is so easy when both of you can see it and do something about it, but not for us. Simon usually finds it first, followed by a loud scream and some very unmentionable words, as he hobbles to the bathroom on one leg! I am not able to pick up anything from the floor, so it's a two-person job: one to explain where it is, and the other to retrieve it! I should have known that this was just a small indication of what would surely follow.

In the early days of our marriage, I was dreadfully homesick and found things very hard to cope with. Thankfully that passed before the real nightmare began. As Simon became more unsighted, things spiralled into a terrible morass of temper tantrums and shouting and calling each other appalling names, none of which were truly deserved. The neighbours had a field day, all but selling tickets if things kicked off in the garden or, worse still, in the middle of town! Luckily for me I had the ace there, as I could just disappear at full speed in my chair, leaving a very angry man – who wasn't aware that I had left him! (I only ever had to do that once, I'm happy to say.)

Things became very strained for a long time, until I finally found a solution. (This is very effective if there are only the two of you, but don't rely on the animals to understand.) Whenever things got too anger-fuelled I found that I could completely hide from Simon by just sitting still and saying nothing. It is a wonderful way of calming the situation, and I have spent many a peaceful time reading a book or playing cards in full view of him. It is a catharsis on so many levels, as it is a very restful and angst-free way of avoiding shouting, and brings both of you to a reasonable level of peace. But it also put a different perspective on our behaviour and handling of his sightlessness, and thankfully our arguments were more along the lines of cats scrapping in the yard rather than bull and bear fights in a pit!

One thing that has to be addressed almost from the onset is the trail of destruction that accompanies practically everything in the home. Simon has never been a tidy man, and has no concept of clearing up. We were constantly trying to find things that had been put somewhere specific, according to Simon, when in actual fact they were somewhere completely different. The usual culprits were his watch and his wallet. Imagine how that was when he became blind!

When he does any washing up and drying up,

I have to dig everything out of the cupboards and put them in the dishwasher. Our teacups, mugs, dishes and plates are all now chipped. It's usual to be given half a cup of tea and find the rest all over the floor in the kitchen. These may seem minor issues, but when they are a twenty-four-hour-a-day issue, it is surprising how it affects us.

Some of the saddest aspects are that so many things we used to share are now lost, and even little things of no apparent importance will be expanded into a huge feeling of loss. Simple things like playing cards or Yahtzee together, or even watching television. If audio descriptive subtitles are available, it's a boon for Simon, but very hard for me to cope with, as I find myself listening to the narrative and losing the whole plot of the show. Added to this is the usual "What's happening?" in the quieter parts, and me losing the plot even further as I try and fill in the gaps.

It's also very rough when you want to share anything visible with a blind person. For example, photos of the grandchildren, or something silly that the animals are doing. And sadly, more often than not, I find myself becoming more unkempt, and wearing less make-up, as he can no longer tell me how nice I look. He also has no idea if the clothes he is wearing are appropriate for whatever occasion, drops his clothes on the floor when he undresses, and puts yesterday's jumper back on with gravy down the front, or inside-out.

Again, these may seem minor issues, but it is the small irritating things that develop into huge ones if allowed. He may go into moments of deep despair when he realises he will never know what his grandchildren look like, or see spring budding again, or our dogs playing with the kitten. But sharing these small, seemingly inconsequential, things will become an untenable issue if you are not aware that they can (and WILL) happen.

For instance, minor issues will suddenly turn into somewhat larger ones because we are both grieving his sight loss. Quite often, because he has no focus point to interest him, he will simply fall asleep. There will be times of such frustration for me while watching him struggle with something, and it's so hard not to get impatient or, worse still, try and interfere. Having said all this, bear in mind that nothing lasts forever, and the really hard times will pass as you learn how to cope with them.

Luckily Simon is a very active man. He thinks nothing of setting off every Christmas on his 'Santa Run', where he is gone for four days, travelling about from place to place, mainly on local transport. This I class as my annual holiday, as I have a wholly peaceful four days – and it refuels me for the whole year! His journey starts from Ashbourne to Leicester (Market Harborough) to be with his sons and grandchildren, then it's on to Bedford, where he stays with my daughter overnight, before moving on to Ludlow and Bristol, before heading back to Ashbourne. Bearing in mind that he generally does this the week before Christmas, it is no mean feat for a sighted person, let alone a blind man with a huge backpack, his companion dog, white stick and no idea which direction is the right way! At this point, I can't begin to say how much help and information he receives, both from the bus drivers and the general public, and I would like to mention that a sight impaired person should never be afraid to ask for help. Most folk will respond in the best possible way; some, sadly, will simply brush past or ignore you, but they are greatly in the minority and don't deserve anymore of a mention. A very few will initially be a bit 'verbal' if they are bumped into, but this generally changes when realisation occurs.

It is very important to try and continue activities, and not fall into the trap of feeling that blindness is a finality of normal life. Our mottos are that "Sightlessness is not helplessness" and "I don't take prisoners!"

There are countless times in these past five years, as Simon became completely blind, when we've both wondered if it is worth it all the extra effort to do anything resembling normal. The answer is YES! My man is first and foremost a man, a husband, a companion and a carer, and his lack of vision, although devastating at the beginning, is now developing into an acceptance that there is life beyond, and we are (still) learning to cope with it.

This might be a good time to tell you about this year's Christmas. In the past he has mostly received clothes, or gadgets, or books for his Kindle. It is unimaginably difficult to buy things for an unsighted person. However, this year, I decided that things were going to be different!

This year he will be tackling two separate zipwire trips, one through trees in four stages, an indoor skydiving experience, a deep sea fishing trip, and not one but TWO flights in a little plane doing loop the loops and other daredevil stunts! I might add that Simon is seventy-two years old! My only problem now is what can I do for an encore?

Kelly Mahoney

Sadly the answer was nothing. Kelly suffered a major stroke and died not long after writing that. The really sad thing is that we had just emerged out of our joint and separate hells. The old magic was coming back, and life was looking really good.

CHAPTER TWENTY

THE GREAT LEVELLER

*'When you reach the end of your rope,
tie a knot in it and hang on.'*
– Franklyn D. Roosevelt

Life can be great. Sometimes it can also be an absolute pain. It is rarely boring. Just when I settled down to a comfortable routine of looking after my disabled wife, the dogs and cat, and the campaign to get my life back after sight loss, something happened just to see if I was still paying attention. Life threw me a curve ball. I lost Kelly, my wife.

We had only been married for six years. During that short time she had become my rock and inspiration in my fight to manage my descent into darkness. In spite of her own difficulties she was constantly encouraging and cheerful. Between us we managed pretty well. She was my eyes and I was her legs. At her passing the whole ball game changed.

Suffice it to say that the fight for normality was probably harder at that time than when my sight went. On top of that I was faced with a whole tranche of urgent practicalities. I was suddenly living alone in a house organised for a sighted person. This meant that, at the very least, there would have to be some immediate remedial work if I was to manage.

On my return from the hospital that last time my thoughts, as you can imagine, were verging on the desperate. I freely admit to performing the old conjuring trick with a bottle of Writer's Tears Irish Whiskey. The next morning, however, I woke with a clear head, which would have really annoyed Kelly, and I knew I had to stop feeling sorry for myself and get a grip on the situation. Whilst it felt unbearably painful and utterly devastating I had to recognise that I was not the first person to whom this had happened, neither would I be the last. Being totally blind was just a twist in the tale.

There are hundreds of totally blind people living successfully on their own. My task now was to learn how to do it too, and quickly. I had to make my home accessible so that I could manage as well as I did when I could use Kelly's eyes. But it is one thing to live successfully as a blind person when there is a resident set of eyes. It is quite another to do it without.

In spite of the emotional turmoil and grief it was a matter of urgency to make the house safe and habitable. When Kelly and I married we each had our own property. The trick was to accommodate the contents of both into a small three-bedroomed house. On top of this, my wife was a hoarder. I accepted the hoarding and the clutter as I felt she had lost enough through my sight loss. Add to this that I am not the tidiest or most organised of people, and I knew I had an interesting project to contemplate.

The first job was to inform everybody, and this involved going through all her notebooks and computer to find addresses. This task took a couple of days, and fortunately my daughter came across for a few days and was of great help. In fact I could not have done it without her.

Amongst those I informed was my support group, Blind Veterans UK. I knew they would provide emotional and practical help as required. Indeed their phone calls and emails were a great comfort. As time passed they, at my request, expanded my voluntary work so that I would have something else to occupy my mind. My big fear was that I would end up brooding, and possibly slide into depression. This possibility was something that Kelly and I had discussed shortly before her death.

The second job was to identify the elements that would enable me to live on my own without difficulty. We'd had a lady cleaning for us for the last five years, and had been fortunate in that she had become a good friend and, more to the point, utterly trustworthy. I immediately asked her to double her hours, to which she thankfully agreed. I also asked a friend to maintain my garden on a quid pro quo basis. He agreed to drop in every evening for half an hour. I later agreed to pay him, which made it more regular. In addition to this I also ensured that both these people had a communication link to Blind Veterans as they, in the final analysis, would provide a fall-back position. As much as I hated to admit this, I felt it important to have this level of oversight. This was later expanded to join the community connections scheme. I now wear an alarm pendant which can summon help day or night. Being blind and on my own this seemed a seaman-like precaution.

There are times when you have to accept your limitations and pride, and falling were something I did not wish to consider. In a curious way the new circumstances emphasised the need to be practical, forget pride and ask for help. It would mean the difference between sinking into chaos and creating order out of turmoil and thriving.

As time went on I came to appreciate the

thought and foresight shown by Kelly. It was clear that before her death she had set up a support network for me for when she died. This network was both extensive and a great comfort. It was also non-intrusive. Thus, with the bit between my teeth and a network of support, I set about the task of reorganising our house.

Reorganisation phase 1

The fight to regain some semblance of emotional stability in such circumstances is hard enough without the added problem of physical hazards. Whilst a reference to physical hazards may sound a little dramatic, when you are totally blind it is real enough. Apart from the obvious measure of eliminating trip hazards, choke points and generally making the house safe, there were also other matters. Amongst these were the safe administration of my medication, which Kelly had done, and the proper rotation of perishable food. Get either wrong and you could find yourself in serious trouble. Fortunately I had taken over the basic administration of the home some years previously, and as far as the medication was concerned I opted to have it put in blister packs by the pharmacy. The food rotation developed into a routine with the lady who cleans for me. Between us we made sure that everything in the fridge was edible and unlikely to growl at me.

The major practical task, of course, was to reorganise my home. I 'looked' over the entire house to see what had to be done. I had to take into account everything I would be unlikely to need or use. We had an enormous amount of surplus bedding, ornaments, furniture and bits and pieces. On top of this, I also took the heartrending decision to get rid of my books. Being blind there was no point in keeping them. I reckoned all this would take the best part of two years if it was to be done properly.

The first phase would be to create a safe environment in which I could operate with ease and comfort. This meant I would have to make safe areas where I could cook, relax and sleep. The kitchen, living-room, bathroom and master bedroom were identified as the immediate subjects for reorganisation, and was clearly a job that would require the use of someone's eyes. Fortunately both the lady who cleans for me and my daughter were up for it and we accordingly discussed and agreed a plan of action. There are always sources of help, if you just ask. No one should ever feel there is no one. Local volunteer organisers may be able to find help. Similarly the local church if family simply live too far away.

The task of reorganising requires discipline and a degree of un-sentimentality. It should, however, be combined with a degree of sensitivity. It could be easy to end up with a soulless accommodation area instead of a home. I was careful to make sure that my wife's influence was still there, but not to quite the same extent. I have, in other words, made the place habitable for me and yet managed to retain the stuff she really loved. It is still a home, and she is still present. To put it another way, the task is not to eliminate all trace of your departed spouse, it is recognising where you have compromised in the past and reshaping the home more to your needs.

Having faffed about discussing the theoretical side of the mammoth task of reshaping my home, we embarked, as outlined in chapter sixteen, 'Establishing your base'. The cupboards were crammed with who knows what, much of which had probably not seen the light of day for years. For one thing, I counted over forty mugs! There were only the two of us! Everything had to be thinned out.

At the end of this basic trawl we had reduced the kitchen gadgets from over thirty to six, baking tins from fifteen to four, cooking dishes from thirty to four, and pans from nine to four. The overarching criterion was whether I could use the object and whether I would use it. At the end of the exercise we had a conservatory full of stuff to go to the charity shops. We also took a carload of rubbish to the tip, and my daughter took a carload home to sell on the internet.

It was at this time I purchased my electronic pen, both for food and for cleaning products, as it is vital not to get the two mixed up. Without labelling it is too easy to clean your windows with bleach and your worktops with window cleaner. The same goes for food. If it is labelled then there is less chance of curry paste on your toast or beans on your trifle. Some things are easily recognisable by their shape. A marmite jar, for example, has particular shape and does not need a label. The same goes for a bottle of washing up liquid.

Once the kitchen was reorganised the next job was the living-room. Kelly had organised the room so that she could see the television, and every surface had something on it, usually breakable, usually precious. For me this room had always been a nightmare. Without extreme caution it was only too easy to sweep things onto the floor in passing. We moved the furniture back to maximise the floorspace. The TV was put out of the way as I only needed to hear it. There was now a clear route into the kitchen from the living-room, and a clear route to the hall. The room felt twice the size, and I could move around without the risk of yet another breakage.

A major part of the work was to locate, label

and safely store most of the documents Kelly had been safeguarding. Once they were labelled – insurance documents, TV licence etc – I felt we had made a huge step towards being me being independent.

The DVDs and CDs were all labelled and, perhaps even more important, so was the booze! I also simplified the television control down to one button and voice activated commands. Another item that was changed was the telephone. Previously we'd had a cordless phone with close-set and small buttons. I found this almost impossible to use. I therefore exchanged it for a model with bigger buttons, which I still struggle with but it's a lot better. The addition of a rubber bump on the number five, so I could navigate the other numbers around it, made making calls even easier.

After the living-room came the master bedroom. Removing Kelly's clothing into the spare bedroom was a massive job, and not a little poignant. But once her clothes were gone I was able to reorganise mine. We also needed to locate, identify and dispose of Kelly's prescription drugs. There were a lot. These were returned to the pharmacy for destruction, and at the same time I informed them she would not be requiring more.

I suppose I could have waited to reorganise the house, but my feeling was it was important to start immediately as my fear was that it would never be done at all if I delayed.

The number of people who asked me how I was going to cope without Kelly was surprising. Apparently the opinion was almost universal that I would not. If I had not reorganised the house they may well have been right.

One of the things people expected was that I would get rid of the animals. Why would I do that? I had been looking after them from the beginning and saw no problem in continuing. To be alone without the animals would have been unbearable. Apart from which, they have clear ideas about how they want the house to be, which do not coincide with mine, and the resulting contest of wills keeps us all honest and amused!

There is one last aspect to consider here. When managing my descent into darkness there was always a tension between the impairment and life itself, and there was a similar tension here. In the former it was, I felt, important to achieve an impairment to life balance. It now seemed equally important to achieve a grief to life balance. This does not lessen the hurt, but it does make it more bearable. Not only that, it prevented a slide into depression or other form of mental ill health. This, surely, is what those who love us, including the departed, would want for us? It is up to us to do this.

LEVEL FIVE

SIGHT LOSS AND SOCIETY

CHAPTER TWENTY-ONE

THE TOLL OF DIVERGENCE

'Sight loss is our burden, not our sin.'
– Author, 2019

I sometimes feel that disability, particularly sight loss and blindness, is a bit like the Tardis in *Doctor Who*. From the outside there is not a great deal to see, and it seems to be quite minor in the scheme of things. Once you are inside, however, the picture changes radically. The landscape is enormous and the implications huge. Those of us with any kind of disability have to get boss of the Tardis very quickly if we are to understand all of its ramifications. Failure to do this condemns us to a lifetime of being side-lined and possibly not even appreciating there are battles to fight we can win.

A useful place to start might be to understand how society views those who are different, and to appreciate how deeply we are conditioned to respond negatively to others not in our group. Until we have some understanding of this we cannot even begin to recognise the need to detect negative behaviour, let alone take steps to overcome its affects.

One of the great strengths of the human race is its enormous diversity. A major weakness is that diversity is punished at an individual level. Most, if not all of us, belong to a tight little group with its own values, customs and rituals: the 'in group'. Everybody else belongs to the 'out group'. It seems to me that anyone who has anything that distinguishes them from others become consigned automatically to the out group. They are singled out for special treatment. In the case of those with perceived flaws, the treatment can all too often have a deeply negative affect.

There is nothing new in this practice. The Spartans were known for placing any flawed infant out on the mountain to die of cold or to be eaten by wolves. The Third Reich in the 1930s and 40s pursued this as a policy of state to an extreme degree. More recently we can point to ethnic cleansing in the Balkans and Far East.

From where does this rejection and even persecution of those who are different come? I can only speculate. I guess that from earliest times the solidarity, and therefore survival, of any group was rooted in conformity. The family would have its norms to which members would subscribe. The different families would join together as clans and they in turn would form tribes and then nations. At each point along the line conformity, with perceived norms, was a necessary criteria for membership. It can only be assumed that any deviation from that conformity was viewed as a threat to the group and universally rejected.

A failure to conform by being obviously different due to impediment or behaviour would be punished in some way. That an individual with a difference would have far more in common with their tormentors than not would be largely ignored. The ability of people to detect the slightest variations from conformity is quite extraordinary.

One of the important drivers in both the recognition and persecution of difference is fear. Something different introduces the unfamiliar or unknown, and it is this fear of the unknown that is a major driver in the persecution of any divergence. On the whole this is dealt with by removing or destroying the threat represented by the unknown. In the eighteenth and nineteenth centuries that fear was extreme enough to manifest itself in pregnancy impression. It was the belief that if a pregnant woman saw someone who, for example, was blind, then the child would be born blind. This was not merely superstition of the ignorant, but a firmly held view of the educated, including medical doctors.

In the early stages of social development, the hunter gatherer stage, anybody with a physical or behavioural impediment would be considered as a liability in the core activities of hunting, gathering and fighting. They would thus be not valued and probably be ostracised. It is not unreasonable to assume that this marginalisation of the different became a core value which was carried forward as society developed into what we see today.

This persecution is exacerbated by the simple fact that those who do conform will be eager to distance themselves from anything remotely different. This will not only confirm their orthodoxy, it will also prevent them from dealing with the unknowns of difference. The unknown is the source of enormous fear for everybody as it rattles the predictability, and therefore safety, of daily life.

Whilst conformity can be a source of comfort and stability, it can be based on emotions and irrationality, and the irrationality of conformity and orthodoxy is amply illustrated by the idea of fashion. The underlying assumption of fashion is that a person can consider themselves better than another because of the clothes they wear. As those clothes will often have come from the backs of animals or from plants like cotton it makes you wonder exactly how facile humankind actually is.

To my shame I have to admit to similar behaviour, remembering as I do, the enormous pride I took in wearing yellow flares back in the seventies! Also not forgetting the pride I took in my uniform as a Royal Marine officer. If adherence to fashion, however facile, was the limit of our quest for orthodoxy it would not be a problem. But once adherence to norms and being 'normal' becomes linked with approval, success and the creation and retention of wealth, the situation changes. Unfortunately this trait has a far more sinister side.

I recall reading *The Pillars of the Earth* by Ken Follett. A cracking read. I re-read the book after the onset of my own departure from orthodoxy, that is becoming blind, with use of my Kindle. It is a story of greedy, powerful, corrupt and ruthless men doing what they like, to whom they like, when they like, in a land where the population is kept down by savagery and self-interest with only the occasional pocket of decency. This was set at the time of Henry II and the murder of Thomas Beckett. After re-reading the book I have to ask myself if things are really any different today.

It could be that perhaps some things have

changed in degree but not really in kind. The behaviour of many of the great and the good during the pandemic, the exercise of naked greed and the exploitation of the population, has been truly staggering. Having no sight I find my clarity of vision is hugely enhanced. Every time I hear certain members of the establishment on the TV or radio, apart from wanting to throw something heavy, I am inevitably reminded of Imelda Marcos's comment that 'only the little people pay taxes'.

If you look around it is clear that savagery is the order of the day in huge areas of our world. Closer to home in the recent past we have had the incident in Leicestershire of a mother being driven to murdering her handicapped child and committing suicide because of the cruelty of her neighbours. Prior to the pandemic, our TV screens were filled with reports of violence, terrorism or domestic postcode or drug-related knife crime. At a much minor level, I have quoted various minor incidents that have happened to me since losing my sight. Looking around we have to conclude that the world is not a uniformly nice place. Indeed, I would go so far as to observe that the world is largely savage or indifferent. This of course has huge implications for anyone who is 'different'.

I was born in 1947, and it is quite shocking to reflect that there would still have been people born as slaves in the Land of the Free. It comes as no surprise that the Black Lives Matter campaign has arisen. Its mere existence can only be considered as a disgraceful and shocking indictment on human nature. It is clear that we still, in the nuclear age, have a Stone Age mentality. This affects everybody who is different in any way, whether due to race, culture, faith, sexual orientation or impediment. In other words, this has enormous implications for people with disabilities, including sight loss.

As stated, it seems to me that one of the major drivers of the continuous persecution of those who are different is fear. This fear is embedded into the lives of people by the language used to describe those who are different. At a very basic level the negative words associated with difference of any kind, including disability, only serve to confirm its alienation from mainstream society – words that are regularly bandied about either in thought or deed.

In addition to this there is a general sense that anything to do with disability is best shovelled out of sight. I recall very vividly the parents of one of my day centre clients bemoaning that the centre was in the middle of town and highly visible. The fact that we used the town itself as a major resource drove some of the parents into almost incoherent rage. With something as terrifying as sight loss the feeling is even worse. It is definitely something that people do not want to consider, let alone accept as a fact of life.

There are of course many people who would be mortally offended if their attitude towards others was pointed out to them. A curious aspect of the allegedly kinder world which we inhabit is that one of the core values is to be kind to those who are less fortunate. But this core value is not universally accepted, never mind acted upon. Often it is the case that kindness receives approval provided it is exercised elsewhere or requires no effort. The NIMBY, or Not In My Back Yard, movement is a real and frequent aspect of providing for less fortunate people. Many of those who may express kindness as a core value would also be of the view that they would rather not be involved if at all possible.

There are also those who have set themselves up as moral watchdogs in an attempt to put a stop to the persecution of the different. Sadly, in my view, they have dealt with symptoms rather than the cause by tackling the language people use rather than the attitudes behind negative and discriminatory behaviour. I am, of course, referring to the politically correct.

On the whole I feel they have managed to alienate rather than influence many people. It is certainly the case that those I have met manage to obscure their message under a cloak of self-righteous certainty which only serves to alienate rather than persuade. Many of their pronouncements have either attracted derision or have made no sense at all. I have worked in places where you could not ask for a cup of black coffee as that would supposedly offend people with African origins. We used to refer to brainstorming when trying to come up with ideas. Now this has been replaced by thought showers, as the other might offend those with epilepsy.

A more recent howler has been the attempt to replace clapping with 'jazz hands', as the sound of applause might upset people who have a nervous disposition. As a blind person I do not find that particularly helpful or inclusive.

When I set up my day centre all those years ago the client group were referred to as 'mentally handicapped people'. I felt very strongly that this emphasised the handicap element and we determined that we would refer to our people as 'people with a mental handicap'. This has now been changed to 'people with special needs'. This last phrase is utterly meaningless, as I would argue that most, if not all, of us have special needs of some description.

In their haste to make sure nobody is offended it seems to me that the politically correct have only succeeded in provoking anger and derision. I certainly think some of their pronouncements are laughable and, more importantly, pointless. In addition to that, their consistent attempts to strip my native language of meaning and richness often drives me to fury.

The current trend of lumping people into communities is, in my view, one of the most damaging own goals by the politically correct. This clearly not only encourages, but also legitimises, the use of stereotypes. This is discussed at much greater length in the next chapter, 'Community, the new C word'.

The failure of the politically correct to persuade the general population is important. They are absolutely correct in their contention that use of language is significant. Language sets the tone of every encounter; it can set up expectations and it can encourage or deny the use of stereotypes. Language is vital. It is also subtle. The uncouth attempts of the politically correct do little to alter the social climate and infuriate many. I have had first-hand experience of their unyielding insistence on the use of language. For example, when I refer to myself as blind, a word with which I am quite comfortable, I do not need some sighted zealot telling me I am 'sight impaired'. My sight is not impaired. It is absent. I am blind.

There is no argument that the language we use is important. It can influence how others view us. But the language we use about ourselves must come from us. If it is imposed by some self-appointed guardian of public morality we will not own it and it will have no meaning.

One of the factors we must consider is that our difference, in this case sight loss, is not the sum of who we are. It is only a part of our life, not its entirety. The language we use must reflect this. In order to do this effectively we have to believe that our difference is only part of us and that we have more in common with everybody than not. In my own case, as frequently mentioned, I am completely blind, but that is only a small part of who I am.

As stated earlier in the book when discussing stereotyping, I could describe myself as a blind writer, but this makes little or no reference to the fact that I am also a person, and sets up a whole load of expectations about me, few of which would be positive. As such it is a deeply negative statement. Bottom line, if I cannot present myself in a positive light why should anybody else?

If on the other hand I describe myself as a writer who enjoys walking, sailing and talking to people who also happen to be blind, that will set up an entirely different set of expectations. It stresses the normality of having interests rather than the abnormality of being blind. It emphasises possible commonalities rather than differences.

Those of us who have any kind of disability, including sight loss, have an interesting path to tread. I feel we have to achieve a balance. On the one hand is our disability, and to totally ignore or deny it is not only dishonest, it is also denying all the hard work done to counter its effects – work that should be recognised and honoured. On the other hand there is also the need to stress the similarities between ourselves and other people.

One of the ways we can achieve this balance is to be acutely aware of how we describe and refer to ourselves. We must be sure to place ourselves firmly in the everyday world. If the matter of our disability is raised it is important to be matter-of-fact about it and to return to the everyday framework as seamlessly as possible.

We inhabit a world which is socially confusing and sadly hostile or indifferent to anyone who is markedly different in any way. Fortunately scattered amongst the hostility and indifference are swathes of decency. These are the majority who we encounter, as the rest cannot be bothered. But even these decent individuals will have pre-conceived ideas about our abilities and behaviour. They will label us as blind and act accordingly. (This is also discussed at length in the next chapter.) One of the first things we have to do is to break out of the mould into which they have unconsciously cast us. It takes very little to do this. I have found that one of the ways of breaking this spell is to ask how they are because:

- This is a very 'normal' thing to do.
- It is contrary to expectations.
- It breaks the spell of their pre-judgements.
- It provides an opportunity for a conversation.

All this contributes to breaking down barriers and placing you firmly in the everyday world rather than the disability bubble.

Another way to break the spell of the 'disabled' stereotype is to listen to other people. The expectation is that you will bang on about your own problems, but if you listen carefully to the woes of others this will go a long way to enabling people to forget you have a disability. In other words, social acceptance. This can be expanded into finding opportunities to help, taking on leading roles, and meeting your responsibilities as discussed at length in this book.

Many years ago my brilliant mentor – who started as a psychiatric nurse, progressed to managing services for people with disabilities and mental health issues, became a director of RNIB, and finished up as a hypnotherapist – would often repeat his view that "Everyone is afraid of everyone else, which means everyone is afraid of you." My experience throughout most of my life has borne out this point of view to a greater or lesser degree. But this very powerful approach gives us yet another way to nullify the effect of our disability. We can actively seek to reassure other people that we are not a threat. This has to be done extremely carefully, however, and never made explicit. Often it is the case that just being aware of the need to reassure others will achieve this.

If you can do this, it not only tackles the issue of anxiety and fear, it also has enormous implications for the status of the individuals within the encounter. It is quite possible to go into an encounter with an individual with the unspoken assumption that disability equals inferior status. If, as a person with a disability, we manage to reassure the other person then the whole question of status is turned on its head.

Overall the strategy has to be to engage in atypical activities, to challenge the expectations of others, to demolish stereotypes and to make any encounters as positive and everyday as possible. Stress the commonalities rather than the differences, and to all intents and purposes ensure that your disability is regarded, if at all, with proportionality.

Once you are recognised as having a disability the odds are stacked against you. This is simply human nature, always has been, and probably always will be. The fact that it is necessary to have laws to prevent discrimination is a clear indication of the imperfection of human nature. The law, however, is one thing and practice is quite another. When even the very ministry tasked to look out for people with disabilities is itself, allegedly, renowned for its discriminatory practices, then it seems clear that in the end the only people who are really going to make a difference are those with the actual problem.

As my blindness approached and established itself I thought long and hard about how to conduct myself. I found that a no-nonsense approach has served me best. This has required more work than I imagined, but here is the breakdown of the work:

- I have had to learn about every aspect of sight loss.
- I have had to cope with the grief of losing my sight.
- I have had to learn a host of new skills.
- I have had to relearn how to communicate.
- I have had to learn to be patient.
- I have had to be consistently assertive.
- I have had to learn how to deal with bullies and unpleasantness.
- Above all, I have had to radically alter what I thought was possible.

Coping with the covert persecution of society is only one part of the cost of having a disability. If we are to counter this persecution we have to recognise the part we ourselves play. We too, who are part of society, take on the mainstream views. This means that we are the most influential factor in our side-lining. Not only do we accept it, we actively collude with it. We, like everybody else, perhaps have the sneaking suspicion that we have done something to earn our disability. We feel guilty, at numerous levels, about having a handicap, about being useless, about being a burden, and this guilt is possibly the major obstacle in achieving proportionality with reference to our sight loss. It has to be dealt with if all the other work is to firstly take place and, secondly, be affective.

Understanding how and why disability, or any divergence from the mainstream, is punished is an important part of getting a handle on our sight loss. It is something we must investigate.

CHAPTER TWENTY-TWO

DISABLED OR DISENABLED?

'It is what others do
or not do that disables us.'

– Liz, ROVI, 2018

'Non quam illigitimi carborundum' loosely translates as 'Never let the bastards grind you down.' This should be the rallying cry of the downtrodden and underclass, and I have an overwhelming sense that the disabled are ranged among their ranks.

My first contact with disability was as a trainee social worker. At the time I was far more interested in what my client could do, rather than what he could not. I took this attitude with me when I set up a day centre for people with disabilities a few years later. We created a unit where the emphasis was on life skills and re-integration within their local community. I was determined to establish a horticultural model of care that nurtured and developed what they could do as a base for real growth, a centre where there was no place for work being brought in from factories and others. The notional dignity of working sat very uneasily with the payment of pocket money rather than wages.

Indeed, prior to being interviewed for the role, I visited a day centre in the same authority and was shown around by the manager. I spotted a middle-aged client sorting out coloured beads. (The sort used for the Master Mind game.) I asked the manager what he was doing. I was told he was learning colours. I walked over, introduced myself and asked him if he could tell me what the colours were. He replied he didn't know, but he knew they were different. This was pretty much what I had anticipated, so I then asked him how long he had been doing it. His reply staggered me. Expecting him to say an hour or so, his response of "Twenty-seven years" was truly shocking. It was a brutal introduction to the reality of the warehousing model of care.

I was successful in the interview and appointed to set up and run the new day centre. Not long after we opened, the director of Social Services came to visit. He asked me, rather frostily, what I made at the centre (meaning product or revenue). His mood was not improved when I replied "People." As the local councillor was also present and enthusiastically agreed with me, it was not a good day for the director.

Either coincidentally, or consequently, a vociferous local self-advocacy group for people with disabilities sprung up, but unfortunately this movement was hijacked by the politically correct luvvies. They understood everything, apparently, about rights, but nothing about obligations and responsibilities. The self-advocacy movement thus became a very negative pressure group instead of a genuine move to self-assertion and a fairer slice of the cake.

Sadly these vulnerable people were written off with condescending smiles as 'Little tinkers', or worse. Even now, more than thirty years later, whenever I hear people talk about disability I want to squirm. I detect a deep-rooted vein of patronisation, condescension and hypocrisy. My discomfort with how I felt about the way in which the disabled were viewed only increased when I became 'disabled' myself.

This was not a bad thing. If nothing else it has forced me to look at the whole issue with a much sharper focus. It is one of life's little ironies that when you become blind you can sometimes see so much more clearly, and it suddenly seemed so obvious that people with disabilities are marginalised and written off as 'dead weight'. The very term disabled has enormous negative loading attached to it. But not only that. The very word is an astonishing example of the intellectual laziness of people. A laziness that results in inaccurate and harmful use of language.

I, for example, do not feel that I am disabled. I consider that my eyes have become disenabled, and that not being able to see is an infuriating inconvenience. (As there are many friends who consider I am probably barking, I shall stop short of claiming that all that is wrong with me is that I cannot see!)

When I look back at the time when I was young, fit and up for anything, I have to recognise certain things. There was no way, at any point in my life, I could have even remotely approached the achievements of the Para-Olympians, which includes the time when I was training to be a Royal Marine commando officer. And at no time, in spite of having a Masters degree, have I had the intellectual capacity of Stephan Hawkins, the political skill of David Blunkett, or the ability of one of my day centre clients to play chess for his county. I could cite endless further examples, including Douglas Bader and Colin Hodgkinson, who were both successful fighter pilots in the Second World War.

Going further back in time it is recognised Vice Admiral the Lord Horatio Nelson was probably the finest naval tactician, leader of men and commander the Royal Navy has ever had. What all these people have in common is that they are, or were, disabled. Really?

It seems to me that the very idea of disability is in need of a radical rethink. The notion that an individual is not disabled, it is what other people do or not do that disables them, points to one aspect of disability.

So often when someone has an obvious otherness there is an assumption by those around that the individual has a flaw. It is also assumed this flaw is incorporated into the entire person. In other words, the whole person is disabled rather than a particular function. It is why I always insisted that my clients were people with disabilities rather than disabled people. But even to this day many people do not see the distinction. Worse, they do not see its importance and certainly do not consider it worth bothering about.

A quarter of the population have sight loss to a greater or lesser extent. By sight loss I mean less than perfect sight all the time. Do we as bystanders attribute imbecility, deafness and incapacity and patronise those who wear glasses? No, we do not. So why when an individual progresses to the use of a white stick does everything change?

When on a Monday someone comes back from

a walk and takes the decision it is time to use a cane, his eyesight has not altered radically when he goes out the next day with his cane. What has changed is that he has crossed the Rubicon. He has privately and publicly declared he is now 'disabled'. That simple act can take enormous courage, and it can have a demoralising affect which significantly influences how they view themselves. Suddenly they become a disabled person rather than someone who cannot see very well.

The effect on the public perception is even more profound. The person with the cane becomes invisible and, when they cannot be ignored, they become objects of pity, patronisation and a painful reminder of things best not thought about. There are, I believe, two major factors at work here. The first is the power of stereotyping and labels in combination with the inherent intellectual laziness of most people, which has already been discussed but in brief is the immediate assumption of a host of expectations in terms of abilities, values and attitudes. They basically refuse to see a person outside the parameters defined by the stereotype of 'blind' and, by extension, a member of the blind community. The current fashion of lumping everybody into communities has, in my view, made stereotyping not only easier but also acceptable. But how people who say they are dedicated to the recognition of diversity can also plonk people into communities is totally beyond me. As far as I am concerned, the use of this term is symptomatic of extreme mental laziness and, worse, deeply disrespectful.

The second force at work here is the person with the white cane. They too are lodged somewhere within society, and they too can be guilty of being lazy in that they will conform to the expectations of everyone else and exhibit the behaviours and dependence predicted by their perception of their disability. In other words, they conform to what society expects of a blind person and thus collude with others in the almost inevitable process of making them disabled. This gives us a clear view of one of the major sticking points within the field of disability: we allow ourselves to think of ourselves as disabled. This encourages others to continue the process of disabling us.

The truth is, we are not disabled at all. We merely have a particular function disenabled, a part of us that is not working. This does not mean that the rest of us is useless.

I have known people who cannot walk, have difficulty in talking, and need help with their personal needs, yet they wheel themselves into a room and their sheer joy of living and smile light up the entire place. I would be very hesitant to refer to them as disabled. I believe that whilst an indomitable spirit and an ability to communicate to others exist you are not disabled. It is only when these qualities are crushed that you become such.

I feel very strongly that whilst individuals have the spirit and guts to engage in the struggle for life, and communicate with others, they are like anybody else. They only become disabled when they give up and allow others to force them into the cage of disability. It is so easy for this to happen. You are looked after without lifting a hand for yourself. You have no decisions to make, and need take no responsibility for anything. In reality you abdicate from life. Who could resist such a deal?

The alternative is constantly reviewing, with brutal candour, who you are and striving to challenge what you think is possible, and change it. It hardly sounds a cushy billet. I pride myself on being independent and highly motivated not to be disabled. My campaign to remain a full human being is proactive, conscious and unremitting. The lovely lady who cleans for me always insists on making me some toast and a cup of tea when she comes in. She says a little pampering does no harm. One part of me is fiercely resistant to the whole idea. A much larger part of me loves it! I justify it by telling myself that she loves doing it and that I do not wish to offend her. This is so much eye wash:

for just a short time I am lazy. It seems that a surrender monkey can lurk in the breast of any of us.

On one occasion I was tested for Covid-19 at my home. There was a knock on the door. I asked who it was and the tester announced himself. I opened the door and a large rustling presence with a muffled voice stood there. Clearly he was wearing a bio hazmat suit with a full helmet. All three of my dogs shot out of the door and off down the street. "Oh," said the presence, "your doggies have run away." "Some twit must have left the gate open," said I. Pause. "That was me," said a small voice. "Off you go then," said I, and I and the rest of the close were treated to this chap in a bio hazmat suit and helmet clumping up and down calling, "Come here, doggies! Come here, doggies!" There are occasions when even zealots like me will play the disability card. I do not excuse it; sometimes the temptation is too strong!

If we look at this motivation to live a full life within the context of needs, then some things become clear, which we will now discuss based on the evidence of my own experience. I hasten to add the evidence is anecdotal, and perceptual, because it is located within my own experience. If someone can produce hard evidence to the contrary, nobody would be more delighted than myself.

There was a psychologist called Maslow who suggested that individual needs were hierarchical in nature. What that means in English is that we all have needs, and these needs are layered so that until one set of basic needs are met no attention will be paid to higher and less practical ones. A clear example of this is that as a social worker I recognised there was no point in talking to clients before lunch. In other words, no one is going to listen to discussions about behaviour and future plans when their stomachs are growling. Similarly, every student knows that the worst time to pawn your watch is just before lunch.

Maslow suggested that there were five distinct levels of need, and are referred to as 'Maslow's hierarchy of needs'. They start with the very basic needs, and the basic levels have to be met before you can consider higher ones. That is, animal or brute needs have to be met before we consider the needs that distinguish us as human beings.

I found the whole concept highly useful, and over the years it has informed much of my management practice and work as a social worker, artist and Trades Union representative. Now that I am managing my blindness, the same applies. Indeed the structure of this book, to a large degree, reflects this hierarchy – a hierarchy of sight loss, if you like.

The first and most basic level of needs are physiological, or maintenance of the body, and I have created an adaptation of Maslow's model to suit the context of our discussion about disability in general, and blindness specifically. At first glance the model seems pretty straightforward. Drill down into it however and it is evident that the limiting of life opportunities for people with disabilities start right here. The basic physiological needs are food, drink, shelter and sex. If we look at them in turn a pattern begins to emerge.

The first level of needs

Food

Whilst many people with disabilities are capable of shopping for food, preparing it and generally keeping themselves fed, as far as people with sight loss are concerned, this task is not straightforward. Selecting the food is fraught with difficulties, and on top of that the sheer level of organisation, planning and preparation for even the simplest of meals makes the whole exercise more than a little daunting. Is it any wonder that it is easier for everyone if the person who is disabled is fed like a chick on a branch? Apart from which, the constant cry of "Look at the mess you have made! You just make MORE work for me!" by genuinely outraged carers and partners does little to encourage activity in the kitchen. Drink is the same as no one wants a blind person tottering around in their kitchen whilst they prepare a drink for themselves.

Shelter

Shelter should be simple. However, ask yourselves how many people with disabilities live in accommodation which is not suited to their needs. Often, because money is in short supply, the conditions may well be cramped, of poor quality, expensive to run and with no suitable storage or room to move about. Therefore there is always a possibility that this basic need will not be met adequately, let alone in full. Frequently it is the case that venturing forth is considered to be too dangerous. So often we are confined to the home cave where our every basic need can be conveniently met. This is an enormous price to pay as it negates any notion of having any control over your life and making choices. It also puts your mental health in jeopardy in terms of meeting other higher needs. This is a sure-fire route to terminal decline.

Sex

The last category of need in this first level is sex.

Or, more accurately, sexual satisfaction. Putting aside the notion that you do not have to have disabilities for this to be an issue, the overall attitude to this is quite extraordinary. Having worked in the field, this subject is enough to scare the horses and frighten the children. It is beyond taboo!

To this day I hold very fond memories of the utter confusion and speed of retreat exhibited by my seniors whenever the subject of sex was raised. This squeamishness has had serious consequences. Opportunities for people with disabilities to meet a sexual partner of their preferred gender are limited. And even if people chance to meet, their opportunities to actually do anything will probably be severely limited, what with support workers bobbing in and out like a fiddler's elbow. In addition, there seems to be the view that people with disabilities do not need or want sex or privacy! The attitudes will range from an aghast "Good grief, do they do *that* sort of thing?" to "Oh, they don't need to bother with *that*, do they? Do they even *feel* anything?" and almost anything in between. Worst of all there is a general sense that it is everyone's business and should be prevented at all costs.

For just this occasion I shall don my disability hat. You will recognise it; it is conical with a large 'D' marked on it. And I will state categorically that, YES, people with disabilities do need and want to have our sexual needs met, and we get as much enjoyment as anyone else when we do!

As we can see, even the basic needs of food, drink, shelter and sex are, or can be, poorly met, and those that are met are often at the cost of the independence, aspirations and hopes of the person concerned. It is said that man (or woman) cannot live by bread alone, which brings us to the next level of needs.

The second level of needs

The second level of needs is emotions, sense of identity, and attachment or belonging to a group. The desire to meet these needs is pretty consistent, universal and pressing. This was graphically illustrated during the long lockdowns of 2020. I spent time talking to people who were isolated and one of them said one of the saddest things I have ever heard. We were chatting on the phone and, out of the blue, she said, "You know, all I want is a hug." This demonstrated so clearly just how powerful these needs are.

Emotions

As far as emotions are concerned, those with disabilities are expected to be in a continuous and unwavering state of gratitude and supplication, constantly needing to negotiate for the use of someone's help. This, as discussed in chapter thirteen 'Help, the poison chalice', is an incredibly complex area of activity. Gratitude burnout is always a possibility, and we have to be on our guard in case gratitude is replaced by frustration, rage and resentment. So often I have heard people say, "What are you so angry about? You should be grateful for all these people doing things for you!" which, to my mind, sums up the kindly intentions of those who would strip us of any feelings, sense of identity or self. The lesser needs are more or less met, but this is at the cost of higher ones.

Identity

People with disabilities are often regarded as objects, as meal tickets, as a nuisance but very rarely as people. Any attempt to meet higher needs is almost bound to be tokenistic, without considering the person in any shape or form. Or if they are considered, there may be no real understanding of why the higher need is such an important part of their identity.

Belonging to a group

Group membership is a significant part of

defining yourself. If you cannot achieve full acceptance as a valued member of a group then you can become ambivalent or confused about who you really are. The sense of belonging can come from an unexpected quarter sometimes.

If you take, for example, Blind Veterans, which is a huge organisation with nearly six thousand members, at first sight such an organisation might not be able to offer much towards meeting second level needs. But because of its ambiance, because of the nature of its active members and the attitude of the ground staff, you only have to reach out to be included and valued. I imagine that membership of a church, mosque or temple, or any kind of group where more than just the basic needs of life are considered, would have much the same effect.

The third level of needs

The third level of needs are the aesthetic needs, things like the appreciation of beauty, natural, artistic or musical. I suspect that a fair proportion of people with sight loss are frankly past caring for reasons discussed in chapter two, 'The great disconnect'. Those who go to a day centre may have the occasional and prescribed opportunity to daub some paint on some paper or listen to music, but how much this meets any aesthetic needs is anyone's guess. I felt we approached meeting these needs in my centre by getting people to do a group picture and then talk about their individual contribution and the picture as a whole. With music, we were lucky to have a very talented music tutor, and he got people playing music that culminated in periodic public concerts. He definitely helped people satisfy this level of need. In a similar vein, I was fortunate enough to stumble across a drama student on a barge passing through a lock. I offered her work and some of the work produced by some of our people was stunningly beautiful.

As for me, I was once a professional artist. I no longer paint as I would derive no satisfaction from it, and now write instead. As I tend to write about disability in general and sight loss in particular, I have to be careful not to disrupt the disability to life balance discussed in chapter nine, 'Managing the descent into darkness', however.

I also obtained an Amazon Alexa. Apart from trying to wind it up by asking it on whom it is spying, it is great for music. A single command will summon an extensive range of music, and this has afforded me a huge amount of pleasure. The only fly in the ointment is that she flatly refuses to play anything by the massed bands of the Royal Marines! Watch this space! The struggle continues!

As far as meeting aesthetic needs are concerned, you must first have the will to recognise this as a level of need. Secondly, you have to be prepared to think outside the box to make it easy to meet that need. If there is too much faffing about involved then it becomes a chore and not pleasurable. In my case, although initially keeping all my CDs, finding the right CD out of hundreds, locating the CD player, loading the CD, hitting the right button only to find the CD was upside down was just too much bother. Saying, "Alexa, play a selection from Queen, please!" means I can sit back and listen without the preceding stress. Just saying.

The fourth level of needs

The fourth and penultimate level is the need for esteem, our own and that of others. This is, to say the least, problematic. As the Iron Duke himself once remarked, 'Every man needs esteem to set him up.' This is a clear recognition that without a measure of self-esteem life is pointless.

When you lose your sight one of the overwhelming emotions is an awareness of being helpless and useless, and everything around you will conspire to set these feelings in concrete. Even the well-meant, "Don't you worry, dear, let me take my coat off and put the shopping away and I will make you a nice cup of tea," is the death knell of any aspiration for self-esteem. This and some of the background dynamics discussed in chapter ten, 'Loss, change and relationships', demonstrates the unremitting assault on our sense of self.

The invariable long wait for basic, let alone specialised, support and help with sight loss is also less than helpful. You can almost hear the joyful clatter of hammers as the nails go into the coffin of your self-belief, hope and aspirations.

I also feel very strongly that self-esteem is linked to the need to be needed. We all need to feel that we belong to the hive and that our efforts make a difference. If we are honest with ourselves, most of us have the notion that our contribution would be missed in its absence. One of the natural acts of most people is to offer help to others. Let me give you an example.

One day I was in town and I heard a vehicle pull up next to me. A voice said, "Can you direct me to the market, please?" I turned towards the voice and said, "Straight on, over the bridge and up to the traffic lights. Then turn right." What came back was: "Sorry, mate, didn't realise you were blind. I will ask someone else." My reply was: "As I was saying, turn right at the traffic lights...no don't interrupt...move into the left lane, then go left up the hill. The market is immediately on your left. You will be lucky to park, however. You'd be better off walking from here. How dare you deny me the opportunity to help you! What were you thinking of?" There was a startled silence. The voice explained he had not really thought about that, apologised, thanked me, and drove off. Fortunately I was able to shout after him that he was going the wrong way!

When this sort of thing happens it does little for your sense of self-worth. Even when I wrote the book *A Descent into Darkness* and people were telling me how good it was I could not accept it. I still sensed a silent…'for a blind man'. I felt slightly less paranoid when it was nominated for the Blind Veterans Founders Award, even though it did not win.

The long and the short of it is that people with disabilities have few opportunities to feel good about themselves. Not only that, any praise we might receive is regarded as a little suspect and possibly riddled with concealed caveats. It always seems there is a constant pressure to deny life-affirming opportunities, particularly at this level – that is, of course, if people have any spirit left to fight for their sense of self-worth. Sadly, for most people, and not just those with disabilities, a sense of self-esteem is generally terra incognita.

The fifth level of needs

The last and ultimate level of need is that of self-actualisation. This is quite a difficult one to describe. Basically it is when everything in life is perfect and there is no room for improvement. Herein, of course, lies the very seeds of the destruction of the meeting of that need.

Very few people achieve self-actualisation, and then only for fleeting moments. The cynic would observe that anyone who thinks they have met this need does just not understand what is going on. It is probable that top contestants, when they win a gold medal, experience a sense of self-actualisation, but by its very nature it can be only transitory.

One of the best descriptions of self-actualisation is, "When the inner world is at one with the outer, and the outer world is at one with the inner." That is the nearest I can get to having a handle on self-actualisation. Very few people ever achieve it and it is always fleeting. Because of its almost sublime nature, I would speculate that those who do achieve it may never even realise that they have.

Looking at disability within the adapted framework of Maslow's hierarchy of needs does, I feel, lend a degree of illumination to issues surrounding disability in general and sight loss in particular. Not only that, it allows us to consider parallels with other sectors of the population. This is where the lines between disability and disadvantage become blurred.

My instinct is that there is a clear connection between deprivation and disability. A cursory trawl through the internet would seem to confirm this. In particular glaucoma, age-related macular degeneration, diabetic retinopathy and cataracts appear to have clear links with deprivation. This does not, of course, preclude these conditions being present outside these areas. The poorer diet, lower standard of education, poorer living conditions and greater level of pollution make this almost inevitable. Therefore, the preponderance of sight loss in poorer areas is likely to continue. At some point it is almost inevitable that sight loss will become a political football. Having said that, I accept that this is a sweeping generality with no supporting evidence. It is merely my impression, which of course may be incorrect. But it may be that the link between deprivation and sight loss will need a book of its own.

As a social worker I encountered many people who not only lacked the get up and go, but also the means to fight for a full and meaningful life. If you are brought up in a one-parent family, in crowded and poor housing, with a poor diet and education and surrounded by squalor, abject poverty and criminality, you clearly do not have a good start in life. These sorts of conditions break people, and all the systems we have are designed to keep people in their place. Very few scramble free.

The over-riding emotions you meet are hopelessness and despair. There is also a background of simmering rage, which is quickly crushed by the authorities as soon as it manifests itself. I believe that this adds up to disability. The difference is that the disadvantaged are referred to as the 'feckless poor' (and why should they give a feck?), or the underclass. Those with nominal disabilities are the 'unfortunate poor', or the disabled. To me, these terms are distasteful (and nothing to do with us). They summarise something unimportant, something to be put on the back burner and subjects of pious, pedantic, pointless and promissory prattling when they do rear their ugly heads and become too much of a nuisance to be ignored.

I refer to the disabled as the unfortunate poor, as I feel those who are born into wealthy families either never see the light of day or there are resources enough to counter any apparent disability. Harry Enfield's character, 'Tim, Nice but Dim', whilst a parody, does point up a fundamental difference. An unprivileged person would be classified as having learning difficulties (which used to be called 'non-specific mental handicap') and shoved into a day centre.

Tim, on the other hand, would probably be given a couple of directorships. The poor chap would have to subsist on 50k a year or so, for turning up a couple of times a quarter. The contrast is staggering, but not unrealistic.

This clearly raises a simple question: Is it only the non-wealthy who are deemed to be 'disabled'? If this is the case then it could be argued that disability and all its connotations of being part of the underclass is a matter of established public perception. The fact that many causes of unnecessary sight loss are associated with those who are less well-off only gives weight to this impression.

It seems to me that whether you are disadvantaged or disabled, the only way of fighting clear of the underclass is to have the sheer guts and chutzpah to fight clear and succeed against all the odds. There are two examples that spring to mind that demonstrate this.

The first was a client when I was training to become a social worker. He was under fifty years old, yet going on ninety. (Having said that, I know many ninety-year-olds with loads of get up and go.) This man had nothing wrong with him. His spirit had been broken by life. He simply did not have any motivation to do anything, and consequently had retired to his bed from his early thirties. He was truly stuck in his inability.

The second example was a cheeky fourteen-year-old scallywag I met when I was an intermediate treatment group social worker. I ran groups for kids 'on the edge of the justice system', in other words, and he was one of my group members. I met him recently, some forty years later, and in spite of the most horrendous odds he has fought clear of the underclass. He is now a successful management consultant with his own business. He had the sheer guts to overcome the limitations of his background and the accompanying labelling to successfully stand on his own feet.

It is clear that inner resources are a major factor in overcoming both disadvantage and disability. It is also recognised that not everyone has that innate fire in the belly to lift them out of a bad situation. However, timely and appropriate intervention may well act as a substitute. If you teach an individual the right skills, they will have the confidence to trot off and slay dragons.

If we refer to the rules of engagement with sight loss, it may be a good point to remember one of the basics: 'Obstacles are an opportunity to adapt, improvise and overcome.'

If we look at the matter of public perception, it seems clear to me that sight loss per se is too horrific for the general public to think about.

As frequently noted, it is probably everyone's worst nightmare. As such it is almost taboo to mention it. So often, when there is a response, it is one of pity. Let me assure you that we feel enough pity on our own behalf without others joining in! We do not need pity. What we need is some understanding and a willingness to cut us a little slack.

As far as having the wherewithal to fight clear of disability, there are two major hurdles. The first is the appalling disconnect between eye care and support for sight loss. This has been discussed at some length in chapter two. Just to reiterate, the delay reduces many sight loss patients to such a state of dismay and horror that there is almost an inevitability to giving up.

The second major hurdle is the nature of the available support. Sight loss is something that affects every single aspect of someone's life, and the support offered should reflect this. In many respects becoming blind is like being new-born. Initially you are totally de-skilled and you have to learn to do almost everything again. It is not until much later that there is a transference of the old skills into the new reality. That is if you fight, work hard, and tolerate almost unendurable frustration, anger and emotional pain.

Any support package should recognise this.

The starting point for the acquisition of any skill has to be the willingness and courage to try. For this reason, people should have a clear warning of all the things that could affect them, which we discussed in chapter six, 'The totality of sight loss'. This would go a long way along the road of enabling people to be calm and therefore receptive within the new reality.

The next stage would be to make people confident with the information that comes from the proprioceptive sense, as discussed in chapter seven, 'Getting it back together again'. Once people know what their hands are doing they can then begin to work at basic living skills. At the same time there should also be input on interpersonal skills. Interpersonal skills are the key to re-inclusion and fighting clear of the cage of disability. This is discussed at length in chapter twelve, 'Communication skills and assertion'.

Summary

As far as I am concerned, although I am completely blind, I do not consider myself to be disabled, but this was not always the case. To begin with my balance and proprioception were all over the place and, to be candid, my mental state was probably not much better. As time went on, as a result of bloody-minded determination and the unstinting support of a loving wife, I learned to do more and more for myself.

The final part of the struggle to fight clear of the cage of disability was the sudden loss of my wife. When Kelly died I had a clear choice. I could give up and say it was not possible without a sighted carer/companion/spouse. I could declare myself disabled and throw myself on the mercy of Social Services. (But as my care budget had been assessed at less than ten pounds a week this had little appeal.) On the other hand, I could honour all the pain, tears and tantrums that Kelly and I had gone through to get me where I was and make the final push out of the cage. I chose the latter, and am now getting a handle on living as an independent adult.

Not being able to see is a detail. Sometimes an infuriating one, but still only a detail. It is certainly not a valid cause to give up and declare myself disabled.

People tell me I am amazing. What they mean is they believe they could not do what I do if they lost their sight. My answer to that is no one knows until they have to try. I firmly believe that anyone can achieve what I have, given the right support, training and determination. The vital key is of course determination. I was so lucky. Looking back over my life it is almost as if everything had led to my coping with blindness.

I was born with a silver-plated spoon in my mouth. I went to a good school, which made for a good start in life. I joined the Royal Marines as a young officer. What followed was the most excruciating fifteen months of character-forming training you could imagine. I did not make it as a warrior, but I did leave with an innate desire to constantly question what I thought was possible. This, whilst a frequent source of grief, has never left me. In combination with a basic knowledge of psychology and interpersonal skills, it has enabled me to be true to myself throughout my life.

I fully recognise that not everyone is gifted with that level of determination. However, if people do not have the fight knocked out of them by the unnecessary delay in support in the form of knowledge and training, then they have a good chance of fighting through. This training has to be radically improved and made relevant. As intimated throughout the book, I believe the key is good solid interpersonal skills training. This will provide both the confidence and the weapons to fight out of the cage of disability.

There is absolutely no point telling you that it was a walk in the park. It wasn't. It has probably been the most savage battle of my life. Furthermore, it will continue until I am no more. This is something that has to be understood and willingly accepted.

The choices are clear. On the one hand you can accept a rather shoddy freeride, playing the disability card and forfeiting any right to a fulfilling life. You can, on the other, choose to stand up, fight and stake your claim to be a fulfilled person. Those are the choices and, guess what? Yes. The only person who can make that choice is you.

CHAPTER TWENTY-THREE

COMMUNITY, THE NEW C WORD

'We are here for but a second; our impact ripples through eternity.'

– Amit Ray

We are all heroes of our own story, and how we define ourselves within it largely determines our physical condition, mental health and self-regard. These are also influenced by the view of those around us and also the wider world. Within the framework of that story, every one of us judge others and form an opinion of them. These judgements are rarely accurate. We are all inherently lazy and when regarding others we use stereotypes, which is the best rational guess in the absence of any other information. Unfortunately we tend to ignore anything which alters the image and only attend to that which supports it. This is called confirmation bias, and this type of perception of the social world has the very flimsiest of foundations, and it leaves no room for the appreciation of diversity.

As I understand it, the appreciation of diversity encourages us to view those who have a different culture, faith, gender preference and world view than us with unprejudiced regard. It provides the opportunity to understand, recognise and celebrate what others have to offer. Everyone has the right to be regarded with such an open heart and mind.

Recognising and appreciating diversity has a profound influence in creating a kinder world and improved lives for all. The polar opposite of this is epitomised by what I perceive to be the continuum of approaches to people who are perceived as different, including those with disabilities, mental health issues, and clearly recognisable otherness. This continuum ranges from implacable hatred to indifference to a pretence of socially acceptable tolerance to genuine positive regard. We all fit somewhere on that continuum. However, nothing is ever set in stone, and education can generate a degree of elasticity and movement along the continuum. Unfortunately for the advocates of diversity, education can create movement in either direction.

Messages of hatred and intolerance are easier to understand than those of accepting diversity. I also believe the indiscriminate use of the word 'community' is a clear internal obstacle to the recognition of diversity. I feel very strongly that this smothers any idea of individual differences; indeed it could be considered a classic case of shooting oneself in the foot or an own goal.

I know a man who is a highly successful management consultant. He is very intelligent, hardworking, has great personal integrity and a wicked sense of fun and humour. I am privileged to call him my friend. You now have an image of this man. If I now tell you he is black, gay, a little plump and middle-aged, the image will shift. For most people there will only be a slight shift, as they are only referencing non-specific and non-directional stereotypes in passing.

If I now tell you he is part of the Black community, something far more profound happens. The stereotypes become focussed and directional, and we are invited to use them. Suddenly we feel compelled to dig out a photofit kit of stereotypes. These could be based on people as diverse as Cetawayo, Nelson Mandela, Stevie Wonder and Frank Bruno, for example, or none of these. They have no relevance to my friend, but they will inform our view of him.

If I go on to tell you he is part of the gay community, the same happens, and the stereotypes could be based on Alexander the Great, Oscar Wilde, Julian Clarey or Tom Daley. What if I now tell you he's also part of the plump/obese community, or the middle-aged community, or the business community? How do you categorise him now?

Now let me tell you I met this man forty-five years ago. He was my client when I was a social worker dealing with juvenile delinquents. Are you instantly forming the notion of a bad boys community?

The use of the word community of any kind can be both inconsistent and unhelpful. It smothers diversity and individual differences under an anodyne layer of irrelevant stereotypes. In effect this highly vibrant, personable and delightful individual has been drowned in a vat of generalities.

There is, however, another consequence of the word community which may or may not be an unintended consequence. By referring to the population in terms of gender preference, disability, race, creed and so on we are being split into separate groups. In the same way the authorities kettle or split up demonstrations, we are being sociologically kettled. In this way we are separated into competing factions with the potential of fighting both within and between groups. Coherent opposition to the extreme behaviour of others can develop. In addition to this, the 'communities' can be easily isolated, picked off, persecuted and exploited. This is classic divide and rule.

In a way this is due to human nature, and human nature drives us all. The word community naturally triggers that response in us, and it is time to reject its use in its current context because sometimes it leads us into some strange places.

In London there are three particular statues. The first statue is that of a disabled man who was frail with ill health. The second is that of an emotionally immature rebellious gay man who failed dismally in his allotted life task. The third is that of a grieving and angry mother whose daughters were brutally raped. I am, of course, referring to Lord Horatio Nelson, brilliant leader and darling of the Georgian Royal Navy, then to Richard the Lionheart, rebel, brutal soldier and failed monarch, and finally to Boadicea, Queen of the Iceni and brilliantly successful freedom fighter against the Roman occupation.

These three examples tell me it is so important that we view others with an open heart and mind. This will allow everyone, regardless of their perceived otherness, including disability, to get a fair crack of the whip.

Coming back to how we view ourselves, this has a direct influence on how we see others which, in turn, will affect how they regard us. Their impression of us and their subsequent behaviour has a huge influence on our self-esteem and self-image. In the final analysis, we are all locked into a perpetual and symbiotic merry-go-round where words like community and the reckless use of stereotypes places a harmful constraint on openness.

Knowing this, everything alters. All of us, particularly those of us with disabilities or an obvious otherness, have a golden opportunity because this knowledge can enable us to begin to really understand ourselves and, as a direct consequence, others. When we can take control of what we project to others without fear or favour, this will influence how they see us; that is, as real people and not some formless stereotype part of some stereotyped community. With this openness we can create a level playing field and claim our rightful place in the sun, no matter who we are.

CHAPTER TWENTY-FOUR

RENAISSANCE OR LIMBO

'All my life I have been in my own shadow, now is the time to seek the sun.'
– Author, 2021

Throughout the book the subject of acceptance has been a recurring theme. It is the first, and possibly one of the most important, of the rules of engagement and crops up in different guises. This, I guess, is because it is the central pivot upon which everything else hinges. It is also the one area where endeavour does not always guarantee success.

When catastrophe strikes in the form of disability it as if the world is ending. The old customary capacities and skills can no longer be trusted and certainly not taken for granted, yet we still take those abilities, and the consequent self-image, as a given. But we find the transition from comprehending what we could do before to what we can now do extraordinarily difficult. Until acceptance kicks in we refuse to believe that we are de-skilled.

So often the default position is to continue as if nothing has changed. As noted elsewhere, change is the one thing upon which we can rely. We spend our entire lives adapting and responding to change, both within ourselves and the world in which we are located. The five-year-old child is very different from the two- or ten-year-old. The ten-year-old is different from a young adult of twenty, and they are different from the same person in their middle years. We spend our entire lives reinventing ourselves, undergoing a continual process of renaissance. In short, change is the default position for each and every one of us.

Change can be challenging and even difficult in the best of circumstances; profound change combined with being in a bad place is invariably intolerable. Therefore change never alters in kind, however it can in degree. It is when the degree of change is severe that we can experience difficulties.

We define ourselves by who we believe we are. A large part of this belief is rooted within our perception of our capabilities and a confidence in those skills and attributes. In other words, we largely define ourselves by what we can do. Fortunately, what we can do is not the total sum of who we are.

A dozen years or so ago I took one of my periodic breaks in the Peak District. I recall walking to the top of Jacob's Ladder in time to catch the sun just before it peeped over the eastern horizon. As the sun came up the hills to the right were outlined against the light, the valley floor of Edale was shrouded in mist, and the tops of the lower trees were tipped in silver and those of the higher in gold. I cannot remember such a stunning sight anywhere. It was sublime, and it had a profound affect upon me. Even though I am now blind the memory of that experience stays with me. The reason is this.

It is accepting that each day you are redefined in the light of experience, and that each day is a new beginning, that is the beginning of a renaissance, if you will. This just does not require any special wisdom or even mental fortitude. All it requires is the determination to not let circumstances overwhelm you, and the requirement to be both willing and able to recognise the renaissance for what it is: a chance to create something new from the old. This, I feel, is much a matter of attitude as anything else.

It is said that if you give a man a fish then he can eat for a day, but teach him to fish for himself and he can feed himself forever. The treatment of sight loss is not dissimilar. Cook a meal for a man and he can eat, but teach a man to cook and he can feed himself. Further to this, teach him to redefine himself and achieve some kind of rebirth in his new persona, then he can compete on a level playing field in almost any arena. This is particularly so if he is equipped with communication and assertiveness skills.

I have found after two years of total blindness that things have changed radically. Instead of constant tension and preparedness to fight I feel curiously calm, aware and content. It seems that I have come to an accommodation with my blindness. Perhaps, more to the point, I feel I have incorporated it into who I am. It is now part of me without fear or favour. Having said that, there is the usual parade of distressed and distressing people who try to make life more difficult than necessary, but I find the application of humour and finely developed communication skills soon puts a stop to that kind of nonsense.

When I look back over the last two years, losing the last vestige of my sight, my wife and best friend, my dog and shadow of the last eight years and the final blow of my youngest son, I should be angry and raving. But I am not. Perhaps it is too much to comprehend, or, like the volunteer, I do not understand the question! There is no avoiding the initial denial, anger, confusion and the general emotions associated with loss and change. This is what happens until the dust settles and you incorporate what happens into yourself and acknowledge that the task before you is to get on with the rest of your life.

In many ways I believe that this is what acceptance is about. It is not just understanding and grimly putting up with what has happened, it is coming to a realisation that your disability (or any other change) is a non-issue. This level of acceptance allows you to recreate yourself and be comfortable with who you are now.

The question, of course, is how do we know we have arrived at this sublime point? It is through recognising what are apparently insignificant thoughts and feelings. For me one of the signs was when I was thinking about my life as an artist. Without warning the feelings, without any noticeable process, changed from embittered resentment to pleasure. Suddenly I found myself remembering past achievements with warmth and, perhaps even more importantly, glorying in what I can do now. This is not a matter of lowering the bar of achievement, it is redefining its nature and extent.

As stated previously, one of the ways I used to define myself was to sail. Shortly after losing the last of my sight I took it up again. Once more I was able to drive a boat tight into the wind and feel the sheer joy of achieving that wonderful balance between wind, water and boat. If anything, being blind made it even more intense.

The same joy can also be experienced in seemingly little things. For instance, another time I was sitting in my garden. I had the cat on my lap, the dogs around my feet, and a cup of tea in my hand. The sun was shining. I could hear a blackbird singing its heart out nearby, skylarks high up, and bees coming down to the pond to drink. The whole experience was counterpointed by the sound of the water feature and the smell of the flowers. I sat there, just quietly taking it all in, and gradually it came to me: this was living the dream. There was no need for life's fruitless search for something that none of us would recognise even if we fell across it. This was how to find and actually see true acceptance and your renaissance in the little things. It did not have to be a road-to-Damascus moment; it just had to be what it was: a beautiful, quiet acceptance.

This ties in very closely with the idea of self-actualisation, the thing so hard to define and even harder to achieve. The nearest I can come to it is a sense of fulfilment; a sense of the outer world being at one with the inner, and the inner world at one with the outer. By its nature this is transitory, and a major part of it is actually recognising it when it occurs.

That time at the top of Jacob's Ladder, the sailing and the time in my garden were all such moments. Moments like these are so important in adding richness to our lives. They give us the inner strength and joy to tackle everything else, including the continuous process of redefinition and renaissance.

Renaissance literally means rebirth. It is notable that some Christians have the notion of being born again as a fundamental part of their faith. The Muslims also have the idea of rebirth as a central part of their beliefs. They also take it a little further with the notion of insha-Allah, which basically means 'as God wills'. It may be that I have unconsciously adopted this as my default position.

This is not giving up; it is accepting that some things cannot be helped. Not so long ago I would have been raving against the cruelty of fate. I now appreciate what I have and accept life as it is, and find moments of happiness, in spite of everything, without guilt or anger or a backward glance. It is the transition from pining for the past to that of anticipation of a positive future. It is a letting go. A freeing of the spirit and mind of yearning for the fulfilment of unattainable expectations.

If we acknowledge the idea of renaissance as being central to acceptance this can change everything. Instead of some poorly defined amorphous activity informed by an impenetrable tangle of unfillable expectations, punctuated by struggle and pain rooted firmly in the past, acceptance becomes a gentle transition with clear goals. The goal is to redefine ourselves and to be content with the outcome as a base for further growth. It is here that insha-Allah becomes very seductive. However, let us not forget that 'He (whoever or whatever you personally feel 'he' is) helps those who help themselves.'

In stark contrast is the idea of grim acceptance and getting on with things in spite of everything that happens. Here lies the route to constant struggle, resentment, anger and bitterness. I firmly believe it is struggling over the wrong things that makes the effects of disability so very wearing, creating that deadly limbo between the past and the present and future. The likelihood of moments of happiness, let alone a happy outcome, are increasingly remote with the passage of time if our struggles are focussed on what was, not what is and can be.

In infancy we are shaped by our parents' expectations. We go to school and are influenced by the possibly conflicting wishes of parents, teachers and peers. In employment we are expected to conform to the values and needs of our employer. We fall in love, get married and our spouse invariably tries to mould us into an entirely different person from the one with whom they fell in love! Then we become a parent, with all the expectations surrounding that. Throughout our entire life we are shaped and driven by the expectations and agenda of the people around us. Then something drastic might happen to change that, and suddenly we are regarded as hapless, helpless, hopeless and pointless. In short, others cease to have any expectations of us. This can be viewed as a reason to throw the towel in, or as a golden opportunity.

Some years ago I described my sight loss as an affliction. The ROVI who was training me challenged this, and I have never ceased mulling over that conversation. Consequently, not so long ago I wrote that all my life I had lived in my own shadow, and now was the time to seek the sun. What do I mean by that? The shadow was actually the expectations of other people that I bore, every day, and the sun was the first time to free myself of those expectations now that I had lost my sight.

It was totally liberating. For the first time I was free of the pressure from others to conform to their wishes and agenda. I was free, if you wish, to redefine myself as what I wanted to be, not what others wanted me to be.

There is no such thing as a free lunch though,

as we know, and with this freedom came a cost. I was still bound by the norms, customs and laws of responsibility for my actions, where I could not use my disability as an excuse for transgressions. In short, this is the essential part of being a fully paid-up member of society, and I had no problem with that just because I was now blind.

In a paradoxical fashion, the liberation that accompanied my blindness was, socially and emotionally, the best thing that has ever happened to me. It was not automatic. I had to recognise the opportunity and seize it. And thus began my full acceptance.

Renaissance is recreating yourself post-disability. It is going with the flow. It is looking on the past with pleasure and warmth rather than bitterness and longing. It is accepting the cards you have been dealt and making the best of them. A vital part of this is the anticipation of a positive future. As always, the choice is yours.

CHAPTER TWENTY-FIVE

POINTE FINALE

'Wake up before it is too late.'
– **Author, 2021**

Sight loss and the way it is experienced is unique and highly personal for everyone. It is all pervasive, affecting as it does every aspect of daily life. Sight once gone is generally unrecoverable; its management, however, is perfectly doable. It is clear that whilst sight loss is only one aspect of someone's existence, it is so often the dominant one. It is equally clear that there are as many ways of managing sight loss as there are individuals who have it. There is also a need for a more unified approach to sight loss so that we are all at least talking about the same thing.

Issues such as denial, ignorance and abject surrender are all causing far too much personal anguish and interpersonal paralysis, professional indifference, lack of any willingness to seek understanding, political torpor, and the lemming-like behaviour of many of the population is leading us all to a very bad place indeed.

The situation is simple enough in that the continuum starts with perfect sight and ends, for many, with total blindness. Whilst the two conditions are at opposite ends, they are, nonetheless, part of the same continuum. So why all the mystery and psychological uproar? The short answer is that the prospect of sight loss is so terrifying that people choose to ignore it until it is too late. The fact that we look through our eyes, rather than at them, makes this all too easy. What is needed is a simple framework that allows us all to actively consider our sight as part of us.

Throughout the book I have tried to demonstrate some of the positive ways in which we can change what we think is possible and live with sight loss. It is very clear that with the right support sight loss does not have to be an unmitigated tragedy, and that living an independent and fruitful life is possible.

But consider this. We are one of the richest countries in the world, yet the active operation of disability apartheid is a cause for constant shame. It is a disgrace and a major tragedy that appropriate support is not routinely available, if at all.

I have chosen to end the book with a case study. Although the facts are in the public domain I shall not name the person concerned. This is because I feel the events described in the case study are not uncommon. But not only are they not uncommon, it is also a clear message about what we have to fight for. With constantly increasing numbers of people with sight loss, ignoring the issues involved is no longer an option. This is on ethical, humanitarian, pragmatic and economic grounds. The sooner we act to put the shameful and dangerous treatment of people with sight loss into the political arena the better.

Case study

An adolescent of mixed-race with sight impairment entered a college for blind people. Shortly before, the grandfather, who was a patriarchal and pivotal figure, died. Not long after entering the college the adolescent's remaining sight was lost, which may have been partly due to the stress of the loss of the grandfather, combined with the new situation. In any event, no counselling for either bereavement – the loss of sight or the loss of the grandfather – was offered by the college. In the fullness of time the student graduated from the college and decided to read for a social work degree. After three years this person graduated with a very respectable 2.1 degree in social work after enjoying their time at university, being lively, the life and soul of any party, and a good student. It was from this point that this very able, vibrant and joyful person began the transition into something very different.

As was noted at the time, even people who didn't want jobs were made offers. None were made to this graduate. Not being a quitter, the graduate spent the next few years applying for jobs and also volunteering in the hope it would lead to work. The caring professions, however, displayed their usual indifference to both their paraded values and equal opportunities policies, and in spite of persistently applying for jobs, still none were offered. (Remembering the storm that broke over my head when I employed a blind clerk at the day centre, I cannot even pretend to be surprised by this.)

Finally an interview was offered at Guide Dogs for the Blind as a communications officer engaging with ethnic minorities. Bearing in mind the mixed-race background, the zest for life and social work degree, the job was ideal. The interviewee was told they had to make a presentation using flip charts, which they were not able to do being blind. They were then told they would not be allowed to use their assistive technology, the consequence being the person was unable to attend the interview.

By this time the subject was using a guide dog, and a wonderful bond developed between them. When it was time for a new dog, the old one was retained as a pet. In spite of the constant knockbacks, the subject remained positive, enjoyed life, and was living completely independently. As employment was still elusive, the focus turned to relationships and the possibility of parenthood. A loving and fulfilling partnership was formed, and life was looking good. Seventeen months later the partner, leaving a barrowload of vodka bottles, vanished with the subject's life savings. At the same time the first guide dog died. On top of everything else, this was just too much. After years of being knocked back, yet remaining positive and cheerful, the point arrived when specialist mental health help was needed. Counselling was sought, and following an initial assessment, and after a considerable waiting time, the first counselling session was attended. It lasted eighteen minutes. The counsellor identified that bereavement and grief counselling was needed, and not behavioural cognitive therapy. Another long wait ensued, and then the subject was called for another assessment meeting. At the meeting they were accompanied by a companion who was a trained and qualified rehabilitation officer for the blind.

The first issue was whether the tick box questionnaire had been completed. The response that it was not possible to see the questionnaire let alone the boxes was not well received. Indeed, it was apparently interpreted as lack of cooperation rather than capacity. This set the tone of the meeting.

When the companion offered her skills and knowledge as a ROVI, the offer seemed to fall on stony ground. The psychologist made it clear that vision loss was not up for discussion as it had nothing to do with the current situation. (In my day talking therapies tended to be guided by the needs of the client, not dictated by the therapist. Clearly things have changed.) When the companion questioned this, as the psychologist was herself sight impaired, the psychologist demonstrated that she had not resolved her own sight loss issues by becoming angry. As might be imagined this meeting also finished before time.

This abject failure by the helping professions was a desperate disappointment, and too much to bear. Three days after, on the fourth attempt, the subject died by suicide.

When I heard about this case I was so angry I could hardly breathe. This is why I write. This is why, as long as there is life in my body, I will continue to shout the odds about sight loss.

The subject of the case study – and the link to the full study is in the footnote below – was not someone who had just given up because they were blind. Like myself, sight loss was regarded as more of a nuisance than a disability, and in spite of horrific setbacks life was lived to the full with positivity. When a brick wall was encountered, all that was needed was some help and, above all, some indication that someone actually cared. The absence of both made the bad situation intolerable. As has been said frequently throughout the book: we are not disabled; it's what others do or not do that disables us.

What happened to this person, a real person, graphically demonstrates what could happen to any one of us. Furthermore, this occurred only recently, not in some archaic past.

For the sake of thousands in the present and millions in the future, issues such as this *must* be addressed as a matter of urgency. The ignorance, indifference and abject failure to even attempt to understand the issues of sight loss cannot be allowed to continue. We are heading for a huge increase in sight loss. This is not some vague future threat. It is happening right now.

Whilst the pandemic may have culled many future candidates for sight loss, this may well be countered by many others not attending routine eye appointments. It seems inevitable that many people will lose their sight simply because they have not had their eyes checked for over a year. At the time of writing, there are about ninety thousand people beginning to lose their sight a year. This is three and a half times the number when I first encountered the sight loss world five years ago. Will another five years see three hundred thousand, and in ten years a million a year? Taking into account all the relevant factors that does not seem fanciful.

There are many people with sight loss leading useful and productive lives. Given appropriate and timely intervention and training, many more could do the same. At the moment a combination of delay, inappropriate training, societal attitudes and ignorance are condemning many people to a slow and tedious wait for death. Apart from the personal cost to the individuals involved, we cannot afford this loss of talent as a country.

I am blind already. What I see coming truly terrifies me. We all need to be very aware that there is a person with sight loss coming close to us soon.

Wake up, people, before it is too late.

POSTSCRIPT

This book has taken more than two years to write. During that time I have lost my wife, youngest son and some good friends. Halfway through the pandemic hit us. So many of us have become acquainted with loss, grief and deep sorrow.

I feel the negligent treatment of people with sight loss is a totally unnecessary addition to this toll of grief. This book was written as a genuine attempt to prevent this and fill some of the gaps. It was structured at five distinct levels to introduce in increments the subjects discussed:

- Essential foundation knowledge
- Management and adaptation
- Engagement with the real world
- Practical steps towards independence
- Sight loss and society

It is my hope that people will find this helpful

in managing and overcoming the consequences of their sight loss. I also hope that professionals in the field may also find it useful in their vital work.

Simon Mahoney, 2021

APPENDIX ONE

SIGHT LOSS, THE LURKING MENACE

Sight loss is more common than we imagine. It is also increasing at an alarming rate, yet there appears to be official indifference or disinterest in this. Unless it is pure ignorance. In either case, the lack of action is going to turn around and bite us in the not too distant future. I believe there are four broad reasons why there is an increase in sight loss. They are as follows:

- Our toxic lifestyle
- Our toxic environment
- Our attitude to our eyes
- Increasing longevity

Some or all of the causes of sight loss can be addressed. Failure to do so can only result in a massive increase in the frequency of eye problems. As indicated elsewhere, this increase is not a myth or a fantasy. It is happening now.

Ap.1.1 Toxic lifestyle

With increasing relative wealth has come increasing leisure. This has afforded opportunities for self-indulgence and unhealthy activities. This adds up to a toxic lifestyle for many people.

Ap.1.1.1 Food

We overeat and we eat too much of the wrong food. A shocking example of this was provided by a teenager who recently lost his sight. This was because he had allegedly eaten nothing but Quavers and chips since an early age. A more usual outcome of poor diet is the development of diabetes and/or obesity. Both are linked to sight loss. Both are at epidemic levels and increasing. Diabetes can lead to serious eye complications, such as diabetic retinopathy. Diabetes is the leading cause of preventable sight loss in the UK.

Diabetic retinopathy

This is an eye disease that people living with diabetes are more at risk of developing. If your blood glucose (sugar) levels and blood pressure are consistently high, you can seriously damage your blood vessels. There are many important blood vessels in your eyes, which help supply blood to the retina. When these blood vessels are damaged, they can get blocked, leak or grow randomly. This means the retina can't get the blood it needs and so can't work as it should, the result being your sight will be badly affected and you won't be able to see properly.

Types of diabetic retinopathy

Diabetic retinopathy usually develops in stages. When you get your eye screening results, you should see a letter and a number which tells you the type of retinopathy you may have. For example, an 'R' stands for retinopathy and the number tells you how much damage, if any, has been done. These letters and numbers may vary in different parts of the UK, so check with your consultant.

Here are the three types:

Stage 1. Background retinopathy. This means your eyesight isn't affected yet but you need to prevent the problem getting worse. You might hear this called R1 when you get your eye screening results.

Stage 2. Non-proliferative retinopathy. The damage is more serious and you'll need to get your eyes screened more often to check for any changes. This is called R2.

Stage 3. Proliferative retinopathy. This means you're now at a very high risk of losing your sight and you'll be offered treatment. This is R3.

Diabetic maculopathy

This is a different type of retinopathy that affects the middle of the eye, which may mean that you won't be able to read or drive. You might hear this called M0 if there's no maculopathy found in your eyes, or M1 if fluid is starting to build up in your eye and is affecting your sight.

Other eye problems

Having diabetes can mean you are two times more likely to get cataracts and one and a half times more likely to get glaucoma. Although not types of retinopathy, they can both lead to blindness. A cataract is when your vision gets cloudy. Glaucoma is when fluid builds up in the eye. The pressure, if not treated, can result in the crushing of the optic nerve and eventual blindness. It can be very quick, which is why glaucoma is known as 'the thief in the night'.

Obesity

Obesity has strong links with sight loss. It

can lead to diabetes, with the risks to sight outlined above. It can also be a strong causal factor in its own right. Research in the USA has demonstrated links between obesity and cataracts, age-related macular degeneration, retinopathy and glaucoma. As stated above, both diabetes and obesity are a growing problem in the UK, and it is pretty obvious that the increase in either will have an accompanying growth in the frequency of sight loss.

Ap.1.1.2 Smoking

Smoking is linked to sight loss. Whilst it is on the wane the damage has already been done to millions of people who used to smoke. In addition to this, seven percent of secondary school children admit to smoking. Smoking may as much as double the risk of developing diabetes. There is also a causal relationship between smoking and both the development and progression of diabetic retinopathy in addition to numerous other diabetes complications.

Smoking and dry eyes

Smokers are up to four times more likely to go blind in old age. Dry eye syndrome is described as insufficient tears on the eye's surface, which are needed to keep the eye lubricated and healthy. Sufferers of dry eye can experience eye redness, itchiness, a 'foreign body' sensation, and even watery eyes.

Tobacco smoke is a known eye irritant and worsens dry eye even among second-hand smokers, particularly for contact lens wearers. Smokers are twice as likely to have dry eye. Smokers significantly increase their risk of developing a cataract compared with non-smokers. In fact studies show that people who smoke double their chance of forming cataracts, and the risk continues to increase the more you smoke.

Smoking and macular degeneration

Age-related macular degeneration (AMD) affects the centre of the retina, which is responsible for sharp central vision needed for everyday tasks such as reading and driving. Macular degeneration causes 'blind spots' and often severely impairs central vision. AMD is the leading cause of permanent vision loss aged sixty-five and older. Studies show smokers can have a three-fold increase in the risk of developing AMD compared with people who have never smoked. And female smokers over the age of eighty are five and a half times more likely to develop AMD than non-smokers of the same age. However, because smoking is the biggest controllable risk factor associated with AMD, quitting smoking at any age, even later in life, can significantly reduce your risk of developing AMD.

Smoking and uveitis

Uveitis (inflammation of the eye's middle layer, or uvea) is a serious eye disease that can result in complete vision loss. It harms vital structures of the eye, including the iris and retina, and can lead to complications such as cataract, glaucoma and retinal detachment. Evidence shows smokers are more likely than non-smokers to have uveitis, and smoking appears linked to the development of uveitis. One study found smoking was associated with a 2.2 times greater than normal risk of having the condition.

Smoking and infant eye disease

Women who smoke during pregnancy transmit dangerous toxins to the placenta, potentially harming the unborn child. Smoking while pregnant increases the chance of many foetal and infant eye disorders, among other serious health problems. These include strabismus (crossed eyes) and underdevelopment of the optic nerve, which is a leading cause of blindness in children.

Ap.1.1.3 Alcohol

Excessive use of alcohol can have a detrimental influence on sight. It can both exacerbate existing eye conditions and be a causal factor for sight loss. Everyone who's ever had too much to drink knows that alcohol can give you blurry, distorted vision.

Short-term vision-altering effects

Slower pupil reaction

Alcohol causes the iris to constrict and dilate at a much slower speed. This becomes an issue for drivers who have been drinking as they cannot adapt as quickly to oncoming headlights.

Decreased contrast sensitivity

Being able to make distinctions between different objects based on lightness and darkness, a very important ability when driving at twilight, is impaired by alcohol. A new study from Western University in Ontario, Canada, shows alcohol reduces the ability of the eye to adjust vision for brightness and contrast by thirty percent at a blood alcohol level around the legal driving limit.

Eye twitching

Eye twitching (myokymia), which is actually the eyelid twitching, can be triggered by excessive alcohol intake.

Increased dryness

Findings from a study by the Hallym University College of Medicine suggest consuming even a small amount of alcohol can increase and exacerbate symptoms of dry eye.

Long-term damage

Increased cataract formation

Multiple studies have shown increased cataract formation in patients with higher alcohol consumption.

Increased risk of AMD

The American Optometric Association identifies excessive alcohol intake as a risk factor for AMD (age-related macular degeneration).

Decreased vision due to vitamin deficiency

Heavy drinking affects the absorption of vitamins

in the liver, vitamins needed to maintain healthy eyesight. For example, a vitamin B1 deficiency due to alcohol consumption can cause a weakness or paralysis of the eye muscles. A vitamin A deficiency due to alcoholism can cause night blindness, thinning of the cornea, corneal perforation, dryness, and even blindness due to retinal damage.

Tobacco-alcohol amblyopia

Also referred to as optic neuropathy, people who drink excessively can develop this condition which results in a loss of vision.

Prenatal alcohol exposure

Excessive exposure to alcohol in the womb can permanently affect the eyesight of the baby. According to a review by the Emory University School of Medicine, many eye problems are associated with Foetal Alcohol Syndrome, including underdevelopment of the optic nerve, difficulty with eye coordination, and the tendency for eyelids to droop.

Ap.1.1.4 Chlorinated water

A burning sensation or red eyes after being in a swimming pool are the result of chlorinated water. While chlorine is a necessary sanitizing agent in pools, it is still a chemical and dangerous to your eyes. It strips away the tear film that protects your cornea, making your eyes vulnerable to the dirt and bacteria floating around not eliminated by the chlorinated water. This can result in the following:

Pink eye or conjunctivitis

This is one of the most common eye infections swimmers can get, as it can be either viral or bacterial and spreads quickly and easily through the water.

Red, irritated eyes

This is a result of your eyes becoming dehydrated due to the chlorine and the removal of your tear film. Sometimes you may also experience blurriness and distorted vision, though this is usually only temporary.

Acanthamoebic keratitis

This is a severe eye infection caused by amoeba becoming trapped between the cornea and the contact lens. It can begin to live there, which can result in ulcers on your cornea and permanent damage to your vision. The use of eye drops, basic lens hygiene and tight fitting goggles can either alleviate or prevent most conditions from this source.

Ap.1.1.5 Chronic stress

Modern long-term stress is increasingly being associated not only with sight loss but also as a causal factor. A recent review of studies on sight loss and stress found three major strands.

First, that the onset of sight loss can cause stress. Although this is blindingly obvious it is still a valid finding.

Second, that stress can cause an increase in the rate of deterioration in existing sight loss conditions. This is significant as it highlights the importance of acceptance and the cessation of stressing about sight loss.

Third, that prolonged stress can cause sight loss. This of course is yet another reason to avoid chronic stress if at all possible.

If we look at the basic manifestations of stress then it is possible that any one of them could be a factor. In combination they could be very influential.

Increased blood pressure could cause structural damage to the blood vessels in the eye.

Adrenalin and the production of cortisol could cause damage to the central nervous system. Both the optic nerves and the visual cortex are part of the central nervous system.

Downgrading of the digestive system could possibly cause the eyes to be malnourished. In other words they are not getting enough nourishment to operate and sustain themselves.

The downgrading or absence of the immune system could leave the eyes, like the rest of the body, open to any infection. They would also be poorly equipped to fight any of the hundreds of eye conditions that can result in significant sight loss.

The above is part research, part speculation and part logic on my part. As such you will need to check it out for yourself. There is, however, the makings of an interesting PhD study.

Ap.1.1.6 Excessive exposure to blue light

The use of mobile phones, tablets and computer monitors for social media, game playing, general entertainment, information seeking and work has an overlooked side effect. The one thing all these have in common is that they emit light in the blue spectrum.

Blue and ultraviolet are shortwave light. As the photo receptors in the eye respond to every peak of a wave of light this means that they have to work harder. This in itself is not a problem. The production of a unit of waste for each unit of cellular activity, however, is a real issue. The waste disposal system in the eyes cannot cope when the eyes are operating in the blue spectrum. They become clogged with waste. This can have serious consequences in the long term for people who have an existing eye condition, or for young children.

As most adolescents seem to spend a huge amount of time on social media or playing games, and even very young children have a device of some sort propped up in front of them for much of the time, this is a matter for huge concern. We could speculate that perhaps we could be producing a generation of which one in four could experience serious sight lost before they are fifty. I very much hope that I am letting my imagination run away with me. The use of yellow filters can counteract this affect.

Fluorescent lighting

This is a cheap and economical form of lighting. As such it is used widely in industry, commerce and public buildings and this includes many schools. Cool white fluorescent light also happens to operate mainly in the blue spectrum. As stated above, this can make existing conditions worse and cause damage to the eyes in the long term. Children are particularly vulnerable to this.

Ap.1.2 Toxic environment

We have poisoned, and are still poisoning, our air, water and the very ground upon which we stand. In spite of pious utterances from the great and the good there is relatively little preventative action.

Ap.1.2.1 Air pollution

Particulate air pollution caused by motor vehicles in inner cities is linked with sight loss. People in the worst areas are twenty percent more likely to suffer sight loss than those in the best.

Long-term exposure to air pollution has been linked to glaucoma. These were the findings of a major study published in *Investigative Ophthalmology & Visual Science* and undertaken by scientists at University College London. In England, about 480,000 people have chronic open-angle glaucoma. The participants were asked whether they had glaucoma, and they underwent an eye examination, which was then measured against where they live. The results revealed that neighbourhoods with higher amounts of fine particulate matter pollution were at least six percent more likely to report having glaucoma than those in the least polluted areas. The research team found that people in the most polluted twenty-five percent of areas were eighteen percent more likely to report having glaucoma than those in the least polluted quartile, and they were also significantly more likely to have a thinner retina, one of the changes typical of glaucoma progression.

Eye pressure was not associated with air pollution, which the researchers say suggests that air pollution may affect glaucoma risk through a different mechanism. Professor Paul Foster (UCL Institute of Ophthalmology and Moorfields Eye Hospital) said: 'We have found yet another reason why air pollution should be addressed as a public health priority, and that avoiding sources of air pollution could be worthwhile for eye health alongside other health concerns.'

A recent report claims that twenty-five percent of schools are situated in areas that have air pollution in excess of WHO (World Health Organisation) legal limits (UNICEF). This could be another concern for the future eye health of children. Any study involving air quality has many other factors which make any findings difficult to justify. A major problem is that poor air is often present in areas of deprivation. Deprivation of itself can also contribute to sight loss from social as well as environmental factors.

Ap.1.2.2 Water

Our drinking water is contaminated by fluoride, oestrogen and micro and nano plastic. These contaminants have been associated with sight loss. Doubtless there are other interesting contaminants in the water, the ground and food chain that can also be associated with sight loss.

Fluoride is a toxin. As such it can alter the chemical balance in the eyes and has been associated with sight loss. It can cause degenerative eye diseases such as cataracts, glaucoma and AMD. (Published Mar 18, 2019, New York/PRNewswire in the *International Journal of Environmental Research and Public Health*.)

Although research has consistently shown that it is the optimal application of fluoride to teeth, not its ingestion, that reduces tooth decay, it is difficult to avoid ingestion as fluoride is routinely added to the water supply. Claims of safety from long-term ingestion ignore hundreds of studies showing the potential for harm, including to the eyes.

In a study by Waugh he identifies, for the first time, the key biological pathways and mechanisms by which fluoride contributes to degenerative eye diseases. He suggests minimising fluoride exposure to reduce the occurrence or severity of AMD, cataracts and glaucoma. 'It's well known that excessive fluoride exposure is associated with dental fluorosis and musculoskeletal disorders that cause chronic pain,' said Waugh. 'However, my study's goal was to gain insights into how fluoride may contribute to degenerative eyes, a finding also documented for decades. I show how fluoride ingestion renders eyes more susceptible to degeneration by identifying how fluoride fundamentally alters biological pathways and modifies the expression of genes, proteins and cytokines responsible for development of cataracts, glaucoma and AMD.'

Oestrogen

Oestrogen, both within the womb and in the drinking water, can have long-term effects on eyesight, including sight loss. Oestrogen can make the cornea more elastic which, in some cases, render the cornea useless and result in sight loss. This particularly affects women as the changes in oestrogen levels at puberty, pregnancy, childbirth and menopause can cause permanent changes in their eyes. With the level of oestrogen in the water it is highly likely that not only the sperm count but also the sight of males could be affected.

Plastic

Micro and nano plastic is present in the water we drink, the food we eat and the air we breathe. As far as plastic is concerned, we are all severely compromised. Research so far has found no direct causal link between the ingestion of plastic to general health. There is, however, a growing body of research that is examining the effect of the toxins that can attach themselves to plastic, particularly nano plastic. These include both toxic organic material and heavy metals.

Heavy metals such as lead, mercury and arsenic are toxic to the body. They attack the central nervous system (CNS) and the organs. An important part of the CNS are the optic nerves. Damage to these can lead to conditions such as AMD or age-related macular degeneration. Heavy metals can also adversely affect the visual cortex along with the rest of the brain. Cataracts, AMD and glaucoma are all associated with heavy metals toxicity.

These contaminants have been associated with damage to both organs and the vascular system. We know from the effects of obesity and diabetes that any compromise to the vascular system can have negative consequences for eyesight. I feel it is fair to say that an association between sight loss and the ingestion of the contaminants riding on plastic has been clearly demonstrated.

Ap.1.2.3 Sunlight

UV light from the sun is far fiercer than when I was a child. This damages the skin and the Met Office warn us so we can slap on sun cream. UV light is also incredibly damaging to the eyes and there is a direct causal link with sight loss. Conditions such as cataracts, glaucoma, AMD and damage to the cornea and the iris can all be attributed to UV light. Ask yourself a simple question: How many children do you see wearing sunglasses or even hats when out in the sunshine? It would seem that this is yet another area where we are building a huge increase in sight problems for the future.

Ap.1.2.4 Climate change

I feel it is fair to say that climate change is happening. It can no longer be dismissed as a myth or the bleating of croakers. Research is being undertaken on the effects of temperature and barometric pressure on the body. As far as I know there are as yet no conclusive results. I do not anticipate that that will remain the case for too long.

In the meantime, many friends with sight impairment tell me that low barometric pressure can reduce their remaining vision considerably. It is unknown whether this can cause permanent damage. With climate change and extreme barometric pressure incidents I guess we will find out soon enough.

Ap.1.3 Our attitude to our eyes

There seems to be a general sense that our eyes are somehow disassociated from our bodies, with little or no comprehension that what affects our bodies also affects our eyes.

We know that chronic stress can have a terrible influence on our general health and state of mind. It never occurs to us that it can also contribute to sight loss. Why should we think that when our bodies are taking a hammering that the eyes miraculously have a free ride? The answer is simple.

Sight loss is so horrific that none of us, and I include myself, give it a thought until it happens to us. This disconnect between our bodies and our eyes can be seen to operate at an individual and an institutional level.

As individuals we protect our bodies from strong sunlight. We are nothing like as careful with our eyes. How many parents routinely put sunglasses or a hat on their kids to protect their eyes?

At an institutional level, the huge disconnect

between eye care and support for sight loss is, I believe, indicative of the medical profession not relating seeing with the eyes in any meaningful fashion.

There is of course a more obvious reason for the disconnect between our eyes and our consciousness: we disregard our eyes for the simple reason we look through them rather than at them. As such they literally fade into the background of our general consciousness of our bodies. This too operates at both an institutional and a personal level as, after all, institutions are made up of people.

Ap.1.4 Increasing longevity

There is no doubt that people are living longer, although there is some evidence that this is beginning to stall. Our eyes, like any other part of the body, have a limited shelf life. As they grow from the inside out there is a limit to how far the outer limits of the eye can be removed from the source of nutrients. Apart from that, our eyes were not designed to put up with all the factors mentioned above. Currently one in five of seventy-year-olds have sight loss and the proportion increases with age, as indeed is the proportion of older people.

Summary

It is my belief that in the not too distant future a sizeable and growing portion of the population will have significant sight loss. Taking into consideration all the factors, and the apparent lack of action, it seems not unreasonable to predict a sight loss epidemic of almost biblical proportions.

Apart from the quite appalling personal cost, there is also an economic factor. There will be a huge burden in the cost of treatment and care. There will be a huge demand on mental health provision both for those with sight loss and their significant others. In addition, the majority of people with sight loss will become economically inactive. This will significantly add to the benefit bill whilst reducing tax revenue.

If there is going to be the increase I predict then there is a real problem. No country can afford to have a greater number of net beneficiaries than net contributors to the commonwealth.

Occasionally Guide Dogs for the Blind run an advertisement stating that half of sight loss is unnecessary, yet I am unaware of any public sector campaign to raise awareness of sight loss. Considering the consequences of mass sight loss this is appalling at best, and gross neglect of the governmental duty of care to the population at large at worst. The solution is simple. Not only is it simple, it is in our hands. All we have to do is eat properly, avoid light in the blue spectrum, clean up the cities and take pains to protect our eyes. Above all, we have to start thinking of our eyes as part of us. Surely that is doable.

Sources

- Burkes Eye Physicians and Surgeons Ltd
- RNIB website
- Guide Dogs for the Blind website
- Diabetes Association website
- AMD website
- 'The Effects of Fluorescent Light on the Ocular Health of Persons with Pre-Existing Eye Pathologies' By Elaine Kitchel, *American Printing House for the Blind*
- 'Investigative Ophthalmology & Visual Science', the *International Journal of Environmental Research and Public Health*

APPENDIX TWO

TIPS FOR DAILY SURVIVAL

When we develop vision loss we have no idea how we're going to cope, whether indeed we are even expected to cope, or the best way to adjust the way we do things to make life less of a drama.

Colin Green, another blind veteran, and I wracked our brains to try to identify all the tips we can share with you. Having said that, the list is far from complete!

Ap.2.1 In the early stages

Ap.2.1.1 Preparation

The first major tip has to be to not lose a minute. From the moment you know that you have sight loss, start to prepare for the possibility of entire loss of sight. In short, whilst you have some sight learn the skills you will need if and when it finally disappears.

Ap.2.1.2 Significant others

Next is to tell your nearest and dearest what is going on, immediately. They need to know so that they can understand and offer appropriate support. Make it as matter-of-fact and rational as you can and not a whine.

Ap.2.1.3 Pre-empting stress

Sight loss is stressful, so another tip is to make sure you get a grip on the stress before it gets a grip on you.

Ap.2.1.4 Protection

Sight loss can mean you become an accident waiting to happen, so learn to move defensively. If you are going to place your head outside the line of your body, such as bending over to pick something up, ensure you check the space first with your hand. When moving or setting off check, either with your hand or cane, that you have the room to do so. There is nothing worse than stepping boldly off only to find you collide with something. Spoils the effect somewhat! When carrying something in a confined place, carry the object in the hand away from the nearest obstacles.

Ap.2.1.5 Home navigation

When moving about in your own home, make a point of noting any features that will help you navigate. In my home, for example, there is an invisible track in the carpet which I can detect with my feet. This takes me safely across my living-room.

Ap.2.1.6 Attitude to sight loss

It is important to appreciate that sight loss is an impairment and that it is what others do, or do not do, that turns it into a disability. In recognition of this, it is now a requirement of law that all service and transport providers, retailers and healthcare premises take all reasonable steps to ensure that every person, whatever their impairment, has full access to their services. This also applies to their duty of care to their customers. I was once put in danger by a service provider, and in my complaint their responsibilities were pointed out, and the local paper and Blind Veterans were copied in. Both the reply and remedial action were immediate. Remember, we are not alone! Also remember that expectation is everything. Expect to succeed and you will. (The reverse is also true, so don't expect to fail!)

Ap.2.2 Hints and tips for daily living

This next section deals with different aspects of daily living. Living without any sight is perfectly doable, you just have to stay aware of all the available aids and remember to take them into consideration.

Ap.2.2.1 Communication

There may be other things that you think of to do with communication, but here are some of the key issues.

If you need to post a letter, books of stamps have notches on the edge of the cover: one notch for first-class and two for second-class. These notches also indicate orientation of the stamps. There is some help available with postage under the Articles for the Blind postal service. You can check with your local post office for rules, regulations and restrictions. The labels are available from the RNIB.

Buy a mobile phone with a touch screen, audio navigation and feedback. Some also have a colour detector, scanner and GPS. Many mobile phones can be upgraded to become blind-friendly with an appropriate application installed. I have a synaptic application on my android phone. Some iPhones have an audio feedback function.

Most of us have a laptop, tablet, iPad or PC. Once we begin to lose our sight, if we wish to continue using these gadgets then three things have to happen:

- We have to learn to touch type if not already able to do so.
- We must learn how to work without a mouse.
- We need to fit an audio application to each device we use. A normal QWERTY keyboard has blips/bumps on the keys 'F' and 'J' that means you can navigate the keyboard.

Make use of audio text scanners to read documents. As far as I am aware there are no scanners that read handwriting yet.

Many telephones and cash machines (ATMs) have the number five distinguished by a blip/bump on the key. It is often hard to feel, but it is there to help navigation. We suggest you learn how to find your way around the keypad with your eyes shut as quickly as possible.

Be aware that you have to listen harder when communicating verbally, as you can no longer read faces, gestures and other non-verbal behaviour. Attending a course on basic communication and assertiveness skills may be useful, particularly as we have to learn how to communicate effectively without these cues.

Ap.2.2.2 General tips

This list is long, but by all means not exhaustive, as life can throw up new challenges every day. These are the things we thought of:

- Check and double-check before doing anything.
- Be careful that your sleeves do not sweep objects onto the floor or trail in water.
- Operate on the 'broken glass' principle. In other words, if you come across something that needs doing, do it immediately. For reasons discussed earlier in the book, you might forget if you do not.
- If living with someone, make sure you communicate so that both of you know what the other is doing. There is nothing worse than trying to operate in a shifting land (or kitchenscape)!
- Get used to the idea that everything is going to take more time. Rushing plus sight loss equals chaos.
- Do not leave doors and cupboard doors open or even half open.
- Keep living space as uncluttered as possible.

Ap.2.2.3 Tips for the kitchen

Regularly wash and dry your hands thoroughly, especially after handling meat or fish.

- Keep blades of knives pointing away from you.
- Always work within the confines of your work tray to prevent food or equipment escaping onto the floor!
- Have regular checks made on your equipment – the oven, hob, microwave, electric wok, kettle, for example – to make sure it is in full working order.
- Have a low rail fitted in front of the hob.
- Keep separate chopping boards for meat, fish and vegetables to prevent contamination.
- Close cupboard doors and drawers immediately.
- Turn off heat on hob between tasks.
- Dispose of food often to prevent maggots.
- Do not overthink anything, but stay mindful and focussed.
- Do not touch plugs with wet hands.
- Do not rush. Ever.
- Enjoy it, it is fun.
- Freeze any surplus food in labelled, dated airtight containers.
- Handle raw chicken carefully and wash hands immediately afterwards.

- Keep saucepan handles parallel to the worktop to prevent knocking them onto the floor.
- Heat once applied cannot be undone, so increase heat slowly so as not to burn what's in the pan.
- Keep your worktop uncluttered.
- Pasta swells half as big again when cooked.
- Prawns and fish cook very quickly.
- Prick potatoes and pierce any coverings on ready meals before putting in microwave.
- Read instructions at least twice.
- Replace tops of jars immediately, like mayonnaise, so lids don't get mixed up.
- Reverse engineer each meal. In other words, think about the end result and work backwards to see how to achieve it.
- Rice swells to twice its size when cooked.
- Put scalds and burns under cold water as quickly as possible.
- Smell ingredients, and if any doubt about freshness discard.
- Stir sauces all the time otherwise they go lumpy.
- Timing is everything, so keep practising.
- Turn food from the edges of the pan into the middle of the pan.
- Use water from vegetables for gravy, it's tastier.
- Use your imagination with ingredients! And have fun experimenting!

- Use a clean tea towel for hot ingredients like potatoes as oven gloves can get grubby.
- Use oven gloves for hot pans and oven dishes.
- Use sharp knives as blunt ones, believe it or not, cause more injuries.
- Keep a large bowl nearby for rubbish. A mixing bowl works well.
- Listen for sizzling butter or boiling water to let you know when it's ready for cooking.
- Your sense of smell will quickly recognise when food is cooked, or burnt, which you'll learn to avoid if you don't like the taste of carbon!
- Use a digital or voice recognition timer for cooking times. Talking watches, Alexa or Siri (or other timing app) work perfectly well.
- Always remember to turn the hob and oven off when you've finished cooking.
- Warming your plates and dishes keeps food hotter for longer when completing the final bits of cooking. Covering food with foil helps too.
- WASH HANDS IMMEDIATELY AFTER HANDLING FRESH CHILLIES!

A few things that worked for me:

- Buy a tray to work in. A silicone pet eating tray is perfect for this. It does not move about and is easy to keep clean.

- Use wire food baskets for cooking. There is a film on YouTube showing a blind person using a wire basket in a saucepan to boil eggs. I think this is a brilliant idea, and it could also be extended to boiling vegetables. The use of a basket removes the risk of scalding when you cannot see. I now use a small chip basket for all work involving saucepans.

What to do if a pan catches fire

- Do not panic.
- Turn the heat off and remove the pan from the heat if safe to do so.
- Wet a clean tea towel in water, squeeze out the excess and drape over the fire to cut off oxygen.
- Let everything fully cool down before cleaning up.
- Only open the windows when you are sure the fire is out.
- **DO NOT THROW WATER ON A FAT FIRE!**

Most fires can be controlled in the first minute. Any longer than that, get out, **but do not rush.**

Other tips:

- Have a place for everything and try to stick to it.
- When doing a task, get organised so that

you are in a fixed and recognisable point, for example the intersection point of two work surfaces, and arrange what you need in easy reach around you.

- Replace tops of jars immediately, and certainly before opening another jar.
- When removing bottle tops, make sure you place them in an easy-to-find location. I put mine next to my tray so I do not have to search the worktop for it.
- Restore your sense of balance by carrying jugs of water.
- Restore your sense of proprioception by sorting small objects into separate containers and keep practising the exercises in chapter seven, 'Getting it back together again'.

Ap.2.2.6 Eating

When you cannot see the act of eating can be quite an adventure. Indeed, you can often recognise people with sight loss as they have food stains on their clothing – if you can see that is! Below are some basic tips to make it less of an adventure.

- The backs of knives are usually flush with the handle.
- Find a way of recognising the backs of forks and spoons.

- Use jelly (rubber) mats to anchor your food plate as there's nothing worse than trying to eat from a moving target you cannot see!
- Ask people to tell you where different food is located on the plate either by using the clock system or top, bottom, left and right.
- Consider using high-sided plates and bowls. It makes eating less of an adventure.
- Take your time.
- Do not be embarrassed. Consider how other people would manage if they could not see.
- Difficulties are part of the territory, so accept you have to find solutions.

Ap.2.2.7 Personal care

- Put toothpaste directly into your mouth instead of on your brush.
- Keep toothpaste separate. Brushing your teeth with Savlon or cream for piles has little to recommend it!
- Keep your false teeth, if you have them, in the bathroom.
- Wash your face *after* brushing your teeth, as this prevents getting toothpaste on the towel and the nearest and dearest getting vexed.
- Learn to shave without a mirror.
- Consider a frame around the Seat of Ease (the toilet!).
- Men, consider changing the habit of a lifetime

and sit down to use the toilet, for all occasions.

- Fit a grab rail in the shower.
- Keep shower gel separate from cleaning products. Using bleach or toilet cleaner as a body wash is not generally a good option.
- If you do not have a nonslip floor put a towel on the floor.
- The Be My Eyes app can help you with hair and makeup.
- Consider using a local hair salon who also have a nail care section or nail bar for getting toenails and fingernails trimmed.
- Medication can be put into blister packs. Discuss this with your local pharmacy.
- Administer eye drops yourself if at all possible. Find consistent points on your face from which to administer the drops. In my case, being right-handed, I rest the back of my thumb on the bridge of my nose when putting drops in my left eye, and the first knuckle of my forefinger on the end of my right eyebrow when putting drops in my right eye. My left forefinger is used to pull the lower eyelid down so as to form a pocket into which I put the drops.
- Keep up checks with the optician as they can also use your eyes to help monitor your general health.

Ap.2.2.7 Care of clothes

- Use sock locks to control your socks. These also prevent the washing machine ambushing and devouring single socks, and means you can hang socks in pairs on the washing line.
- Peg your shoes together, as it can be embarrassing to go out in odd shoes!
- Be very disciplined about keeping clean and dirty clothes separate.
- Learn to tie a tie without a mirror.
- Group and label outfits in the wardrobe.
- Thin clothing down to those in regular use.

Ap.2.3 Entertainment

- Audio description on a TV can be accessed through the TV menu. This is something you may wish to organise/negotiate with your spouse or carer.
- A Sky Q Box can be operated on voice command.
- Text can be switched to speech and audio navigation on a Kindle HD Fire, but not on all models, so you need to check before purchasing.
- Amazon’s Alexa will read from your Kindle, access radio programmes and play music on command.
- Talking books are available through libraries

and local blind organisations.

- Talking newspapers are also available, and there is a newsstand option on Kindle.
- Mobile phones fitted with a synaptic application will enable you to use your phone easily, even when blind. I have it on my mobile and it has given me back my independence.
- In Touch on Radio 4 is a weekly programme concerning sight loss.
- The RNIB have their own radio channel called Radio RNIB Connect.
- There is also an organisation called VI Talk. They do regular podcasts. I have done one for them.
- Henshaws of Manchester have a website that is well worth investigating as they cater for all sorts of disability, including sight loss.

Ap.2.4 Out and about

- Stand your cane tip-side down in a bowl of disinfectant.
- Strip keys down to the minimum, and keep them on a lanyard.
- Get your purse or wallet properly organised, and only keep working cards, with payment cards in one slot, reward cards in another, bus pass in another, and all others elsewhere. There is nothing quite so embarrassing as fumbling for the right card with everybody

smiling in a long-suffering way at the poor old blind bloke (who let him out anyway?) making a hash of things!

- Remember that your feet, hands and ears are now your main way of gathering information. Therefore, try and have one hand free at all times.
- Look after your feet and pay attention to the suitability of your footwear.
- Have your hearing checked regularly.
- Consider using a backpack for carrying shopping. This leaves your hands free so you can use your cane properly. It is also the easiest way of carrying any load.
- Where there are lights at a pedestrian crossing there is usually an audible signal to indicate it is safe to cross. At a particularly busy junction, there may not be an audible signal, but there is quite often a knurled nut on the base of the button box. This rotates when it is safe to cross.
- Learn the details of your route and try to visualise it.
- Most road junctions have dropped curbs with bubble pavement. The direction of the alignment of the bubbles points the way across the road.
- Occupy the middle of the pavement as there are less obstacles there, and you are less likely to be shoved into the road or the hedge/wall.

- Give way to pushchairs, wheelchairs, mobility scooters and people on crutches.
- It is very difficult to walk in a straight line, so if you tend to drift then lead with the left leg. This is not fool-proof, however, so constant checking is vital. An alternative is to follow your nose. This works but requires self-discipline not to move your nose away from the direction of travel.
- Turning corners can also be a problem as you have no idea how far you have turned. Again, care and checking are vital. Where you know the corner is short and sharp you can try squaring it.
- Try and use the sun (if it is out!) as a way of maintaining your direction, as it is only too easy to get turned around and end up walking back the way you came. If there is no sun, use a specific noise like a road on your right-hand side, for instance, to guide you, or the wind.
- If you have one, use your long cane without diffidence or embarrassment. It is the best friend you will ever have when properly used.

Ap.2.5 Shopping

As a general rule, do as much of the shopping as you can before asking for help. Newspapers, milk, vegetables and bread are usually in the same place and getting these will demonstrate willingness to be independent. This will make both fellow customers and staff happier to help you when it is really needed. Most people are only too happy to help and need only to be asked.

Ap.2.5.1 Assisted shopping

Most supermarkets are happy to provide an assisted shop. This is covered in chapter thirteen, 'Help, the poison chalice'.

Ap.2.5.2 New equipment

When buying new equipment, make sure that it can be used without sight. It needs to have knobs and switches rather than buttons and digital readout.

Ap.2.6 Some useful gadgets

- Audio timer
- Talking scales
- Penfriend labelling system
- Talking microwave oven
- Talking induction hob
- Talking watch
- Talking compass

As stated at the beginning, these are not all the possible tips. Some we learned from other people with sight loss, some from sight loss professionals, and some you find out from experience. Only you can really determine what works for you. If you discover a new tip be sure to share it with as many people as possible, including me! My email address is:

simon@wingingitblind.com

APPENDIX THREE

SOME BASIC STATISTICS ABOUT SIGHT LOSS

In this section I'll take a quick look at the basic statistics concerning sight loss. In spite of the data I believe that there is a gross underestimate and that nobody has an idea of what the true figures may be. I would speculate that if there was an accurate count the data would not be for public consumption on the grounds of not terrifying the public. I also suspect that sight loss primarily concerns the little people, like you and me, and the government will not want to spend the money. But we'll see...if you'll pardon the expression.

Ap.3.1 Sight loss population and registration

'More than two million people living with sight loss' is an estimate based on how commonly different eye conditions and resulting sight loss occurs. The figure takes into account actors such as age, gender and ethnicity, and builds up a picture of the numbers of people who are living with significant sight loss in the UK. This picture not only includes people who are registered, but also those who are waiting for treatment, those whose sight could be improved, those who have not registered, and people whose sight loss is not at a level that allows them to register. Registration is a vexed issue. See chapter two, 'The great disconnect'.

Ap.3.2 The register

Each local authority holds their own register of blind and partially sighted people. The local authority registers include people who are registered as severely sight impaired (blind) and sight impaired (partially sighted).

Economic impact report

As of 2017, there are around 350,000 people on the registers of blind and partially sighted people in the UK. A total of 173,735 are registered severely sight impaired, and 176,125 are registered sight impaired. This is approximately 290,500 in England, 17,000 in Wales, 8,000 in Northern Ireland and 34,500 in Scotland (Scottish figures were last published in 2010). Visit the Sight Loss Data Tool for more local data and information on sources that publish the register data. (Source: Sight Loss Data Tool)

Ap.3.3 The future

The number of people in the UK with sight loss is set to increase dramatically in the future. As we get older we are increasingly likely to experience sight loss, and the UK population is ageing. In addition, sight loss is strongly linked with certain medical conditions such as diabetes. Lifestyle and environmental factors in combination with basic attitudes means that, without action, the numbers of people with sight problems in the UK are likely to increase dramatically over the next twenty-five years. The number of people with sight loss is estimated to rise to 2.7 million by 2030. By 2050, the current figure will double to over four million. (Source: Economic Impact Report.) For reasons outlined in Appendix Three, I believe this to be a gross underestimate.

Ap.3.4 Main causes

Age-related macular degeneration is by far the leading cause of blindness in adults. Other significant causes of sight loss are glaucoma, cataracts and diabetic retinopathy. (Source:

Economic Impact Report)

Ap.3.5 People who have it

Sight loss affects people of all ages, but as we get older we are increasingly likely to experience sight loss. One in five people aged seventy-five and over are living with sight loss; one in two people aged ninety and over are living with sight loss. (Source: Economic Impact Report)

Nearly two-thirds of people living with sight loss are women. People from black and minority ethnic communities are at greater risk of some of the leading causes of sight loss. Adults with learning disabilities are ten times more likely to be blind or partially sighted than the general population. (Source: Eye Health and Sight Loss Stats and Data)

Ap.3.6 Some basic realities

- Only seventeen percent of people experiencing sight loss are offered emotional support in response to their deteriorating vision.
- Only twenty-seven percent of blind and partially sighted people of working age are in employment – a fall from thirty-three percent in employment in 2006.
- Thirty-nine percent of blind and partially sighted people of working age have problems

making ends meet.

- Thirty-five percent of blind and partially sighted people say that they sometimes, frequently or always experience negative attitudes from the public in relation to their sight loss.
- Thirty-one percent of people are rarely or never optimistic about the future.

(Source: *My Voice*, 2015. Information last updated 1 September 2019)

The above is only what is thought to be the case. It is also important that most of the people have significant others who are also directly impacted.

APPENDIX FOUR

COOKING ECONOMICALLY

As money, for all sorts of reasons, is often in short supply I have included this section. Please use and copy and share.

There are many people who find themselves having to choose between eating and heating. There is little you can do about heating, but there is something you can do to reduce the cost of eating. The expenditure on eating falls into two areas: the cost of cooking and the cost of food. There are clear steps you can take to radically reduce the expenditure on both.

Reducing the cost of food can be achieved by buying fresh ingredients rather than expensive ready meals. For example, for the price of a ready meal you can buy a whole basket of fresh vegetables which can be roasted in the oven with herbs and sprinkled with cheese. With a hunk of bread, this dish of roasted veg can last a few days, and is so much better for your health and your wallet/purse. Tips like these, and many more, can be found in my cookbook, *First Catch Your Rabbit*.

So let's now look at how we can reduce the cost of cooking. When you are cooking you are essentially buying power to make your food eatable. We need to increase the proportion of the energy taken to cook and reduce the amount of energy we waste. In other words, we need to look at how as much of the energy as possible cooks the food rather than flying out the window as heat.

Main assumptions

I am assuming you have an oven and a hob, and basic pans and simtple tools. I am also assuming that the person reading this has never cooked before. For this reason it may seem insultingly simplistic. However, no one knows it all and even the most experienced cook may pick up some hints of worth.

Equipment

Oven

Whatever oven you have there are a number of points to be made.

- The oven is an extremely economic way of cooking. It is not just an additional cupboard.
- If it is clean it will be more efficient. A dirty oven can waste up to a fifth of the energy used for cooking.
- Make sure the seal on the oven door fits properly. A poorly fitting seal can cost you up to half the energy you use for cooking.
- If the oven has a glass panel keep it clean. This prevents you opening the oven to check how the meal is progressing. This is not only a poor idea as far as cooking is concerned, you can also waste up to a fifth of the energy used for cooking.

Electric hobs

Keep the hob clean. You can lose up to a fifth of the energy if you are heating grime as well as the hob.

Saucepans

- The smaller the saucepan the less energy needed to bring water to the boil.
- Only use the minimum of water in saucepans, it takes less energy to bring to the boil.
- If the saucepan is warped it can lose up to two-fifths of the energy.
- Ensure bottoms of pans are clean and shiny.

Dirty bottoms can waste up to one-fifth of the energy used.

- Do not use bigger saucepans than are needed.
- Keep pans covered to keep heat in.

Saving money using the oven

The trick here is to use as much of the energy as possible. For example, if you are cooking something like a pasta bake which requires forty minutes cooking time, turn the oven off after thirty minutes. If it is clean and the seal fits properly the oven will keep its heat for ten minutes. Doing this you save twenty-five percent of the power for that meal.

If you really want to save money put a spare quilt into the cupboard next to the oven. Bring the meal up to heat in the oven, probably for ten minutes, then turn off the power and leave in the oven for fifteen minutes. Then put the dish into the middle of the quilt. Providing the dish is well covered it will keep its heat for a good forty minutes, if not more. If you leave the dish in there for an hour it will come out perfectly cooked and ready to eat. This can save up to seventy-five percent of the fuel for a single meal, and works even better if you wrap the dish in foil or a space blanket and then put it into the quilt.

If you have a freezer, when you cook

something in the oven do more than you need. You can then freeze the rest. It takes less energy to allow something to defrost and then be reheated than to cook it from scratch.

Cooking on hobs

The trick with hobs is to use them as little as possible. For example, if you are cooking three vegetables, use the same pan. Different vegetables need different cooking times, so follow the instructions below. (I use a chip frying basket in my saucepans to stop unnecessary messing about and greater accuracy.)

If you are cooking carrots, leeks and peas, for example, then you do the following:

- Cut carrots up, batons or rounds, and put them in the basket.
- Put boiling water into saucepan from kettle and put on the hob.
- Put carrots in the water on simmer for five minutes.
- Dice leeks and put in the basket with the carrots.
- Turn off the hob.
- After two more minutes add the peas and cover the saucepan.
- After three more minutes all the vegetables will be perfectly cooked using only ten

minutes-worth of electricity.

Always use the heat of the water to continue the cooking after turning off the hob as you can save more than half the power. Another example is when doing pasta. You can halve the cooking time by putting the pasta into a pan with boiling water from the kettle. It only needs a little water and a couple of minutes, and then you can finish the cooking on the hob.

Other ways of cooking vegetables

Using the example of new potatoes, put the potatoes into a vacuum flask and add boiling water from the kettle. Seal the flask. Replace the water after ten minutes and reseal the flask. Leave for half an hour. Experiment with other vegetables.

Slow cookers

These cost the same to run as a light bulb and are brilliant for stews, curries, risottos, chicken and rice.

Defrosting

Allow food to defrost in its own time. This requires planning. It is better for the food than defrosting in the microwave and costs nothing.

Planning and organisation

All the above tips are common sense when you think about it. If you plan your meals you not only waste less food you also do not waste power. With a little thought the cost of cooking can be more than halved. Better the money in your pocket than the gas or electric companies! But it does mean you have to be organised, and willing and ready to try and change the habits of a lifetime.

First Catch Your Rabbit can be found on Amazon and also on my website www.wingingitblind.com There is no copyright associated with this appendix. Share freely.

APPENDIX FIVE

ADDITIONAL RULES OF ENGAGEMENT

Rules of engagement

When you first begin to lose your sight it is vital you recognise you could be in for a pretty torrid time. The creation of a set of rules of engagement is, in my mind, essential if you are to come through the experience relatively sane and upbeat.

In the course of time those rules of engagement should become incorporated into who you are and how you deal with your lack of sight. The one thing that has to be appreciated is that the struggle with sight loss does not end; it does, however, change over time. Therefore, the management of your sight loss changes and develops over time, and the rules of engagement become a bit more sophisticated or reach a higher level. This is not to abandon the original rules, but merely bolting an additional set onto your consciousness.

Such additional rules could be along the lines of the following:

Be aware acceptance is double-edged

We talk about acceptance as being important. We must, however, be aware that acceptance can be acknowledging that something has happened and just hunkering down and hoping it goes away. On the other hand, it can be recognising that something has happened, taking positive steps to live with it, and moving on to living your life to the full. Having a disability does not make you disabled; and just because you cannot see it does not mean you cannot feel, hear, smell and think. It is the eyes that are disenabled, not the person.

Foster patience

Because of issues of status and assumed inferiority by others we have to foster patience, reasonableness and determination.

Constantly challenge what is possible

We do this all our lives. Having sight loss just ensures that we do this more consciously. Challenging what is possible allows us to make progress.

Do not look back in anger, value what you could do, glory in what you can do now, and eagerly anticipate what you will be able to do. In short, live in the present and work for the future.

Regularly review your progress

Looking back and seeing what you could not do but can now is possibly the most important way of motivating yourself to keep growing and developing your abilities as a person with sight loss.

Develop systems and methods that work for you

Even with advice you still have to work out how to do things in practice.

Work out how to do things for yourself. This way they will have meaning and relevance for you.

Do regular psychological housekeeping

It is helpful to constantly check that your self-image and how you present yourself is up to date with the learning and development that is taking place. We spend all our lives redefining ourselves in the light of experience. With sight loss it is important to make the process both more conscious and regular.

Challenge the expectations of others

Other people will expect you to behave as a disabled person, but the degree varies with every person. Do not accept this under any circumstances and challenge any attempt to stuff you in the box of disability.

Be aware of the responsibilities that go with any rights

Too many people bang on about their rights, but with any rights go responsibilities and duties. To ignore those is to be just another free loader and as such you cannot expect to be regarded with respect.

Look after your body. It is the only place you have to live.

Eat well, sleep well and keep fit. Having a disability takes a great deal of energy. Make sure that you are fit and well to deal with it.

The above are, of course, not the only additional rules of engagement you might think of. The point of outlining the above is to show that nothing remains the same for long. Everything has to grow and develop with us, including our guiding principles and rules.

Remember the wise words of Douglas Bader: 'Rules are for the direction of fools and the guidance of wise men.' In other words, they are there for your guidance, not your dominance.

Simon Mahoney
Ashbourne, 2021

ABOUT THE AUTHOR

Simon Mahoney was born into a service family in 1947 in Portsmouth. He was educated at Plymouth College, ITCRM., West London College, Aston and Leicester universities. He has business, psychology, social work and teaching qualifications.

After leaving school he joined the Royal Marines as a young officer. He left at the end of training and after drifting became a social worker. He took early retirement in 1996 and worked as a freelance artist for a number of years.

In 2005 he accepted that the bills were not being covered and took up work as a supervisor and trainer in a service centre for one of the big supermarkets. He also held the role of Union Representative and Union Educational Representative. He is quite clear in his mind that all the roles required a not-infrequent suspension of disbelief.

He moved to Derbyshire in 2012 with the

intention of finally retiring and spending his time walking and improving his landscape painting. A year later his sight started to deteriorate, and three years later he had no effective sight and was stone blind by 2018.

He is now a member of and volunteer for Blind Veterans UK. He began a new career as a writer with the release of *A Descent into Darkness* followed by *First catch your Rabbit*. He has also written articles for *Health is your Wealth* and *The Blind Veterans Review*. He has featured on BBC Radio 4, In Touch, You and Yours and The Food Programme. He also featured on the World Service Food Chain, BBC News, British Forces Broadcasting Service, RNIB Radio Connect, UCB and numerous local radio programmes, along with *I* newspaper and on a VI Talk podcast. His previous books are being serialised on Talking Newspapers. *A Descent into Darkness* is an audio book available on Calibre Audio, and in paperback or for Kindle on Amazon. *First Catch Your Rabbit* is on the RNIB sound library, and in paperback or for Kindle on Amazon. All three books, including this one, are also available via Simon's website www.wingingitblind.com

He is a passionate campaigner for sight loss awareness, but freely admits he is terrified at the prospect of the coming sight loss epidemic. He intends to continue writing and campaigning for "as long as there is breath in my body."

He lost his wife Kelly in 2020, and now lives on his own in Derbyshire with three dogs and a cat called Spitfire.

A DESCENT INTO DARKNESS

This book is intended as some kind of comfort and guide in the new and frightening world experienced by recently diagnosed individuals who are facing the unknown territory of vision loss. It is my account of losing my sight over three years, and includes some basic techniques that have worked for me. It outlines many of the things that people new to sight loss need to know but are rarely told and, as such, it is intended as a guide for those with sight loss as well as those who care for and love them.

There is no doubt that not being able to see is only a fraction of sight loss. Therefore, the physical, social and psychological implications, and the emotions and thoughts whilst facing the horror of sight loss are also discussed. It is all these other bits which transform the experience, if you so choose, into an adventure. The unspoken question is whether what happens to us is garbage to bury, or fertiliser to stimulate growth within us.

I claim no expertise other than that of becoming blind. Throughout this account there is a tension between independence and the need for assistance. Similarly, there is a continual balance between fear and endurance on the one hand, and determination and calmness on the other. Above all, the book points out that good things can and do happen – for example John Bishop coming from the stage to talk me through his slideshow – and emphasises the need to be positive and cheerful in the face of adversity.

www.amazon.co.uk/dp/1916446302

FIRST CATCH YOUR RABBIT

When you are entirely alone and completely blind crying is not an option. That is the quick route to the helter-skelter of depression, helplessness and surrender to fate. As a former Royal Marine, I chose to laugh in the face of adversity. This was not hubris, ignorance of the implications, machismo gone mad or even hysteria! It was the only rational route out of what could otherwise have been a comprehensive disaster.

How I regained the kitchen so I could feed myself is outlined in this book. To be able to cook what you want when you want is a major element in the path to independence and reclaiming your life after sight loss. But how I did it, entirely alone, blind and dodging three dogs and a cat called Spitfire is anybody's guess!

The equipment, techniques I reinvented and level of organisation are all described in the book. Everything was learned on the hoof. The result is not just a cookbook. It is a survival manual for working in the kitchen when you are totally blind. There is nothing mysterious or exceptional here, it is all reasonable, logical and, above all, doable.

Note: No rabbit was harmed or even caught whilst writing this book.

www.amazon.co.uk/dp/1916446337/

USEFUL WEBSITES AND PHONE NUMBERS

Blind Veterans UK
www.blindveterans.org.uk
Helpline: 0800 389 7979
London: 0300 111 22 33
Llandudno: 01492 868700
Brighton: 01273 307811

RNIB
www.rnib.org.uk
Helpline: 0303 123 9999

Henshaws of Manchester
www.henshaws.org.uk
Helpline: 0300 222 5555

Glaucoma Association
glaucoma.uk
Helpline: 01233 648170

Macula Society
www.macularsociety.org
Helpline: 0300 3030 111

4sight
www.4sight.org.uk
Helpline: 01243 828555

Partially Sighted Society
www.partsight.org.uk
Helpline: 01302 965195

NHS helpline: 111

POLICE helpline: 101

Printed in Great Britain
by Amazon

78015279R00294